JAI SIXTH!

By the same author:

Charge to Glory
Scarlet Lancer
The Barren Rocks of Aden
From Sepoy to Subedar (Ed.)
Bokhara Burnes
John Burgoyne of Saratoga
The Duke of Wellington's Regiment
The 16th/5th The Queen's Royal Lancers
Imperial Sunset
Glubb Pasha
'A Hell of a Licking': The Retreat from Burma 1941–2
Hussein of Jordan
*The Scarlet Lancers: The Story of the 16th/5th The Queen's
Royal Lancers 1689–1992*

FRONTISPIECE – Her Majesty The Queen by Commander Denis Fildes RN (Retd).

"There was great rejoicing early in 1959 when Her Majesty The Queen conferred on the Regiment the title of 'Queen Elizabeth's Own'. " (p.105)
The portrait, by Commander Denis Fildes RN (Retd), was commissioned by the Regiment in 1960.

BUCKINGHAM PALACE

Next month, the 6th Queen Elizabeth's Own Gurkha Rifles will lose its identity when it merges with the other three Regiments to form The Royal Gurkha Rifles. The Regiment has given loyal service for 177 years, and I am proud that since 1959 it has borne my name - the only Regiment in the British Army to do so.

It is always sad to see the passing of a great Regiment, but I am confident that the indomitable spirit of the Gurkha Officers and soldiers of Nepal, and the traditions and standards of the 6th Gurkhas, will live on in the new Regiment. I know too that the proud history of the 6th Gurkhas will be kept alive in the hearts and minds of its serving and retired Officers and men, and to all of them I send my warm thanks and best wishes for the future.

ELIZABETH R.

June, 1994.

JAI SIXTH!

The Story of the 6th Queen Elizabeth's
Own Gurkha Rifles
1817–1994

by

JAMES LUNT

LEO COOPER
LONDON

To the memory of All Ranks
of the 6th Queen Elizabeth's Own Gurkha Rifles
who fell in action
fighting for Britain
1817–1994

First published in Great Britain in 1994 by
LEO COOPER
190 Shaftesbury Avenue, London WC2H 8JL
an imprint of
Pen & Sword Books Ltd
47 Church Street, Barnsley, South Yorkshire S70 2AS

A CIP catalogue record for this book
is available from the British Library

ISBN 0 85052 423 7

Typeset by CentraCet Limited, Cambridge
in 11/13 Garamond

Printed by Redwood Books Limited
Trowbridge, Wilts

CONTENTS

———◦—◦—◦———

Contents

ILLUSTRATIONS

Illustrations

60. Her Majesty The Queen inspecting the 6 GR Guard of Honour in Hong Kong on 21 October, 1986.
61. Lt Col N. A. Collett and the officers after the 175th Anniversary Parade in Brunei, 1992.
62. Mrs Marie Pett, Mrs Sudha Rai and a group of Gurkha wives and children.
63. Maj Harkasing Rai MC and Bar IDSM MM.
64. "The Almighty created in the Gurkha an ideal Infantryman" – 21164983 Rifleman Budhibahadur Gurung 6 GR.

In addition to the acknowledgments shown above, thanks are also due to the following for permission to reproduce photographs:

The Trustees, 6th Queen Elizabeth's Own Gurkha Rifles, Lt Col D. H. McK. Briggs, Lt Col N. A. Collett, Sgt D. Forsey RMP, Lt Col P. P. A. Gouldsbury, Maj P. Griffin MBE, Lt Col A. S. Harvey OBE MC, Lt Col R. C. Neath OBE, Maj Gen R. A. Pett MBE, Maj P. B. H. Robeson, Lt Col The Viscount Slim OBE, Capt I. N. A. Thomas, Lt Col M.J. R. Wardroper and Maj T. E. E. Whitehead.

MAPS

BATTLE HONOURS

Burma, 1885–87
Helles
Krithia
Suvla
Sari Bair
Gallipoli 1915
Suez Canal
Egypt 1915–16
Khan Baghdadi
Mesopotamia, 1916–18
Persia, 1918
N. W. Frontier, India, 1915
Afghanistan, 1919
Coriano
Santarcangelo
Monte Chicco
Lamone Crossing
Senio Floodbank
Medicina
Gaiana Crossing
Italy, 1944–45
Shwebo
Kyaukmyaung Bridgehead
Mandalay
Fort Dufferin
Maymyo

Battle Honours

Rangoon Road
Toungoo
Sittang, 1945
Chindits, 1944
Burma, 1944–45

The Battle Honours awarded previous to *Burma, 1885–87*, viz: *Arracan*, *Assam* and *Ava* do not appear to have been carried forward in the Army List.

FOREWORD

by
Major General R. A. Pett, MBE
Colonel, 6th Queen Elizabeth's Own Gurkha Rifles

THIS book tells the story of the 6th Gurkhas from their raising as the Cuttack Legion in 1817 to the merger with the other British Army regiments of Gurkha Rifles in 1994. It is an adventure story to rank with any in fact or fiction, here superbly told by James Lunt, who has captured that unique spirit of the 6th Gurkhas.

A curtain of mystique surrounds the fierce hillmen of Nepal. This book lifts a corner of that curtain and illuminates the stoicism and heroism of both the Gurkha riflemen and their exceptional officers, British and Gurkha alike. It tells, for example, the story of the 1st Battalion at Gallipoli, where they alone succeeded in reaching the heights of Sari Bair, but at the cost of every British officer dead or wounded, save only the Medical Officer. Equally enthralling is the account of the 2nd Battalion's hard slogging alongside the 14th/20th King's Hussars in Italy in the Second World War, and the award of two VCs in the Chindit campaign, to Captain Michael Allmand and Rifleman Tulbahadur Pun of the 3rd Battalion.

But this book also fills in the periods in between the big wars – on the North-West Frontier; in the jungles of Malaya, Borneo, Brunei or Belize; on the Sino-Hong Kong Border, or the sports field, or the Century Range at Bisley; or just . . . soldiering. Throughout the book shines that ineluctable spirit of the 6th Gurkhas and the sheer, infectious fun of serving with those

Foreword

"Bravest of brave, most generous of the generous". For to serve with Gurkhas is not just a privilege. It is, truly, a pleasure. Within these pages are to be found the essence of that privilege and pleasure.

Jai Sixth!

ACKNOWLEDGEMENTS

MY principal acknowledgement must be to Major General Ray Pett, Colonel of the Regiment, for entrusting to me this chronicle of the 6th Gurkhas from their founding year in 1817 until their amalgamation with the 2nd Goorkhas in 1994, to form the First Battalion of The Royal Gurkha Rifles. Since we had never previously met, I am afraid he had to take me very much on trust and I hope I have not let him or the Regiment down. I have done my best to follow the remit he gave me.

He told me that he did not want the conventional kind of regimental history in which the movements of Companies, and sometimes of Platoons, are recounted in considerable detail, accompanied by maps liberally spattered with arrows pointing this way and that, but rather an overall account of the Regiment from its first raising until its disappearance from the *Army List* in 1994.

Unfortunately, owing to domestic circumstances, I have not been able to visit the Regiment in Brunei. However, I have, from time to time over the years, met the 6th Gurkhas and can number among their officers several old friends. I have also visited Nepal and met the Gurkhas in their native habitat. Lieutenant Colonel 'Tich' Harvey, Regimental Secretary in his retirement, has been of enormous assistance and it was a pleasure to meet Lieutenant Colonel Nigel Collett who commanded the Regiment from 1991 to 1993,

I have also to thank General Pett for choosing the illustrations, always a difficult and time-consuming task.

Acknowledgements

My GOC in Aden from 1961–63, General Jim Robertson, a 6th Gurkha of 6th Gurkhas, has helped to fill in some of the gaps, as has Brigadier Gil Hickey who organized our unforgettable visit to Nepal 26 years ago. Unfortunately ill-health prevented my meeting with General Pat Patterson, an old friend, and likewise Brigadier Brunny Short. However, I was fortunate enough to have a meeting with John Slim, under whose father I had served in Burma in 1942. Michael Calvert, a friend of many years' standing, has been kind enough to tell me about the 3/6th who served under him as CHINDITS in Burma in 1944 and who covered themselves in glory at Mogaung.

Anne Gonzalez has given me some help on the secretarial side but here my deepest thanks must go to my daughter, Jenny Toyne Sewell, who, despite a terrifyingly busy life, has found the time to type the manuscript in her usual immaculate style and, now and then and from time to time, has corrected my spelling and grammar and improved my punctuation! I am enormously indebted to her.

Finally a word for Lance-Naik Amritbahadur in whatever Gurkha Valhalla he is at present inhabiting. Without his ready aid as my orderly during the retreat from Burma in 1942, I certainly would not have survived to write this book and, to that extent, he must bear some responsibility for what follows. *Syabas!*

J. D. L.

INTRODUCTION

WHEN I undertook to write this History of the 6th Queen Elizabeth's Own Gurkha Rifles, it was in a sense in repayment of a long-standing debt I owe to a Gurkha soldier. Lance-Naik Amritbahadur of the 7th Gurkha Rifles was my orderly during the long retreat from Burma in 1942 and, on one occasion certainly, he saved my life. I have never heard of him again and undoubtedly he will have died. He was an old soldier in 1942.

In this history it will be seen how bravely and loyally the Gurkha soldier has served the British Crown for close on 200 years. Whether storming the heights of Sari Bair on Gallipoli in 1915 or charging well dug-in Japanese machine guns through the mud and blood of Mogaung in 1944 in Burma, the 6th Gurkha Rifles have at all times lived up to the Gurkha philosophy that it is 'better to die than live a coward'. No regiment in the Brigade of Gurkhas has a finer record and I regard it as a great privilege to be asked to tell the Regiment's story in the pages which follow.

Although I have never served in a Gurkha regiment, I have served with Gurkhas often enough, both in Burma and afterwards. In the 4th Burma Rifles, in which I served from 1939–41, our Band was entirely Gurkha and I have had many dealings with Gurkhas, both officers and riflemen, since those days. I have also visited Nepal and know the homeland of these sturdy hillmen, for whom I have always had both admiration and affection.

One of the outstanding advantages of the Gurkha Brigade of

the pre-1947 Indian Army was the similarity of the soldiers. Obviously there were differences between the Magars and Gurungs of Western Nepal, as recruited in the 6th, and the Limbus and Rais from the East, and more so with the higher-caste Chhetris recruited in the 9th Gurkha Rifles. Nevertheless their common characteristics and religious beliefs gave the Gurkha regiments a flexibility not otherwise to be found in the old Indian Army in which Dogras differed greatly from Pathans, as did Sikhs from Madrassis. It made it that much easier to reinforce in war one Gurkha regiment from another Gurkha regiment, regardless of the fierce pride in regiment which was such a feature of the ordinary Gurkha rifleman. What is more it seems to have applied equally to the British officers (BOs). That most famous of all 6th Gurkhas, Field Marshal Lord Slim, commanded a battalion of the 7th Gurkha Rifles, and another distinguished officer of his vintage, Bruce Scott, commanded a battalion of the 8th Gurkha Rifles. There would appear to have been a similar flexibility in the Brigade of Gurkhas since 1948 when the 2nd, 6th, 7th and 10th Gurkha Rifles were incorporated in the British Army.

There already exist three volumes of the History of the 6th Gurkha Rifles, beginning in 1817 and ending in 1982 when the Regiment was about to move from Hong Kong to Brunei, where the 6th are again serving today. In 1969 the 1st and 2nd battalions were amalgamated as a result of the reduction in strength of the Brigade of Gurkhas. Today, once again as a result of the reduction in the strength of the British Army, the Regiment faces amalgamation, this time with the 2nd King Edward VII's Own Goorkhas (The Sirmoor Rifles), to form the 1st Battalion of The Royal Gurkha Rifles.

No one in either regiment can be expected to welcome such a drastic change in regimental identity but I have not the slightest doubt that the regiment which will emerge from this amalgamation will be in every way as successful and as distinguished as were its predecessors. And although there will be, inevitably, sadness at the disappearance from the *Army List* of two such distinguished regimental titles, some consolation can be found from the fact that there will still be Gurkhas serving the British

Crown, as they have done so gallantly in the past. How gallantly will be clear from this story of the 6th Gurkhas which follows.

Regimental history can hardly be regarded as popular reading, apart from those who have a vested interest in the particular story or for military historians engaged in research. The Gurkhas, however, have long had a special place in the affections of the British people and with this in mind I have tried to avoid too detailed descriptions of events and individuals, but rather to convey the *esprit* which made the 6th Gurkhas the fine regiment that it was, and to give some impression of the *panache* and *élan* of the ordinary Gurkha rifleman which has made service with him so worthwhile – and such fun!

James Lunt
Oxford 1994.

TITLES OF THE REGIMENT

1817
Cuttack Legion

1823
Rangpur Local Battalion
8th Rangpur Light Infantry

1827
Assam Light Infantry

1861
42nd Regiment of Bengal Native (Light) Infantry

1865
46th Regiment of Bengal Native Infantry
42nd Assam Regiment of Bengal Native Light Infantry

1885
42nd Bengal Infantry

1886
42nd Gurkha Light Infantry

1891
42nd Gurkha Rifle Regiment of Bengal Infantry

1901
42nd Gurkha Rifles

• 1903
6th Gurkha Rifles

1959
6th Queen Elizabeth's Own Gurkha Rifles

CHAPTER ONE

———⊶⊙⊷———

The Early Years

AS a glance at the opposite page will show, the Regiment has had many changes of title in the close on two hundred years of its existence. These reflect not only changes in organization and role but, equally importantly, changes in recuitment. During the first twenty years of the nineteenth century the Honourable East India Company was fast extending its rule over the sub-continent. The Mahrattas had been subdued and the Pindaris soon after them; and between 1814 and 1816 the war with the Nepalese had been brought to a satisfactory conclusion by the Treaty of Segowli which, among other conditions, permitted the Company to recruit up to three regiments of Gurkhas, hitherto not enlisted in the Company's army.

The 6th Gurkha Rifles, however, did not begin as a Gurkha unit and nearly seventy years were to elapse before the Regiment became all Gurkha. It began life on 16 May, 1817, in Cuttack, one of the principal cities in the province of Orissa in the Presidency of Bengal. Cuttack is 220 miles south-west of Calcutta and 45 miles inland from the Bay of Bengal. The province was both hilly and thickly forested, inhabited by numerous aboriginal tribes at feud with each other and with many petty rajahs who were busily fighting each other in the wake of the break-up of the Mughal empire. Two of the tribes, the Paicks and the Kols, were being particularly troublesome and the Governor General in Calcutta decreed that a 'Local Corps' should be raised to deal with them. It was to be called the 'Cuttack Legion', with a uniform of dark green with black

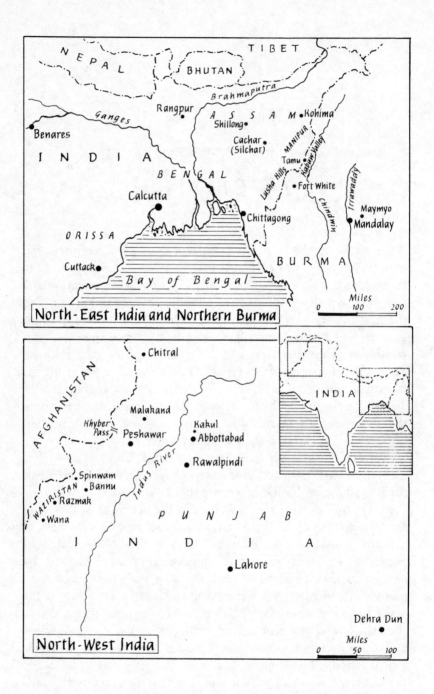

North-East India and Northern Burma

North-West India

velvet facings; the lace was to be silver. It was to be raised by Captain Simon Fraser of the Company's Service with an establishment of ten officers and 656 sepoys. The establishment included two Troops of light cavalry and two 3-pdr, or 'galloper' guns, as used by the horse artillery, as well as three companies of infantry. The role of the Cuttack Legion was more that of military police than that of a regular battalion of the Bengal Native Line, the advantage to the Company being that 'local' or 'irregular' corps could be disbanded once the task for which they were raised had been accomplished. They had a lower establishment of British officers, and the *sepoys* were paid less than the regulars, which was small enough in all conscience. They also provided opportunities for the more junior British officers who might have to wait until their sixties before obtaining command of a regular regiment.

There is no record of whether the Cuttack Legion took the field against the Paicks who had been causing trouble around Cuttack, but, although armed only with bows and arrows and axes, the Paicks gave such a good account of themselves that when the raising of an additional company was authorized, it was composed of Paicks. The Kols proved themselves to be equally stout foemen. In 1820 the Cuttack Legion entered their country to subdue a rebellion against the Rajah of Porahat. In one action when a troop of cavalry was sent to cut them off, the Kols, finding their showers of arrows did not deter the galloping *sowars*, turned and met the charge, axes in hand. The Kols did not give up easily and a great many of their villages had to be destroyed before they agreed to submit, which they did with great reluctance. By then, 1823, it was considered that the province had been sufficiently subdued for the Cuttack Legion to be moved to Rangpur in northern Bengal, where it under-went its first change of title, becoming the 8th Rangpur Light Infantry, but still remaining a 'Local Battalion'.

It was under this title that the Regiment took part in the First Burma War from 1824–26. The origin of this war was a Burmese invasion of what is now Assam, coupled with a similar invasion from Arakan aimed at Chittagong. Two separate columns were organized, in both of which the Regiment was involved, aimed at driving out the Burmese. Augmented by a squadron of Horse,which it was authorized to raise in 1824, the Regiment had several successful encounters with the Burmese, finally driving them out of Assam and Bengal. It was granted the Battle Honours of 'Ava' and 'Arracan'. The Battle Honour 'Assam' had been originally granted in 1826 and was subsequently confirmed in 1861.

The Burma War over, the Regiment found itself localized in Assam, becoming the Assam Light Infantry in 1827. In the following year its establishment was increased from ten to twelve infantry companies, the squadron of Horse having disappeared. This was a significant year for the Regiment since the two additional companies were to be composed of Gurkhas; previously individual Gurkhas had been enlisted but were scattered throughout the Regiment. They were now concentrated in the two new companies, the rest of the Regiment being composed largely of Sikhs. There was certainly plenty to keep them occupied as the Company's rule was extended over Assam and India's North-East Frontier, inhabited as it was by many martial tribes such as the Abors, Nagas, Lushais and Singphos, to name only a few.

This meant jungle warfare of the most testing kind fought by small detachments at the end of long and primitive lines of communication. As in Burma during the same period, it was truly a 'Subalterns' War', involving incredibly long marches through some of the toughest country in the world to come to grips with tribesmen like the Nagas, who were masters of the jungle. It is a sad fact that these skills in jungle warfare, all of them learnt the hard way and at the cost of many lives, came to be forgotten in the years between the two World Wars when the Indian Army's attention was increasingly fixed on the North-West Frontier where the Pathan tribes were equally warlike and skilful, but there was no jungle to be found within hundreds of miles. Consequently, to the best of this author's memory, jungle warfare was seldom, if ever, practised, even in Burma where he was serving before the Japanese invasion; with the result that when war came we were out-fought and out-manoeuvred in the very element in which we ought to have had the advantage. There are no jungles in Japan!

As the Assam Light Infantry the Regiment carried Colours, originally presented in about 1870. As was the custom in the Indian Army, recruits were sworn in on the Colours.* However, when later it became a Rifle regiment, who do not carry Colours, the Regiment petitioned the King-Emperor that the old custom of swearing in on the Colours could continue, and this was granted. By 1927, however, the old Colours had become too fragile and were therefore placed in a frame and the Colonel of the Regiment, Field Marshal Lord Birdwood in his capacity as Commander-in-Chief, presented replicas for the swearing-in ceremony. In 1913 the then Commandant's wife, Mrs Bruce, was repairing the original Colours and encasing them in a gold net. So great was the respect of the riflemen for the Colours that they insisted that a kukri sentry should be present while she worked in order to ensure that she did not purloin any piece of the fabric.

As Assam and its north-eastern marches were gradually pacified, there was a requirement for more troops to provide outlying detachments. In 1844 the Regiment became the 1st Assam Light Infantry. A 2nd Battalion was formed from another 'local corps', the Assam Sebundy Corps. This, in the fullness of time, was to become the 8th Gurkha Rifles, which accounts for the close relationship that long existed between the 6th and 8th Gurkha Rifles. When the 'Wind of Madness' swept through Hindustan in 1857, both battalions of the Assam Light Infantry were true to their salt, receiving the Governor General's commendation for their loyalty in a special Order in 1859. In 1861 there came an even more welcome award when the Regiment ceased to be 'irregular' and was brought on to the regular establishment as the 46th Bengal Native Infantry, renumbered as 42nd later that year.

The Regiment continued to remain 'mixed' until 1885, and indeed it was by no means universally approved when the Sikh and Hindustani soldiers were mustered out and the Regiment

* Known then, and now, as *Kasam Khane*

[5]

became all Gurkha. It was said that Lieutenant Colonel J. P. Sherriff, who had commanded the Regiment since 1873, favoured Sikhs over Gurkhas, but was apparently out-manoeuvred by two of his junior officers.* It now became the 42nd Gurkha Light Infantry until in 1901 this was changed to the 42nd Gurkha Rifles. Under Kitchener's reorganization of the Indian Army in 1903, when the ten Gurkha regiments were numbered separately from the other Infantry regiments, the Regiment became the 6th Gurkha Rifles. This was further embellished in 1959 by the title 'Queen Elizabeth's Own'.

As an example of the kind of operations in which the Regiment was involved during those early years in Assam there follows an account of the Lushai campaign from November, 1871, to March, 1872, in which the 42nd Assam Light Infantry played a distinguished part. The Regiment was commanded by Colonel Thomas Rattray, CSI.

The Lushai Hills are situated between south-eastern Bengal and Burma. It was wild and heavily forested country inhabited by equally wild tribesmen who practised headhunting and, some averred, cannibalism. As the Tea Planters extended their estates in eastern Assam and Bengal, the Lushais started to raid them until at last a little European girl, named Mary Winchester, was carried off and kept by them as a prisoner. This led the Lieutenant Governor of Bengal to declare that a punitive expedition was 'absolutely necessary for the future security of the British subjects residing on the Cachar and Chittagong frontiers'.

Two small columns were formed, one based on Cachar and commanded by Brigadier General Bourchier and the other on Chittagong and commanded by Brigadier General Brownlow. The Cachar column consisted of half the Peshawar Mountain Battery, one company of the Bengal Sappers & Miners, the 22nd Punjab Infantry and the 42nd and 44th Assam Light Infantry. The senior staff officer with the Cachar column was Colonel F. S. Roberts, VC, the famous 'Bobs Bahadur' of later years. Fortunately Colonel Rattray's letters written during the

---

* Sherriff, who retired as Lieutenant-General, was Colonel of the Regiment from 1904–1911.

expedition have been preserved and give an excellent account of what followed.

'My Regiment is under orders to proceed to the Lushai country, an unknown land lying between Assam, Burmah, Munipore [sic] and Cachar. The inhabitants are savages, and have been doing a great deal of harm lately, and won't come in, so an expedition is to be sent against them. One brigade leaves Cachar, in which my Corps forms one, another from Chittagong and we are to meet somewhere on the borders of that country, at a place called Chuttack. The country is described as most difficult, high hills covered with dense jungle and no roads, but we are to get at them somehow. We are to be five months out, only allowed forty pounds baggage, no tents, no mess, to live on rations from the Commissariat . . . Only one servant is allowed to an officer. We must go on the Prussian system, making requisitions on the Lushais! no beer, no wine with us. My men are delighted at the prospect and I am sure will do well. I expect we shall have some stockades to take. The jungle climate will be our worst foe.'

The first part of the journey was by river in a steam launch making little more than two miles per hour against the current. The column eventually reached Chuttack. Rattray's next letter, dated 30 December, 1871, continues the story:

'Since I wrote last, I received orders to march to the General's camp with 200 men; the General sent me word he had a hard day's work in store for me – 28th I marched. Our road lay down the face of a hill 3000ft high. I had been warned to be on the alert, as the Lushais were on our track and we had to search the jungle on each side. Three Sappers were wounded. We had not advanced far when firing commenced just ahead. I went forward to see what it was, when I found a party of unfortunate coolies going back to the Station we had just left, under an escort of the 44th. One coolie had been shot . . . We reached the camp at 3pm. I fell in with Nuttall, who had hard work on the 23rd. He described it as most trying and dangerous. He had had to fight his way into a village and then had to burn it. Any one who moved in camp was fired upon by men posted in the hills. I marched next morning at 8am. The Lushais had got into our rear, interrupting our communications, killing some and had captured 17 elephants . . .

'We were told that we should be most severely tried, as the Lushais would contest every step. We had to cross the river five times and then descend a mountain of 4000ft, commencing with a perpendicular ascent of 1000ft. We passed the night here, and got some breakfast. We had scarcely got out of the camp when they commenced firing from the heights on both sides. We answered them when we could see their firing. We got to the bottom of the hill, when a heavy fire commenced from the rice fields on the side of the hills. My men could stand it no longer and they fired a volley when they saw the smoke. About one hundred shots were fired, apparently without effect, for the worst of it was you never saw the enemy.

'We pulled ourselves up an almost perpendicular hillside holding on to bamboos and tree stumps. As soon as we commenced ascending fire came from the top, and we saw that our work would be cut out to get there. We saw the Lushais crawling off into the jungle on all fours (every Lushai who has a gun has three unarmed men with him to carry him off in case of being wounded). One man was hit; the Gurkhas rushed into the jungle after him and managed to get his musket . . . Roberts VC was heard to say that the 42nd knew their job to the General who replied that they had a very fine leader. Slowly toiling up the hill, the advance guard suddenly came upon a party of Lushais headed by a chief with a splendid topknot of feathers on his head, who called on us not to fire; he wanted to treat.'

After the Political Officer (Edgar) and the Lushai chieftain had discussed terms, the fighting ceased.

'They were a most friendly, good natured lot of men eager to look at our swords and revolvers, etc., and evidently admired us greatly,' writes Rattray.

1. *"The force amounted to 4,800 rifles and nine guns from two mountain batteries."* (p.12) In 1884 the Regiment was issued with two 7-pound mountain guns, known as "Bubble and Squeak". They stand outside the Officers' Mess today.

2. *"By the 1880s the Gurkhas had become something of a class apart in the Indian Army."* (p.10) The Subedar Major (senior Viceroy-Commissioned Officer), 1890.

3. *"The last two years in Shillong were overshadowed by the disastrous earthquake of 12 June, 1897."* (p.12) Captain Jack Chatterton (standing, centre) proposed under the dining table whilst salvaging the Mess silver.

4. *"The Officers' Mess plate was wrecked and the few pieces which survived were melted down to form a silver centrepiece of a rifleman of the 42nd Gurkha Rifles."* (p.12)

5. *"Gallipoli has been described as a 'mincing machine' and within a week of the landings it became a battle of attrition with opposing trenches which in places were within a grenade's throw of each other."* (p.19)

6. *"Among the British officers was Major C.J.L Allanson who took over command of the Battalion."* (p.22) As Adjutant, 1/6th Gurkha Rifles, 1904.

7. *"Major Allanson and Captain Phipson were awarded the DSO. Of the many Battle Honours awarded to the Regiment in the course of its long history, 'Sari Bair' must rank as being outstanding."* (p.25) Colonel E.S. Phipson, CIE, DSO, O St J, IMS.

8. *"1/6th Gurkha Rifles was 'the outstanding battalion of the Gallipoli campaign'. 179 had been killed including seven British and three Gurkha officers."* (p.25) Of the survivors shown here, Captain Bagot-Harte (centre, back) died in Waziristan in 1917, and Lieutenant King-Salter (sitting, left) in Mesopotamia in 1918.

9. *"The battalion acquired an interesting piece of loot from the Ur of the Chaldees ... thought to be the lintel of a doorpost from the Temple of Diana."* (p.28) "The Stone" now serves as a door stop.

10. *"Over 3,000 prisoners were taken, including Nazim Bey, the Turkish divisional commander."* (p.29) 2/6th Gurkha Rifles marching north to the Battle of Khan Baghdadi, 22 March, 1918.

11. *"It has been claimed that the 1920s and 1930s were the 6th Gurkhas' 'golden era'."* *(p.34) Officers of the 1st, 2nd and 3rd Battalions, 1920.*

Rear: Lieutenants E.F. Qualtrough, H. Shuker, R.St B. Emmott, Captains J.G. Bruce, J.K. Jones, Lieutenant S.S.H. Berkeley, Captains E.G. Brown, H.V. Collingridge, Lieutenants H. Robinson, D.W. Belcher, VC, R.Faulkner, MC

Centre: Captains T.C.E. Barstow, OBE, G.C. Strahan, OBE, Major A.B. Rumbulow-Pearce, Lieutenant-Colonel W.C. Little, Majors M. Wylie, F.B. Abbott, DSO, J.M. Whittall, Captain A.G. Fuller

Front: Lieutenants A.E. Armstrong, G.F.X. Bulfield, E.F.W.H. Kevill Davies, W.K. Phillips, W. Anderson, F.G.H. Green, J.F.R. Forman, T.N. Smith

12. *"Four of them — Slim, Scott, Bruce and Cowan — were to become Generals in the next conflict."* (p. 34) Officers, 1/6th Gurkha Rifles, Christmas Day, 1923.
Rear: Lieutenants T. N. Smith, W. K. Phillips, Captain W. J. Slim, MC, Lieutenant I. N. Macleod, Captain H. R. K. Gibbs
Front: Captain J. B. Scott, Mrs Hackett, Mrs Glynton, Lieutenant-Colonel G. M. Glynton, DSO, Mrs Scott, Major H. M. M. Hackett

13. *"The Regiment petitioned the King-Emperor that the old custom of swearing-in on the Colours — known then, and now as 'Kasam Khane' — could continue, and this was granted."* (p.5) Recruits in the 1930s and 1940s marched under the unfurled replica Colours to rejoin their companies as full members of the Regiment.

14. *"...a Rifles regiment, who do not carry Colours..."* (p.5) Even the replica Colours are now too fragile to be unfurled. Recruits are sworn in on the boxed replicas, beside the drums bearing the Regiment's principal Battle Honours.

'They ate our biscuits with great relish. Here the Chief sent one of his followers on to this camp . . . A cry was heard, something between the shout of a dervish and the shriek of an evil spirit. This was answered from all the hills around and all firing ceased. We had to march down the hills again – a most trying business it was. When we reached camp at sunset great were the congratulations. Up came an old Sikh of the 22nd and said: 'Great is your *Iqbal* (fate), up comes your regiment, away you go, we thought you would all be killed, when Lo, you make peace, the rascals come in and all is quiet! Wah! Wah!' 'Oh,' I said, 'not *Iqbal* but faith in God.' You should have heard the roar. Certainly such a happy conclusion could never had been expected . . . I don't object to fighting but I do object to climbing a hill and getting a bullet in my head at the top.'

It was not, however, the end of the fighting. Christmas Day was celebrated in the mountains sitting 'around a table with lighted candles in front of them'. On 17 February, 1872, Rattray wrote his last letter from the Lushai Hills:-

'Sitting on the ground and writing on what is called a bed is not conductive [sic] to letter writing. We have penetrated more than a hundred miles into the hitherto unknown country. Awful hard work making one road up and down mountains from four to six thousand feet high . . . Twice the Lushai tried their luck against us in fight, but both times received heavy punishment; they have not attempted it again. We have lost eight men killed and about 16 wounded . . . I am now located on the side of the hill. My hut is 6000ft above the level of the sea and very cold in the mornings and nights . . . They (the Lushai) came up to us in the most friendly manner . . . The ladies are particularly anxious to see the colour of our skins . . . They saw an officer bathing and were astonished as they never wash themselves and wondered why the Sahibs wanted so much water.'

The Regiment clearly acquitted itself well and Rattray was awarded the CB after the campaign was wound up at the end of

February. Jungle warfare, wherever it is fought in Burma, Malaya or Borneo, does not seem to have changed all that much over the years!*

During the Third Burma War in 1885–86, the 42nd Gurkha Light Infantry occupied Tamu on the River Chindwin and, at the end of 1887, when ordered to Maymyo to form part of the garrison of newly annexed Burma, the Regiment marched every mile of the way from Kohima in 55 days, following the same route as the Fourteenth Army took in 1945 on its way to recapture Mandalay; and as yet another example of history repeating itself, in 1888 and 1889 the Regiment was involved in operations against the Chins, capturing Tokhlaing which was promptly named Fort White after General Sir George White, VC, the GOC Burma at the time. Finally, during those many years of change, one thing must have remained constant, viz: the long years in office of those who held command, such as Lieutenant Colonel S. F. Hannay who was Commandant from 1839 to 1861, until he died and was buried at Dibrugarh.† Nor was it only the British officers. When Subedar-Major Runbahadur retired in 1878, he had completed 45 years' distinguished service and there were other Gurkha officers who came close to him in this respect.

By the 1880s the Gurkhas had become something of a class apart in the Indian Army. British Officers of that Army tended to support the class of Indian soldier they knew best, be it Sikh, Punjabi-Mussalman, Mahratta, Dogra etc., but Gurkhas were in some fashion different. It was not only the character of the Gurkha soldier, brave, loyal, cheerful and mostly free from

---

* In December, 1878, Major General Roberts, who was commanding one of the columns about to invade Afghanistan, wrote to the Viceroy's Private Secretary asking, *inter alia*, for the 44th Native Infantry from Assam, going on to say: 'Assam seems a long way to send for a regiment, but it is worth doing so under existing circumstances; the 44th is a good fighting corps, and is composed almost entirely of a hardy class of Goorkhas.' Presumably Roberts' opinion was formed during the Lushai expedition. He might equally well have asked for the 42nd. Roberts had a poor opinion of the majority of Native Infantry regiments but thought highly of the Sikhs and the Goorkhas (as he spelled it).

† Hannay was named Simon Fraser after the founder of the Regiment.

caste prejudices that, according to his British officers, made him so attractive to serve with, but also the somewhat isolated nature of the Gurkha regimental centres set in the Himalayan foothills in places like Almora, Abbottabad and Bakloh, where Gurkha regiments thrown in on themselves really did become 'Families'.

On its return to India from Burma in April, 1890, the Regiment was stationed in Assam, where it was soon to be involved in a most unfortunate affair in Manipur, then an independent state on the border with Burma. As so often in India, it began with a palace revolution. The ruling Maharajah was ousted by his brother, the commander-in-chief of the State army, who installed another brother in his stead. This was rejected by the Government of India which instructed the Chief Commissioner in Assam, Mr J. W. Quinton, to go to Manipur and restore the previous Maharajah. He set out in March, 1891, via Kohima, with an escort of 400 rifles from the 42nd and 44th Gurkha Rifles, commanded by Colonel C. McD. Skene, Commandant of the 42nd. In addition there was in Manipur a Residency Guard of 100 rifles from the 43rd Gurkha Rifles, some of whom were away on detachment.*

Although the Chief Commissioner was received in Manipur with some state, his escort being equally cordially welcomed, the plan for a Durbar to be held that day was aborted owing to the failure of the commander-in-chief, who had named himself *Jubraj* (or Crown Prince), to attend. Another Durbar was arranged for the following morning. Meanwhile Colonel Skene informed his officers that the Chief Commissioner's intention was to arrest the *Jubraj* and to deport him. The previous Maharajah would then, presumably, be restored to the *gadi* (throne). However, when this plan was put into effect the next day, heavy fighting broke out between the Manipur soldiers and the escort.

Towards nightfall, after much firing which included some Manipuri artillery, a 'Cease Fire' was agreed. The Chief Com-

* The three Gurkha Rifles regiments involved became, subsequently, the 1/6th, 2/8th and 1/8th Gurkha Rifles.

missioner went to meet the *Jubraj*, taking with him the Political Agent in Manipur, the Chief Commissioner's secretary, Colonel Skene and Lieutenant Simpson who commanded the Residency guard of the 43rd Gurkha Rifles. After a lengthy discussion, Mr Quinton and his companions entered the city and were never seen again. They were murdered, presumably on the orders of the *Jubraj*, and very heavy firing again broke out. This included shelling by the Manipuri guns, making the Residency compound untenable. Out-numbered and out-gunned, it was decided to withdraw the escort. The retreat began early on 26 March and did not end until the troops reached Silchar in Bengal. The 42nd Gurkha Rifles lost their Commandant and three riflemen killed; Lieutenant Lugard and 15 riflemen were wounded. It was hardly the most creditable action in the Regiment's history and two officers were subsequently court-martialled.

However, retribution was swift. Three columns were assembled to advance from Kohima, Cachar and Tamu (on the Burma border). The Regiment was split between the Kohima and Cachar columns and the force amounted to 4,800 rifles and nine guns from two mountain batteries. The Manipuris made little attempt to oppose such overwhelming force and Manipur was entered on 27 April by what became known as the 'Manipur Field Force'. The erstwhile Maharajah was restored and the Regent (his supplanter) and some others were transported for life. The *Jubraj* and one of his generals were condemned to death and hanged. The India medal with clasp 'N.E. Frontier 1891' was awarded to those forming the Field Force. Then Manipur faded into the background until it became the scene of General Slim's great victory over General Mutaguchi's Fifteenth Japanese Army between March and July, 1944.

The Regiment left Assam on 15 September, 1899, after a stay of 77 years. The last two years in Shillong, one of India's more attractive hill stations, were overshadowed by the disastrous earthquake of 12 June, 1897. The Officers' Mess plate was wrecked and the few pieces which survived were melted down to form a silver centrepiece of a rifleman of the 42nd Gurkha Rifles. The arms were similarly damaged and the entire regiment had to be re-equipped, this time with the Martini-Henry Mk IV.

There is a delightful and romantic story in connection with the earthquake. On the day that it happened the Officers' Mess plate had been set out on the dining room table for checking. Bent and battered, it had later to be recovered from the rubble and identified. Captain Jack Chatterton was charged with this task, together with a fatigue party of Gurkha riflemen. Soon, however, others came to lend a hand, including the delectable Miss Alice Green with whom Chatterton had become acquainted shortly before. Between them they concentrated on the silver, digging through the rubble above and below the dining room table. After several hours' toil they succeeded in propping up the smashed table in a corner of the room and piled the damaged silver beneath it. Exhausted, they then sat down *under* the table for fear of further falling masonry. According to their daughter Joan, it was there, after a short period of silence, that her father, Jack, proposed to her mother, Alice! Chatterton went on to command the 1st Battalion from 1908–14. His daughter Joan, now in her 95th year, is the oldest member of the Regimental Association and one of the great characters of the Regiment.

Sterling work was done rescuing people and in helping to rebuild not only the barracks but also some private houses. This received the official thanks of government. Despite this sad event there were many regrets when the Regiment left Shillong for Abbottabad where it was to join Punjab Command. Unfortunately its journey there turned out to be a long one. Cholera broke out on the river steamer which was conveying the Regiment down the Brahmaputra. This resulted in everyone being placed in quarantine until pronounced fit to proceed to Benares, where the Regiment was to stage. There were 53 deaths in this epidemic and only by constantly moving camp was the outbreak brought under control. It was six months before the Regiment arrived in Abbottabad in the Hazara province of the Punjab on 25 March, 1900. It was to be the Regiment's 'home' until Independence in 1947, shared with the 5th Royal Gurkha Rifles F.F., the 13th Frontier Force Rifles and the Mountain Artillery Centre. It was still being developed as a cantonment when the Regiment arrived there.

When the three separate Presidency armies were abolished in 1896, regiments were ordered to take into use badges to be worn on the left side of the headdress. The Regiment chose two silver Kukris, 1½ inches long, crossed edge downwards, the figure '42' under the angle, with words Gurkha Rifles on a silver scroll below. The figure '6' was substituted for '42' in 1903. The badge was ensigned with the Crown in 1959 when the Regiment became 'Queen Elizabeth's Own'. The Historical Record is at pains to point out that had the numbering of the Brigade of Gurkhas been done in strict seniority of raising, the Regiment would have come fourth instead of sixth in the order of batting. That distinguished soldier-cum-novelist, John Masters, goes further in his *Bugles and a Tiger* when he writes:

> 'The 1st Gurkhas were earnest, the 2nd idle, the 3rd illiterate, the 5th narrow-minded, the 6th down-trodden, the 7th unshaven, the 8th exhibitionist, the 9th Brahminical (they enlisted high caste Gurkhas) and the 10th alcoholic.'

He omits any mention of his own regiment, the 4th Prince of Wales's Own Gurkha Rifles, presumably because they were paragons of all the virtues. In any case 'down-trodden' seems a curious label to attach to a Regiment which managed to produce a Field Marshal and two Major Generals in a single campaign; but John Masters was, of course, a wonderful story-teller as well as an outstanding soldier.

Under the Kitchener reorganization of 1903, most of the old Madras regiments, with which the East India Company had defeated the French and conquered Burma, virtually vanished. They were either converted into Punjabi or other regiments, or disbanded. This was done on the grounds that the Madrassi soldier no longer possessed martial qualities. It was not only unfair but untrue, as the Madras Sappers & Miners were to demonstrate in many a hard-fought campaign in the years that followed.* The 65th Carnatic Light Infantry was one of the

---

* The 3rd Madras Regiment was re-formed in 1942. When the author visited the Madras Regimental Centre at Wellington in the Nilgiris in 1967, he was shown round by one of the senior Majors who happened to be a Gurkha!

many distinguished regiments to be disbanded and it was ordered to hand over its regimental funds and its mess and band property to the 2nd Battalion of the 6th Gurkha Rifles, orders for the raising of which were received in Abbottabad on 8 November, 1904. Henceforward each regiment of Gurkha Rifles would consist of two battalions. The Regiment was to remain a two battalion regiment (with the exception of the war-raised battalions in both world wars) until 16 June, 1969, when the 1st and 2nd Battalions were amalgamated in Hong Kong.

As will have been understood from the foregoing narrative, Gurkha regiments have long been closely connected not only with Assam but also with Burma. A great many Gurkhas enlisted in the para-military Assam Rifles and Burma Military Police (BMP). In Burma many took their discharge and settled down around Maymyo as market gardeners. In Mandalay in 1939 the band of the 4th Burma Rifles was entirely Gurkha. The 7th Duke of Edinburgh's Own Gurkha Rifles was raised at Quetta from the 10th Gurkha Rifles in 1907. The 10th Princess Mary's Own Gurkha Rifles began life in 1887 as a battalion of military police in the Kubo valley in Burma, becoming the 10th Gurkha Rifles in 1901. This was the fever-infested Kabaw valley up which the retreating Burma Army staggered in May, 1942, and down which the 11th (East African) Division blazed the trail for the Fourteenth Army late in 1944 on the road to Mandalay.

In his masterpiece, *Defeat into Victory*, Field Marshal Lord Slim, the greatest Gurkha of them all, has written: 'The Almighty created in the Gurkha an ideal infantryman . . . brave, tough, patient, adaptable, skilled in fieldcraft.'

He could have added a remarkable capacity to endure. It might be considered only natural that as hillmen the Gurkhas are first-class mountain troops, but they have proved themselves just as good in the jungle – quiet, stealthy and skilled in the setting of ambushes. They demanded no less from their officers which made service with them a testing experience. As a generalization it used to be the case that regiments of the Gurkha Rifles preferred to get their recruits from the mountain villages rather than as offspring of serving Gurkhas born in the

Lines – 'line-boys' as they used to be known. But many in the latter category have proved themselves in war and in the changing circumstances of today there is a much less rigid approach.

In 1907 the felt hat, which will always be associated with the Gurkha Brigade, was introduced; the 5th Royal Gurkha Rifles were the guinea pigs. It soon entered the Ordnance vocabulary as 'Hat, Felt, Gurkha'. Since Gurkha soldiers were expected at that time to shave their heads, the felt hat worn double and with a stiff brim, at an angle and secured by a chin strap, was a smart headdress. Worn single it soon lost its shape. Its worst feature manifested itself in the monsoon; when soaked it became intolerably heavy. Although usually associated with the Gurkhas, it was also adopted by the Royal Garhwal Rifles, Kumaon Rifles and the Burma Rifles and, much later, the single version by the Fourteenth Army where it became *de rigueur*. Australian and New Zealand regiments also favoured the felt hat, either turned up on one side or not, and it acquired considerable popularity among settlers in East Africa and Rhodesia, as well as in the King's African Rifles. Nowadays fly fishermen appear to have adopted it as their headgear.

For a great many years operations on the North-West Frontier of India dominated the tactics and the thought of the Indian Army. There was seldom an operation which did not involve a battalion or more of Gurkha Rifles. Bannu and Razmak became as familiar as Dehra Dun or Shillong. Operations on the Frontier had their own rules of engagement and the Indian Army has often been criticized for giving them undue prominence. Field Marshal Montgomery was one of the leading critics in this respect. But the fact remains that the Frontier did *matter* to those responsible for policy far away in New Delhi and, surely, it is not surprising that regiments like the 6th Gurkha Rifles, who were hammered on the anvil in Waziristan, were later able to give such a good acccount of themselves at Gallipoli and in Italy. The Pathan was a good teacher.

CHAPTER TWO

The Great War

WHEN war was declared on Germany on 4 August, 1914, both the 1st and 2nd Battalions were in Abbottabad. There, at 9 p.m. on 15 October, 1914, orders for mobilization were received. The Regiment was about to take part in a war which would take it as far afield as Greece, Egypt, Gallipoli, Mesopotamia, the Caucasus and Persia, costing the lives of 17 British officers, three Gurkha officers and no fewer than 220 Gurkha rank and file, either in battle or from disease. It is a formidable death roll for just one regiment of Gurkha Rifles. The numbers of wounded were very much higher – 668 at Sari Bair alone.

The 1/6th were the first to leave India, together with the rest of the 29th Indian Infantry Brigade, of which the Battalion formed part. Intended originally to join the Indian contingent in France, the Brigade was deflected to Egypt for the defence of the Suez Canal, under threat from a Turkish force preparing to advance across the Sinai Desert from Palestine.

On 26 January, 1915, there was a brisk little action at Kantara, roughly midway on the Canal between Port Said and Suez, when the Battalion came under fire for the first time since Manipur 24 years previously. The Turks did not, however, press their attack but withdrew after some desultory shelling. They returned early in February, this time with rather more vigour but with equally little success, although the Battalion lost one rifleman killed and one British officer and five riflemen wounded. It was not a heavy loss to pay for defending the strategically vital Canal and it provided an excellent opportunity for the Commandant to shake down the Battalion after so many years of peacetime soldiering.

He was Lieutenant Colonel the Hon. C. G. Bruce, who had come from the 5th Gurkha Rifles F.F. to take command in 1913. He was an excellent soldier and had a particular empathy with the Gurkha soldier; he was also an experienced mountaineer. After the war he led the 1921 and 1922 Everest expeditions. On 26 April, 1915, headed by the band of the 4th East Lancashire Regiment, Bruce led the 1/6th Gurkha Rifles on to the quays at Port Said, where the Battalion embarked on board the *Dunluce Castle*, its destination Gallipoli.

Sir Ian Hamilton, the talented but luckless general who had been appointed the military commander of the Dardanelles Expeditionary Force, had formed a high opinion of the Gurkhas while serving with the Gordon Highlanders in the Second Afghan War in 1878. He asked Lord Kitchener, the Secretary of State for War, for a 'Brigade of Gurkhas', ending his letter by saying, 'Each little "Gurkh" might be worth his full weight of gold at Gallipoli.' Kitchener did not respond to Hamilton's request, although in the end Hamilton did get his 'Brigade of Gurkhas'. The 29th Indian Infantry Brigade comprised the 14th KGO Sikhs and the 69th and 89th Punjabis, besides the 1/6th Gurkha Rifles. Because the Punjabi battalions contained Mahommedan soldiers, the Brigade Commander, Brigadier General Cox, asked for them to be replaced lest they should object to fighting against their co-religionists. In due course they were replaced by the 1/5th and 2/10th Gurkha Rifles, although it is hard to say why General Cox took this particular line. Punjabi Mussulman soldiers fought all the way from Basra to Baghdad and beyond, and again in Palestine and Aden against the Turks, without causing trouble on religious grounds. After all, Mahommedan has fought against Mahommedan just as often in history as Christian has fought against Christian.

The British 29th Division had landed at the toe of the Gallipoli Peninsula at Cape Helles on 25 April, 1915, taking the Turkish defenders largely by surprise. Simultaneously the Australian & New Zealand Army Corps (ANZAC) had landed farther up the west coast of the peninsula at Gaba Tepe. The

1/6th Gurkha Rifles landed on 1 May, 1915 at V Beach without suffering any casualties, although subjected to shelling. Although the Turks were reacting violently to the landings, counter-attacking wherever there had been a foothold, 29th Brigade was the only divisional reserve and, as such, was held back. Nevertheless in the short space of nine days, without having had the opportunity to fire a single round, the Battalion had had one Gurkha rifleman killed and one British officer and 20 Gurkha other ranks wounded. Gallipoli has been described as a 'mincing machine' and within a week of the landings it became a battle of attrition with opposing trenches which in places were within a grenade's throw from each other. On 9 May 1/6th GR relieved the 1st Battalion, The King's Own Scottish Borderers on the extreme left of the British front line. This was to provide the battalion with the opportunity to show the Gurkhas' mettle.

Five hundred yards beyond the Gurkhas' trenches, and jutting out into the sea, the Turks had established a strongpoint which marked the right of their defensive position. It was about 300 feet high, from which machine guns could enfilade any attack from the British-held trenches. Two attempts to take this strongpoint by the Royal Dublin and Royal Munster Fusiliers had failed. Colonel Bruce was determined to improve on this. After careful reconnaissance and close liaison with the Royal Navy, who would provide the close support from their guns, a plan to assault the bluff was carefully worked out. It involved scaling the bluff from the seaward side and, once the strongpoint had been overwhelmed, rapidly preparing it for the Turkish counter-attack.

The sides of the bluff were steep, in places almost sheer, and thickly covered with dried scrub. In order to make the ascent from Gurkha Beach where the battalion had landed, the attacking troops would have to cross the mouth of a ravine (Gurkha Ravine) which could be enfiladed by the enemy. Two field batteries of the Royal Artillery were to provide covering fire, in addition to HMSs *Talbot* and *Dublin*. Early on 12 May Subedar Gambirsing Pun and Havildar Santabir Gurung crawled forward to reconnoitre the ground that led to the summit. 'A'

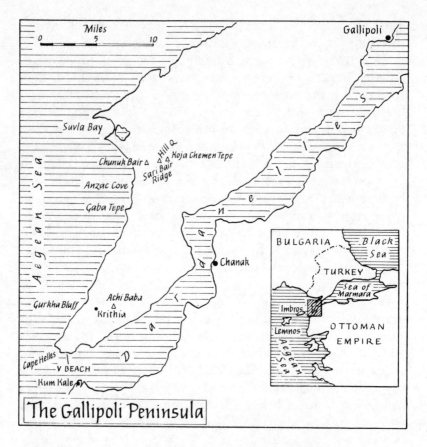

The Gallipoli Peninsula

Company was to make the assault but was subjected to some shelling while forming up just before dusk; one Gurkha was killed. Under cover of darkness the Company moved forward and had scaled the bluff by eight p.m. To everyone's astonishment there was no opposition and immediately the Gurkhas set about preparing to defend their objective, soon to be joined by 'C' Company and the Machine Gun section. By nine o'clock in the morning of 13 May the entire Battalion was deployed on the bluff at a cost of 18 Gurkhas killed and three British officers and 39 Gurkhas wounded. It was a copperplate operation, carefully planned and gallantly carried out.

To mark the Battalion's excellent performance the Army Commander directed on 17 May, 1915, that henceforward the bluff would be marked on the Expeditionary Force's maps as 'Gurkha Bluff'. The 1/6th Gurkha Rifles had certainly justified the faith that Sir Ian Hamilton had in the Gurkha soldier. Despite their casualties, the filthy living conditions, the constant shelling and the ever-increasing heat, the Battalion's tails were high.

Such high morale was not easy to achieve. At Gallipoli, it has to be said, everything that could go wrong did go wrong. To add to the obvious difficulty of obtaining a lodgement on a hostile coast defended by a tenacious and brave enemy, the terrain inland was difficult beyond belief. Long, deep and winding ravines ran inland from the shoreline, their sides sheer in places and covered by thick shrub sometimes as high as a man, making observation over any distance virtually impossible. The ground was rock hard when it came to digging trenches. The weather grew steadily hotter and the only water had to be brought in by barges. Killed and wounded had to be evacuated across narrow beaches, frequently shelled from the high ground above. Maps were in short supply and inaccurate. And everywhere there were flies in their millions, settling on living and dead in swarms. No wonder dysentery was a prevalent complaint.

To add to these problems was General Hamilton's obsession with security. The initial landings had taken the enemy by surprise and Hamilton was determined to continue to play his cards close to his chest. His administrative staff were not taken into the confidence of the operations staff and, as a result, the logistic back-up was inadequate. There was also a shortage of ammunition, particularly for the artillery, and although to some extent naval gun support made up for this, it had its limitations in such craggy terrain and when intercommunication was largely dependent on field telephones, or messages carried by runner down crowded trenches. Finally, Hamilton was opposed by a gifted enemy commander, the German General, Liman von Sanders, quick to react to every British move and ably supported by the Turkish divisional commander on the spot, Mustapha Kemal, later to be the founder-figure of modern Turkey. Without them the Turks may well have lost.

JAI SIXTH!

By August the battle had become one of attrition, with appalling casualties suffered by both sides. Attempts to extend and deepen the original landings had come to a halt in the face of stubborn Turkish resistance. Hamilton, therefore, planned to try elsewhere, aiming to land a fresh Corps, IX, at Suvla Bay, in conjunction with the seizure of the dominating heights of Sari Bair Ridge by an advance from ANZAC. This was to provide the 1/6th Gurkha Rifles with their 'finest hour'.

The Battalion had spent most of July on the island of Imbros after being withdrawn from Gallipoli. Its battle casualties amounted to two British and three Gurkha officers killed, and nine British officers and five Gurkha officers wounded. 91 Gurkha other ranks had been killed, and 369 wounded. While at Imbros reinforcements were received amounting to six British and Gurkha officers and 116 other ranks. Among the British officers was Major C. J. L. Allanson who took over command of the battalion. When ordered, late in July, to return to Gallipoli, eight British officers moved with the battalion.

Writing to Lord Kitchener at the beginning of July, Hamilton told him, 'To attack all along the line is perfect nonsense – madness!' He preferred instead, 'to win some small tactical position which the enemy may be bound, perhaps for military or perhaps for political reasons, to attack'. The 'tactical position' chosen for seizure in early August was the Sari Bair Ridge, the dominating feature in the southern half of the Gallipoli Peninsula. It ran roughly from SE to NW, 4,500 yards inland from the coast and 1,000 feet high at its highest point, Koja Chemen Tepe. Farther along the Ridge to the west were two other prominent features, Hill Q and Chunuk Bair, each of 820 feet. The plan was essentially an ANZAC one, the Australians and New Zealanders being reinforced by the 29th Indian Infantry Brigade and five battalions from the newly-arrived 13th (New Army) Division. Simultaneously the 10th and 11th (New Army) Divisions, grouped as IX Corps, were to be landed at Suvla Bay a few miles farther up the coast. The night of 6/7 August was chosen, both for the landing and for the assault on Sari Bair.

There were to be two assaulting columns; that on the right was almost entirely New Zealander. The left column consisted of the 29th Indian Infantry Brigade and the 4th Australian Infantry Brigade, together with supporting troops. The country to be traversed as far as the lower slopes of Sari Bair was a positive spider's web of ravines, gullies, scrub and boulders. All this had to be covered in darkness with the assistance of local guides. The Australians lost their way and when dawn came the 1/6th found themselves, together with the 1/5th Gurkhas, on the lower slopes of Hill Q, about 500 yards below the crest, having suffered some 64 casualties in killed, wounded and missing. Under constant fire from the enemy, they hung on throughout the night of 7/8 August, attacking again at 4.15 a.m. on 8 August and getting to within 200 yards of the crest. By now they were supported by companies of the North Stafford-shires, South Lancashires and the Warwicks, but all were held up by concentrated enemy fire. With the Warwicks was a certain young subaltern, W. J. Slim, who soon found himself commanding his company the other officers being either killed or wounded. It was his first experience of battle alongside the Gurkhas and the impression made that day never left him. They were superb.

It was their fieldcraft that enabled them to survive throughout 8 August but at a cost of 35 casualties, which included two British and two Gurkha officers wounded. Slim, too, was severely wounded and had to be evacuated. A fresh attempt to seize the heights was to be made at dawn on 9 August. Two companies of the South Lancashires were to take part in the attack. By now the Gurkhas had been without sleep for more than 72 hours and were both hungry and thirsty. Their attack was preceded by 30 minutes of naval bombardment of the crestline which must have been awe-inspiring. What follows is best described by Major Allanson who more than earned the VC that day, although he had to be content with the DSO. His account follows:

'At an angle of about 35 degrees, and only 100 yards away were the Turks . . . I had only fifteen minutes left; the roar of the artillery preparation was tremendous; the hill was almost leaping underneath one. I recognized that if we flew up the hill the moment it stopped, we ought to get to the top. I put the three companies [South Lancashires and Warwicks] into the trenches among my men, and said that the moment they saw me go forward carrying a red flag everyone was to start. I had my watch out, 5.15. I never saw such artillery preparation; the trenches were being torn to pieces; the accuracy was marvellous, as we were only just below. [At] 5.18 it had not stopped, and I wondered if my watch was wrong. 5.20, silence; I waited three minutes to be certain, great as the risk was. Then off we dashed all hand in hand, a most perfect advance, and a wonderful sight ... At the top we met the Turks: Le Marchand was down, a bayonet through the heart. I got one through the leg, and then, for about ten minutes, we fought hand to hand, we bit and fisted, and used rifles and pistols as clubs; blood was flying about like spray from a hairwash bottle. And then the Turks turned and fled, and I felt a very proud man; the key of the whole peninsula was ours, and our losses had not been so very great for such a result. Below I saw the Straits, motors and wheeled transport, on the roads leading to Achi Baba.'

It must have been a wonderful moment but it was not to last for long. As Allanson and his Gurkhas pursued the retreating Turks down the slope, they came under shellfire, causing many casualties. There was no support to right or left and Allanson's only course was to withdraw below the crestline. He always maintained that the shells were naval ones but this has been contested. It was a sad end to a brilliant action which might have made all the difference to the Gallipoli campaign had the Battalion been well supported. As it was, it had to withdraw to the trenches of the night before, but minus the gallant Allanson whose wound compelled his evacuation to a dressing station.

Every British officer had been killed or wounded, the only exception being the Medical Officer, Captain E. S. Phipson, IMS. Captain G. Tomes of the 53rd Sikhs arrived to take command in the afternoon of 9 August but he was killed at daybreak on 10 August. Subedar-Major Gambirsing Pun, IOM, was now in command, but, having no understanding of English,

1. *"It was to be called the 'Cuttack Legion', with a uniform of dark green with black velvet facings."* (p.1)
Sepoy of the Cuttack Legion, 1817.

2. *"The Burma War over, the Regiment found itself localized in Assam."* (p.4)
Captain J.B. Neufville, Commanding Officer, Assam Light Infantry, 1828—1830.

3. *"Lieutenant Colonel Simon Fraser Hannay was named after the founder of the Regiment. He joined on 14 May, 1838, later commanding the Regiment for 22 years."* (p.143)

4. *"On its return to India from Burma in April, 1890, the Regiment was stationed in Assam."* (p.11) The uniform of the 42nd Gurkha Light Infantry, c. 1886. The red pom-pom on the cap will continue to be worn by The Royal Gurkha Rifles.

5. & 6. *"Field-Marshal Lord Birdwood in his capacity as Commander-in-Chief, India, presented replicas for the swearing ceremony."* (p.5) Replica Colours of the 42nd Assam Regiment of Bengal Native Light Infantry, still in use.

he was dependent on the doctor to interpret for him. By 10 a.m. the Turks had regained Sari Bair and the Battalion was ordered to withdraw. Before doing so Subedar-Major Gambirsing Pun ensured that all ammunition, rifles and equipment which could not be carried were rendered useless or scattered around in the scrub. Then the 1/6th Gurkha Rifles withdrew in good order, Gambirsing Pun being awarded the MC for his leadership and gallantry. The total casualties amounted to 204 all ranks in three days' fighting, of whom 45 were killed. Three of them were British officers. Major Allanson and Captain Phipson were awarded the DSO. Of the many Battle Honours awarded to the Regiment in the course of its long history, 'Sari Bair' must rank as being outstanding.

It was not to be the last of the many trials and tribulations suffered by the Battalion at Gallipoli. After the Suvla landings a kind of stalemate settled on the peninsula and trench warfare took over. The Battalion suffered greatly when winter weather set in, the trenches becoming quagmires. Rain was followed by snow and frostbite became a problem. Men continued to be killed or wounded while the sickness rate increased. It came as something of a relief when it became known after 12 December, 1915, that it had been decided to evacuate Gallipoli.

It is a curious fact that in a campaign in which British generalship has been often and justly criticized, the original landings had been remarkably successful, as was the even more difficult operation of withdrawing an entire army under the enemy's guns, with the additional complication of having to carry this out not by land but by sea. In the event the 1/6th Gurkha Rifles lost only one Gurkha wounded and one missing; by 5.30 a.m. on 20 December, 1915, Anzac and Suvla had been evacuated. Helles was similarly evacuated on 9 January, 1916.

The Regiment has every reason to be proud of the record of the 1st Battalion in one of the toughest campaigns ever fought by the British Army, but it paid a very high price. It was the considered opinion of Lieutenant General Sir Reginald Savory, the last Adjutant-General of the pre-1947 Indian Army, who himself served at Gallipoli with the 14th KGO Sikhs (1/11th Sikh Regiment) that the 1/6th Gurkha Rifles was 'the outstanding Battalion of the Gallipoli campaign'. 179 had been killed including seven British and three Gurkha officers; 668 had been wounded. Including the one man taken prisoner after losing his way on the night of the evacuation, the Battalion's total casualties amounted to 848. When it had embarked at Karachi on 28 October, 1914, it had totalled 826!

In a letter dated 19 January, 1918, Sir Ian Hamilton thanked the Regiment for its Christmas card and went on to say: 'It is Sir Ian Hamilton's most cherished conviction that if he had been given more Gurkhas at the Dardanelles he would never have been held up by the Turks.' He was very probably right!

On Christmas morning, 1915, the 1st Battalion disembarked at Alexandria and spent the following month in Egypt before embarking for Karachi. On arrival there at the end of February, 1916, the Battalion was sent to Campbellpore, near Peshawar, where the 6th Gurkhas' depot had been moved from Abbottabad. Their return was welcomed by the 2nd Battalion, already under orders to leave for Mesopotamia, which it did less than a week later. It was very much an occasion of 'Hail and Farewell'. There was an urgent requirement to rebuild the 1st Battalion after the casualties suffered at Gallipoli but recruiting presented a problem. Many of the recruits enrolled in Nepal were under size and many were under age. The custom of the Regiment to enlist only Magars and Gurungs had to be dropped for the time being and almost every class of Gurkha was to be found among the other ranks including Khas, Chhetri, Sunwar and Lohar, as well as Magars and Gurungs.

The 2nd Battalion sailed for Mesopotamia early in March, 1916, spending its first month in Basra building bunds to contain the flooding of the two great rivers, Tigris and Euphrates, which enter the sea there. Things were not going well for the British at the time of the Battalion's arrival. The intention originally for involvement in Mesopotamia was to secure the oilfields at the head of the Persian Gulf, and for this purpose the 6th Indian Division was dispatched to Mesopotamia at the end of 1914. Basra having been secured, and a later attempt by the Turks to retake it having been defeated in the Battle of Shaiba in April, 1915, the decision was taken to push

PERSIA

Kirkuk

Hamadan

Ramadi

BAGHDAD
Ctesiphon
Khan Baghdadi
Aziziyeh

R. Euphrates

Kut-al-Amara

R. Tigris

ARABISTAN

Nasiriyeh

Ur of the Chaldees

Basra

Mesopotamia

Miles
0   50

on to Baghdad. As at Gallipoli, little consideration was given to the difficulties imposed by climate, terrain, the length of communications and the shortage of supplies. What was worse, the fighting qualities of the Turkish soldier were grossly underestimated. Nevertheless, Major General Charles Townshend, GOC of the 6th Division, advanced up the River Tigris as far as Ctesiphon, only 18 miles from Baghdad, before being compelled by superior numbers to retreat to Kut-al-Amara, where he was besieged for nearly six months before surrendering on 29 April, 1916. It was hardly an auspicious moment for the 2nd Battalion to arrrive in Basra only a month previously. On the day of Townshend's surrender the 42nd Indian Brigade, which the 2/6th had joined, was on the march to Nasiriyeh, 148 miles up the River Euphrates.

The march provided an interesting, if unwelcome, foretaste of what campaigning in Mesopotamia would be like. The heat was burning, the track was thick in dust and water was strictly controlled and made unpalatable by chlorination. The local Arabs were unfriendly and quick to murder stragglers. Transport was either pack or mule, camel and cart. Each daily stage was 10–15 miles and Nasiriyeh was reached in twelve days. There the Battalion went into camp on the north bank of the river which was to be its home for the remainder of the year. The marsh Arabs of the Euphrates-Tigris delta were a particularly quarrelsome and treacherous lot and on several occasions the Battalion came into conflict with them.

It was while at Nasiriyeh that the Battalion acquired an interesting piece of loot from Ur of the Chaldees, which was only a few miles away. It was a finely carved basalt slab showing the lower half of an Assyrian figure. It was thought to be the lintel of a doorpost from the Temple of Diana. Eventually it found its way back to India and a home in the Mess at Abbottabad.

One consequence of the Kut disaster was the appointment of a new Army Commander, General Sir Stanley Maude, who had previously been one of the divisional commanders. He came as a breath of fresh air after his predecessors and morale improved remarkably. At the end of 1916 he began a methodical advance towards Baghdad, ousting the Turks from one position after another. Baghdad was taken on 11 March, 1917, but so far the 15th Division, of which 42nd Brigade formed part, had not been involved but remained at Nasiriyeh.

At the end of March, however, the Battalion returned to Basra, this time by train, the railway having reached Nasiriyeh in the previous December. Compared with the march up, it took only twelve hours to reach Basra, where the Battalion embarked on a paddle steamer en route for Baghdad. During the voyage up the Tigris it was hoped to meet the 1st Battalion, newly arrived from India and reputedly stationed at Aziziyeh, but the steamer passed through at midnight without contact being made. On 6 April, 1917, the 2nd Battalion landed at Hinaidi, a few miles below Baghdad, where it was destined to remain for nearly six months, the war having moved on to the north and General Maude having decided to keep the 15th Division in reserve. Unfortunately Maude died of cholera on 19 November, 1917.

It was not until September that the Battalion was ordered to move to an unknown destination. The move involved first crossing the Tigris and then marching due west to cross the Euphrates. There followed from 27 to 29 September the Battle of Ramadi in which 42nd Brigade found itself engaged with a considerable number of Turks. The enemy fought well but the Turkish commander was captured, as were many of his men. The 2/6th Gurkha Rifles had three killed and 82 all ranks wounded.

Although the Turks had still plenty of fight left in them and were as formidable an enemy as ever, they were very short of ammunition and supplies, as well as war weary. 2/6th Gurkha Rifles came into contact with them again at Khan Baghdadi on 22 March, 1918. The weather was bitterly cold and very wet from time to time. Over 3,000 prisoners were taken, including Nazim Bey, the Turkish divisional commander. The regimental chronicler has recorded that the Turks were a fine set of men, but the state of their kit and equipment was appalling. Over 600 animals were captured, all of them skin and bone. The Battalion's casualties were one British officer and four Gurkha other ranks wounded. It had not been a high price to pay for the award to the Regiment of 'Khan Baghdadi' as a Battle Honour.

Having endured yet another Mesopotamian hot weather when temperatures of 120 degrees Fahrenheit continue day after day, the Battalion was ordered to move to Basra: destination unknown. In fact it ended up in Salonika where it arrived in late October, 1918. No one was sorry to see the last of Mesopotamia, which for most of the soldiers was synonymous with flies, heat, dust and the boredom inseparable from war when the bullets are not flying. However, Salonika was to prove but a brief interlude in the Battalion's travelogue because within a few months it was on its way again, this time to Batum and the Caucasus which were in the grip of the Bolshevik revolution. After some months in Georgia the Battalion moved to Samsun on the Black Sea coast, midway between Batum and Constantinople, but after a stay of three months in Samsun they were moved to Constantinople. This was to be the Battalion's last stop before embarking on 31 October, 1919 for India. On arrival at Abbottabad it was discovered that the 1st Battalion had returned from its travels only on the previous day and, not surprisingly, there was every excuse for a party!

The 1st Battalion had returned from north-west Persia where it had been serving since September, 1918. The situation around the Caspian Sea at that time was not unlike the situation there today, after the break-up of the Soviet Empire. There were Armenians fighting Russians, both White and Red; Turks fighting Persians and Persians fighting Persians in the normal course of their tribal affairs. One tribe, the Jangalis, were particularly obstreperous and had to be forcibly suppressed.

The 1st Battalion was sent to Mesopotamia in February, 1917, but was not involved in the fighting, other than against the numerous Arab marauders. The Battalion was deployed to protect the long line of communication down the Tigris. This was dull work but essential, given the lawlessness of the tribes. In September, 1918, the Battalion was ordered to proceed to Persia, part of the way by train and the rest by march route. Detraining at Ruz, the Battalion marched 589 miles to Enzeli in 43 days, the longest stage being 23 miles in one day.

It was after the arrival in Enzeli that Subedar-Major Gambirsing Pun complained of a loss of power in his legs. He had refused to give in during the march but he was now becoming paralysed. This was attributed to the severe head wound he had received at Gallipoli in August, 1915, and on 30 April, 1919, this gallant officer had to be sent back to India. On arrival in India he was invalided out of the service and granted the honorary rank of Lieutenant. It was a cruel end to a brilliant military career and was deeply felt by every officer and soldier in the Regiment, in which he had become a living legend. Fortunately three of his sons followed him into the Regiment.

In June, 1919, the Battalion marched back to Mesopotamia, arriving at Hamadan on 26 June. After carrying out various duties on the Lines of Communication, the 1/6th left Kut for Basra by paddle steamer, embarking for Karachi on 11 November, 1919, one year after the Armistice. If the second half of the war had been less exciting than the first half, the Battalion had done its best at whatever task it had been given. And what is perhaps noteworthy, given the very different circumstances of soldiering today, wherever it went it moved on its feet. It had done a great deal of marching in a very unforgiving climate.

On 5 February, 1917, the 6th Gurkha Rifles formed a third battalion. This was done chiefly by drafts from nine different battalions of the Gurkha Brigade, including Chhetris from the 9th Gurkha Rifles and Limbus and Rais from the 10th Gurkha Rifles. In September the Battalion joined the 5th Indian Infantry Brigade and by the middle of January, 1918, moved to Bannu on the North-West Frontier. There it came under the commander of the Bannu Independent Brigade who was Brigadier General the Hon. C. G. Bruce, who had commanded the 1/6th with such distinction at Gallipoli. There was a great deal to do because the tribes were restless, despite the optimism of the Chief Commissioner of the North-West Frontier Province, Sir George Roos-Keppel, who reported to the Viceroy in January, 1919, that 'Everything on the frontier is so extraordinarily peaceful that it is safe to prophesy a quiet summer'. This was not to be.

Throughout the war relations with Afghanistan had been

good. This had been largely due to the sensible neutrality of the Amir, Habibullah Khan, but unfortunately he was assassinated on the night of 20 February, 1919. In the palace revolution which followed his third son, Amanullah Khan, seized power. His first act was to proclaim Afghanistan's complete independence, an action which the Government of India was slow to recognize. Amanullah's response was to send his troops across the border on 3 May, 1919, and the Third Afghan War began. As might have been expected, the Pathan tribes rose in order to make hay while the sun shone, with the predictable result that the Frontier Militias, on whom the keeping of the peace largely rested, decided in many instances to throw in their lot with their compatriots. The Khyber Rifles, for example, deserted en masse and the Waziristan Militias were similarly disaffected. From Wana to Malakand the tribes were out, while the Afghan Army, under General Nadir Khan, was advancing on Spinwan.

When it was decided to withdraw outlying detachments, 3/6th GR found themselves involved in providing cover for the withdrawing detachments and reassurance for those Militia posts which stood firm. This involved a great deal of marching in difficult country and in great heat. There was a great deal of sniping as the tribal *lashkars* gathered to harass the mobile columns, in one of which actions the Battalion had two men killed and two wounded. The tribes caused a great deal more trouble than the Afghans, who signed an armistice on 3 June, 1919, and then withdrew. Meanwhile the Wazirs, Mahsuds and Mohmands continued in the field.

This was Frontier, or Mountain, warfare of a kind which became familiar to generations of British, Indian and Gurkha troops. It developed its own tactics, amended from time to time as light tanks and aircraft became involved, but the basic rule of always commanding the high ground was forgotten only at the expense of a bloody reverse at the hands of the tribesmen. The Gurkhas, hillmen born and bred, shone to particular advantage on the Frontier and by the time the 3/6th moved to Peshawar on 9 October, 1919, it was a well-trained battalion.

However the Indian Army was fast being demobilized after the war and the axe was swift to fall on war-raised battalions.

On 16 September, 1920, orders for disbandment were received and by 1 February, 1921, the 3rd Battalion had ceased to exist. All those who had formed part of it during its brief existence could pride themselves on the fact that they had, in every way, lived up to the high reputation earned by the 6th Gurkha Rifles in the Great War of 1914–1918. They also added 'Afghanistan 1919' to the Battle Honours awarded to the Regiment.

CHAPTER THREE

Between The Wars

IT HAS been claimed that the 1920s and 1930s were the 6th Gurkhas' 'golden era'. Many other regiments, British and Indian, might well claim the same. It was said by some, not always in jest, that now the war was over it would be possible to get down to proper soldiering again. In the Indian Army there was, fortunately, always the North-West Frontier to keep officers and soldiers up to scratch. The 6th were fortunate in having acquired a very high reputation at Gallipoli. They were also fortunate in obtaining some very high-quality British officers to fill the places of those who had fallen in battle, or who had retired after the war. Four of them – Slim, Scott, Bruce and Cowan – were to become generals in the next contest.

The 6th Gurkha Rifles were not a pretentious regiment and they took their profession very seriously. Whatever they undertook had to be done well. There was a procedure for everything, even for entertainment in the Officers' Mess, as recorded in the Spring, 1989, issue of the *Regimental Association Journal*:

'It was true that the 6th had a prescribed way of doing things. Whether it was pitching a tented camp or organizing a formal dinner in the mess there would be a procedure, a *kaida*, a sensible and practical way of doing it, which was known to all and applied consistently on each occasion. To be sure, if things were to be done well it required a degree of subordination of personal idiosyncrasies in favour of the greater good of the group.'

The 6th were lucky in their regimental centre, Abbottabad, which was not as remote as some of the other Gurkha regimental centres and which they shared with the 5th Royal Gurkha Rifles F.F. and the 13th Frontier Force Rifles, introducing the competition that was lacking in single regiment centres. Abbottabad was a typical Indian cantonment, presenting a marked contrast in orderliness and cleanliness to the hurly-burly of the ordinary Indian town. The roads ran straight between the regimental lines and could only have been planned by the Sappers & Miners. Carefully nurtured trees provided shade. There were well-watered playing fields for every kind of game, not omitting, of course, a polo ground and a golf course. There was a Mall and Clubs for both the British and Gurkha officers, with roads named after such distinguished Indian Army worthies as Lord Roberts.* There were parade grounds, *manèges* for the more horsily inclined, bungalows for officers and the regiment's families, a cinema, St Luke's Church, a *masjid* for the Mahommedans, a *gurdwara* for the Sikhs, a temple or two for the Hindus and, inevitably, a small, or *sadar* bazaar where soldiers and their families could do their shopping. It was a self-contained community, sufficiently high in the Hills to escape the worst of the hot weather on the plains, but not so high as to be unpleasantly cold in midwinter. In fact Abbottabad was considered to be the pick of the frontier stations.

It has to be remembered, however, in the changed circumstances of today that the Indian cantonment was essentially a British creation. It did not necessarily fit into the scheme of things for the ordinary Indian or Gurkha. But in the 1920s and 1930s, although we now know that their days as rulers were numbered, it was still 'British India'. The 'Indianization' of a few cavalry regiments and infantry battalions was only just getting under way in the teeth of opposition from more than a few British officers. Social mixing between British and Indians had still a long way to go and, where the British were concerned,

---

* The Army of independent India has not chosen to change these names, e.g., Roberts Road or Rawlinson Avenue.

any suggestion that the end of the 1940s would see the British out of India would have been laughed to scorn.

Outside the great cities of Calcutta, Bombay and Madras, and manufacturing centres like Cawnpore, the British presence was almost entirely an official one and strictly hierarchical, with the Viceroy at the apex of the social pyramid. There was an official order of precedence and everyone knew their place in it. Beginning with the Indian Civil Service (ICS) – 'The Heaven-born' – it extended through the Armed Services to include the Doctors, Parsons, Forests, PWD, Railways, Canals etc., and society was quick to take offence if anyone infringed rules of etiquette which had almost the sanctity of Holy Writ.

The Army had its own pecking order. The British or King's or Royal regiments, Horse, Foot and Guns, had always claimed precedence over Indian ones. This dated back to the Honourable East India Company's regiments whose officers bitterly resented the fact. They felt, as professionals, that they were made subordinate to amateurs, which was sometimes the case. We are told that in 1823 Cawnpore society was sadly divided on account of a wife of a Colonel in a 'native' regiment. 'The lady had not been handed in to supper by a gentlemen of sufficient rank and the Company's officers were quick to take her side.'* A century later there was much less of this nonsense but it did still exist.

In the Indian Army there was, as in the British Army, a similar pecking order, cavalry regiments liking to think they headed the list, albeit hotly disputed by the infantry. The Gurkha Brigade, by virtue of its recruitment, stood somewhat apart from the rest of the Line but, as John Masters has made plain in his *Bugles and a Tiger*, as repeated earlier (p.14), while all Gurkha regiments were equal, some were more equal than the others. Certainly the 6th Gurkhas had no reason to fear comparison with any of their sister regiments.

The great virtue of the Indian Army was, and still is, that every man is a volunteer. It is a 'Matter of Honour' to bear arms. The warrior stands high in the Hindu caste system and is

* *British Social Life in India* by Dennis Kincaid (Routledge, 1938) p. 182.

similarly regarded in Islam. Men were not driven to enlist by unemployment, trouble with the law or sheer inability to fit in with their home environment. Unlike in the British Army in the Victorian era, when 'to go for a soldier' could bring social disgrace on a family, the reverse was true in India and particularly so with the Gurkhas. The soldier was honoured and respected in his village, both while serving and when on pension. Competition to join was intense, even when the army totalled more than two million, as it did in 1945.

There have been many attempts at describing the typical Gurkha rifleman but perhaps John Masters gets closest to it when he writes:

'Though there are, of course, exceptions, the distinguishing marks of the Gurkha are usually a Mongolian appearance, short stature, a merry disposition, and an indefinable quality that is hard to pin down with one word. Straightness, honesty, naturalness, loyalty, courage – all these are near it, but none is quite right, for the quality embraces all these. In a Gurkha regiment nothing was ever stolen, whether a pocket knife, a watch, or a thousand rupees. Desertions were unheard of, although once the men had gone on furlough to their homes in Nepal they were quite inaccessible to us. There was no intrigue, no apple-polishing, and no servility.'*

Masters goes on to explain that the Gurkha code, 'I will keep faith', best describes the Gurkha and he cites numerous examples of how the ordinary Gurkha rifleman puts this code into practice. We could do with some of it in this nation today.

For the greater part of the Indian Army's history under the British every regiment and battalion was authorized to employ a certain number of 'Followers' or 'Enrolled Non-Combatants', paid from the public purse and pensionable on retirement. In the 6th Gurkhas they included cooks (*babarchis*), water-carriers (*bhistis*), sweepers (*mehtars*), armourers (*mistris*) and clerks (*babus*). Many of the clerks were non-combatants, some were ex-soldiers or line-boys. Some were Mohammedans, others

* *Bugles and a Tiger* by John Masters (Michael Joseph, 1956) p. 92.

Hindus. The Head Clerk in 1/6th GR for many years, was Munshi Mir Ahmed who rose to the rank of Subedar and was the last man to be wounded during the evacuation of Gallipoli. Perhaps the most important of the 'Followers' was the *Chowdry*, or Contractor, who ran the regimental bazaar and served as banker for those who required 'petty cash'. The 'Followers' as a group came under the Bom Police or Provost Havildar and his staff.

In 1940 the term 'Follower' was abolished and their duties were performed by fully enlisted men. *Bhistis* disappeared and all cooks and sweepers were enlisted. British officers' bearers became orderlies. One of the last to go was the CO's chauffeur, Jalal-U-Din, 'who became the local transport contractor . . . He led the local football team . . . It was amusing to see the smaller but determined Gurkhas trying to charge him off the ball, but to no effect – he never minded! He was also a good tennis player and in one year, in partnership with the Commanding Officer's daughter, won the Provincial Mixed Doubles. When in 1947 the last party of the 5th and 6th Gurkha Rifles left Abbottabad . . . it fell to Jalal-U-Din to head the farewell as the men left under the decorated arches, as in former days, they had returned from active service.'

Although the ordinary Gurkha rifleman's background was both simple and unsophisticated, he had all the countryman's ability to judge men, the more particularly where his British officers were concerned. In those days he would not usually respond to an order given in English until first having it confirmed by a trusted superior. A fluency in Gurkhali and Urdu was essential before a young officer would be accepted. We are told that once accepted he was transformed from an unacknowledged nonentity into the Officer Commanding or the OC *sahib*. He would then be closely scrutinized by the riflemen. His speech mannerisms, his gait and posture would all be closely noticed and copied in the privacy of the barrack-room. He would be given a nickname, not always a complimentary one, but it would at least mean that he had been accepted into the 'family'. His men would follow him and, if need be, die for him, as so many did.

In an Indian or Gurkha battalion subalterns had twice or more the responsibility of a contemporary in a British unit. During the leave season he might find himself commanding two companies, as well as understudying the adjutant or quartermaster. His day would begin with parade around 6 a.m. and continue outdoors until 9 or 10 a.m. when a leisurely breakfast would follow. There would follow three or four more hours of outdoor work or administrative duties, before *tiffin* (lunch). In the late afternoon there would be games – football, hockey or volleyball – in which he would be expected to participate with his men, however indifferent he might be at any one of them. Once or twice a week he might sneak off to play polo, but only with the adjutant's permission.

Dinner was a formal affair and mess kit was worn. On Sundays 'black tie' was worn but never ordinary suits. On Guest Nights (or *burra khana*) the band would play, both military and pipes and drums. The 6th Gurkhas had both pipes and drums and a military band, maintained very largely by subscription by the officers, and when playing on outside occasions it was always 'By kind permission of the Commanding Officer and the Officers'. The military band was first formed in 1905 and the Pipes and Drums then in existence were disbanded. However, the Pipes and Drums were reformed in 1924, largely owing to the enthusiasm of Captain (later General) 'Punch' Cowan. The Band was based on Abbottabad but was disbanded when the Regiment moved to Malaya after the war, only the Pipes and Drums remaining. In 1959 a new regimental march, 'Queen Elizabeth's Own', was taken into use, usually preceded by 'Hielan' Laddie' and 'All the Blue Bonnets are Over the Border'. The composer of 'Queen Elizabeth's Own' was Major I. C. Brebner of the Regiment.

For the outsider military bands are hard to justify and their music may be anathema, but there surely cannot be any soldier whose heart is not uplifted when the band strikes up his regimental march. It is, therefore, very sad that individual regimental bands are to be abolished and 'large' or 'corps' bands substituted.. They will not be the same and it is unfortunate that for many years past regimental bands have been the targets for Treasury economies. When this author was serving in the Ministry of Defence in 1970 the file on military bands and the argument for and against their retention was more than 6 inches thick!

Although it seems to have become the fashion nowadays to write critically about the life of the ordinary British Officer in India between the two world wars, or depict it with many snide remarks in films like *Gandhi* or *The Jewel in the Crown*, it was in fact a very active and healthy life and there was not a single British officer worth his salt who was not devoted to the soldiers he commanded. There was nothing patronizing about this. It was the least that was expected of them from the Gurkha riflemen they had the honour to command.

If it may be assumed from the foregoing that life in the Indian Army during the inter-war years was as much play as work, it would be entirely untrue. The frequent tours of duty on the North-West Frontier where real bullets flew would soon put an end to that. Between 1920 and 1939 the 1/6th had two tours in Waziristan and the Kurram, suffering several casualties and receiving three 'immediate awards'; likewise the 2nd Battalion, which arrived in Waziristan in October, 1920, for three tough years during which it suffered several casualties. It was back again in 1936 owing to the activities of the Faqir of Ipi, when the battalion was joined by the 1/6th. Operations continued until April, 1939, when the 2/6th finally returned to Abbottabad.

It may be true that the Indian Army between the two world wars was still more or less armed and equipped as the 1/6th Gurkhas had been when they landed at Gallipoli 25 years previously, but they were probably better trained than most of the regiments in the British Army. The North-West Frontier of India was a hard school in the teaching of most of the military virtues and those who graduated from it, both British and Gurkha, had no need to fear comparison with any other army in the world. They were, in fact, 'top of the class', although it has to be admitted that expertise in mountain warfare did not relate very closely to operations in the jungle!

Service in India was a virtual paradise for the young officer with an interest in field sports but a limited purse. There was

7. *"The Regiment left Assam on 15 September, 1899, after a stay of 77 years."* (p.12) The tomb stone of Major H.W. Priestley at Shillong.

8. *"Cholera broke out on the river steamer which was conveying the Regiment down the Brahmaputra. There were 53 deaths in this epidemic."* (p.13) Kamakhya Temple in Gauhati, where soldiers of the 42nd Gurkha Light Infantry performed *puja* (worship) in 1899, after which the cholera passed.

9. *"The Regiment was particularly proud of the Officers' Mess in Abbottabad which was built in 1911 and continuously embellished, both inside and outside, over the years."* (p.42) The Mess today, now immaculately kept by The Punjab Irregular Frontier Force Regiment ('The Piffers').

10. *"At the top we met the Turks: Le Marchand was down, a bayonet through the heart. I got one through the leg, and then, for about ten minutes, we fought hand to hand, we bit and fisted, and used rifles and pistols as clubs; blood was flying about like spray from a hairbrush bottle."* Major C.J.L. Allanson (p.24). 'Sari Bair' by Terence Cuneo, commissioned by the 1st Battalion in 1980.

11. *"Every British officer had been killed or wounded, the only exception being the Medical Officer, Captain E.S. Phipson, IMS ... Subedar-Major Gambarsing Pun, IOM, was now in command, but having no understanding of English, he was dependent on the doctor to interpret for him."* (p.24) The medals of Colonel E.S. Phipson, CIE, DSO, OStJ, IMS and Subedar Major Gambirsing Pun, MC, OBI, IOM.

excellent shooting to be had almost on the doorstep, black partridge and chikhor for the most part, and usually with the enthusiastic support of the *kisans* (villagers). Fishing for mahseer, a splendid game fish, was to be had in the rivers without having to pay Spey prices and there were trout in Kashmir, in easy reach of Abbottabad. When it came to horses there was polo at a tenth of the cost that it would be at home, and pigsticking for the more venturesome and, of course, there was big-game shooting. It was a young man's world to be lived in the most splendid of scenery and, in the 6th Gurkhas, there was the added incentive of mountaineering, in which the lead had been given by Brigadier General, the Hon. C. G. Bruce. His cousin, J. G. Bruce, who commanded the 2/6th and took part in the Everest expeditions in 1924, later became a Major General. It is, of course, true that these opportunities applied to the British Service as well as the Indian Army, but in the case of the latter there was the added advantage of a knowledge of the language, by no means universal in the British regiments, which made life that much the more interesting.

In 1926 the Regiment was honoured by the appointment of Field Marshal Sir William Birdwood (later Field Marshal Lord Birdwood) as the Colonel of the Regiment. He was at the time Commander-in-Chief, India, but had commanded the ANZAC Corps at Gallipoli when the Regiment's conduct at Sari Bair won for it undying glory. The Field Marshal's nephew, Captain C. W. B. Birdwood, a most promising officer, had been killed when serving with the 1/6th at Gallipoli. The Field Marshal, throughout his Colonelcy, took the closest interest in the Regiment although himself a cavalryman (11th Bengal Lancers and later Probyn's Horse). In 1930 the 2nd Battalion was selected to provide the guards on the Viceroy's and Commander-in-Chief's residences in Simla, then India's summer capital. The combined pipe bands of both Battalions accompanied the escort which was greatly praised for its discipline and smartness. This is hardly surprising since it was commanded by Captain (later Brigadier) J. K. Jones, considered by Field Marshal Slim, no mean judge himself, to be the pattern of the ideal regimental officer.

The Gurkha Brigade, unlike the rest of the Indian Infantry, did not have training battalions where the recruits were trained and time-expired soldiers were discharged. This placed a heavy burden on the active battalions and was not remedied until 1940 when the depots of the 1st and 2nd Battalions were combined to form the Regimental Centre, 6th Gurkha Rifles, at Abbottabad. An account of the Centre will follow later in this narrative; here it is sufficient to pay tribute to Colonels Hugh Walsh and Norman Eustace, successively Commandants of the Centre, for the splendid record of the Centre once established.

The Regiment was particularly proud of the Officers' Mess in Abbottabad which was built in 1911 and continuously embellished, both inside and outside, over the years. It has been said in the British and Indian Armies that the core of a regiment's tradition is to be found in the officers' mess, and that was certainly the case in the 6th Gurkha Rifles. Trophies of war or of *shikar* provided the principal decoration, together with the gleaming silver and pictures of the Regiment in action. It was a masculine environment into which the opposite sex ventured only on invitation, some regiments being stuffier about this than others. Junior officers were expected to behave respectfully to their seniors, except perhaps on Guest Nights when somewhat different rules obtained. General Sir John Hackett probably put it best when he wrote:

> 'The profession of arms is an essential social institution offering an orderly way of life, set a little apart, not without elegance.'*

If that be the test it can be said that the officers of the 6th Gurkha Rifles, both British and Gurkha, and in peace as in war, passed it with flying colours.

Talking of Abbottabad in pre-war days General Jim Robertson, who joined the 1/6th in 1931, has said the 5th and 6th Gurkhas got on uncommonly well, probably better than any two other regiments in the Gurkha Brigade. There was plenty

* *The Profession of Arms* by General Sir John Hackett (Sidgwick & Jackson, 1983) p. 214.

of rivalry on the games field of course but it was all very friendly. However, he recalls being taken to task by one of his senior officers because he had accepted to dine in the 5th Gurkhas' officers' mess. Apparently it was not 'done' for an officer in the 1/6th to dine with the 5th. He does not remember the reason for this – and in any case he ignored it!

CHAPTER FOUR

The 1/6th and 4/6th in Burma

IT is well-nigh impossible to write a continuous narrative to cover the Regiment's remarkable record during the Second World War. It fought in all the main theatres in which the British Army was engaged, France and Germany excepted. Two of its battalions in Burma fought their way from north to south, another won lasting renown while serving in Wingate's 'Chindits', and another fought its way up Italy's Adriatic Coast, scaling mountains and crossing river after river until it triumphantly crossed the Po and swept on to end five years of war outside Trieste. On the side there were campaigns in Waziristan and Persia, the tedium of hot weather service in Iraq, the long and hot drives across the desert to Palestine and Egypt and then back again to the Lebanon and the Syria/Iraq border.

Few regiments could lay claim to such a breadth of experience of war in so many different elements – the mountains, the jungle, the desert, the house-to-house fighting in village after village and town after town up the length of Italy. In every kind of climate from the blistering heat of the Iraq desert to the freezing heights of the Apennines, and the monsoon-drenched and humid Burmese jungles. The Gurkha soldier, fortified by his pride in Regiment and in his country, Nepal, and secured by his loyalty to his officers, British and Gurkha, took it all in his stride and in so doing proved that he is, without doubt, in the words of Field Marshal Lord Slim, 'the ideal infantryman'.

In this chapter there will be told the story of the 1st and 4th Battalions because together they served in the 19th Indian

Division – the 'Dagger' Division under Major-General 'Pete' Rees – which recaptured Mandalay on 20 March, 1945, after very tough fighting. The story of the 3rd Battalion serving with the 'Chindits' will be told in the following chapter; it is a remarkable one, including the winning of two Victoria Crosses in a single action, an outstanding achievement; and finally, the 2nd Battalion's hard slog up Italy which cost 560 casualties before the Germans threw in the towel. All four Battalions added lustre to the Regiment's record and all who served in them, both British and Gurkha, could take pride in the fact that the Regiment was second to none in the British and Indian Armies.

When war was declared on Germany on 3 September, 1939, the 1st Battalion was in the Malakand on the Frontier and the 2nd Battalion was in Abbottabad. The 3rd and 4th Battalions did not exist.* It took a very long time for the war to make much impact in India, apart of course for the 4th and 5th Indian Divisions sent early to the Middle East. For the rest, British society seemed to continue much as before, although admittedly the military tempo quickened as the Indian Army began to expand. However, those of us who survived the long retreat through Burma in 1942 were surprised to find so little changed on our arrival in India, as well as a singular unawareness as to what was happening beyond India's borders. The Japanese were to change all that.

To deal first with the Indian Army's expansion, one of the most remarkable events in British-Indian history. On the outbreak of war the Indian Army was about 183,000 strong, led by 2,978 British and 528 Indian officers. Five years later it totalled 2,250,000 with 37,187 British and 13,355 Indian officers, more than a ten-fold expansion. When war began it differed little

---

* The 3/6th Gurkha Rifles were raised in Abbottabad in October, 1940. The 4/6th Gurkha Rifles were raised in March, 1941. The 3/6th ceased to be part of the Regiment in December, 1947, and became the 5th battalion of the 5th Gurkha Rifles, FF, in the army of independent India. The 4th Battalion was finally disbanded in February, 1947, in Abbottabad. The 1st and 2nd Battalions were transferred to the British Army on 8 August, 1947.

from the army which had fought in the First World War. It consisted of horsed cavalry, unmechanized infantry and horsed artillery. In all India there were only eight anti-aircraft guns and there were no anti-tank guns. With the exception of a few motor transport companies in the Royal Indian Army Service Corps, all unit transport depended on mules, camels and horses.* A plan for modernization and mechanization had been agreed but it was to be a long drawn-out business. Meanwhile a battalion of Indian/Gurkha infantry consisted of 12 King's Commissioned Officers and 17 Viceroy's Commissioned Officers,† and 662 rank and file. It was a very old-fashioned army but an army of high morale.

It is astonishing that, given the difficulties and the requirement to send overseas a large number of troops, between May and December, 1940, the Indian Army increased in strength by 165,000. It was an expansion which was to gather speed year after year while the war continued. In the case of the Gurkhas' expansion, this was dependent on the acquiescence of the Government of Nepal which had always kept a close control on the recruitment of Gurkhas; it had, after all, its own Nepalese Army to keep up to strength.‡ But in 1940–41, as a result of changes in the recruiting organization, larger numbers of recruits were obtained, the Regiment's share by the end of the war amounting to 10,397 recruits. The recruiters were paid pensioners and ex-soldiers. Regimental recruiting parties were no longer sent to Nepal each year.

The 1st Battalion spent the first six months of the Second World War at the Malakand, one of the better of the North-

---

* When the author joined the 2nd Battalion of the Duke of Wellington's Regiment in Multan on 1 January, 1938, the only motor transport in the Battalion was the Commanding Officer's staff car. Hardly any of the officers owned a car. Almost his first purchase was a pony and trap!

† Subordinate officers, viz. 2ic of companies and platoon commanders, in the pre-1947 Indian Army, held the Viceroy's, not the King's Commission. After 1948 in the British Brigade of Gurkhas they became King's Gurkha Officers (KGOs), now Queen's Gurkha Officers (QGOs).

‡ Before the war the Nepalese Army recruited mainly high-caste Gurkhas such as Chhetris, only recruited in the 9th Gurkha Rifles of the Gurkha Brigade of the Indian Army.

West Frontier garrisons, where normal peacetime conditions prevailed. There was plenty of shooting, fishing and polo, and mess kit was still worn on band nights in mess, as were swords and medals when ordered on parade. 'One can hardly imagine there is a war on,' was a common enough comment in India at that time. There was, however, a constant drift away of officers, British and Gurkha, as well as Gurkha NCOs, as the Indian military machine creaked slowly into action. New formation headquarters had to be staffed, new training establishments organized, and soon there would be additional battalions to be raised. In April, 1940, the 1st Battalion changed over with the 2nd Battalion and returned to Abbotabad for what were to prove the last few months of peacetime soldiering.

For some years past the frontier tribes had been kept in a state of excitement by the Faqir of Ipi, a fanatical Moslem cleric who has been described as the best 'trainer' the Indian Army has ever had. Several operations were conducted against him but he always came back for more. Up to his old tricks again in the summer of 1940, the 1st Battalion found itself back in Waziristan in September, where it was to remain until the following April. This was not an easy time. The Battalion was only about 400 strong and only the Commanding Officer had had more than three years' service. Emergency Commissioned Officers began arriving in a steady stream but obviously they required time not only to learn their military duties but also to learn the languages, both Urdu and Gurkhali. On the Battalion's return from the Frontier in April, 1941, it moved to Kakul, the cantonment at Abbottabad being crammed full with recruits being trained for the 5th and 6th Gurkha Rifles. Even so the Battalion was back again on the Frontier in June, the cause the renewed activities of the Faqir of Ipi, this time in the Tochi valley where a combination of great heat, sand-fly fever and a plague of wasps did not affect the Gurkha's cheerful character. It was nevertheless a welcome return to Kakul in September, only three months before the Japanese attack on Pearl Harbor. From then onwards the war came steadily closer to India, although the tempo in India itself took some time to quicken.

On 4 February, 1942, the 1st Battalion marched out from

Abbottabad, as it happened never to return after a connection of 42 years. It moved to Jhansi to join the 64th Indian Infantry Brigade, part of the 19th Indian Division which was then forming. By then the news was almost universally bad. Malaya was about to fall and Burma's time was soon to run out. All the talk was of an imminent Japanese onslaught on India. In November, 1941, the 4th Battalion, raised only in the preceding March, had joined the 62nd Indian Infantry Brigade, also part of the 19th Indian Division. Together the 1st and 4th Battalions were to play a prominent part in the reconquest of Burma, although at the time they joined the 19th 'Dagger' Division* such a prospect must have seemed ridiculously remote. For the immediate future their principal task was to halt and throw back any Japanese attempt to secure a lodgement on the coast of Madras.

Both Battalions were around 1,000 strong with as many as 20 junior British officers, as the OCTUs at Mhow and Bangalore and the IMA at Dehra Dun churned out the Emergency Commissioned Officers. At long last equipment was improving with the issue of 3″ mortars, tracked carriers, trucks and the replacement of the Vickers-Berthier LMG by the Bren. For a period there were even 3.7″ howitzers on the establishment but these were withdrawn early in 1943. The arrival of the battered remnants of the Burma Army in Manipur in May, 1942, had set the tocsin ringing throughout India, softly at first but growing louder as each month passed. At long last there was an enemy at India's gates and the 6th Gurkha Rifles were training hard to repel the attack when it came.

Since there was at first only 19th Division, to be joined later by 23rd Division, to defend the long coastline of the Madras Presidency, to begin with it was more a matter of hope than expectation, with a Japanese battle fleet cruising in the Bay of

---

* Major General J. G. Smyth, VC, was originally appointed to be GOC 19 Indian Division. The divisional emblem of a 'Dagger' was designed by Mrs Smyth. However, General Smyth was switched to command 17 Indian Division, then deploying in Burma, and in due course Major General T. W. Rees of the Rajputana Rifles became the GOC. It was under his dynamic command that the 19th 'Dagger' Division achieved greatness.

Bengal and not a fighter plane nearer than Ceylon. Towards the end of 1942, however, there came a significant change. The emphasis moved from defence to attack, which inevitably meant operations in the jungle if Burma was to be reconquered. Much of the motor transport disappeared to be replaced by that familiar friend of the Frontier, the mule, bolstered by the jeep, a war-winning invention if ever there was one. From January, 1943, onwards the aim was to make the 6th Gurkha Rifles masters of the jungle, of which there was more than enough in southern India in which to train. With the arrival of General Rees as GOC the tempo of training increased still further, and there can have been few better trained battalions in Fourteenth Army than the 1/6th and 4/6th Gurkha Rifles when they arrived in Manipur in October, 1944, after Slim's successful defeat of General Renya Mutaguchi's Fifteenth Japanese Army's disastrous attempt to 'march on Delhi'.

As 1944 drew to a close General Slim's Fourteenth Army was poised to reconquer Burma, but not from the direction originally planned by Headquarters South-East Asia Command at Kandy in Ceylon. It had been thought that an amphibious landing on the Burma coast would be the quickest way to Rangoon, cutting off the Japanese formations in north Burma, but the recall of Landing Craft required for the campaign in North-West Europe made this impossible. Slim therefore planned a battle of envelopment on the North Burma plain, the left-hand pincer aimed at Mandalay, and the right at Meiktila, 50 miles to the south, the hub of the Japanese communications and on the road/rail route to Rangoon. Meanwhile in the north, General Stilwell's American-Chinese Northern Combat Area Command had taken Myitkyina on 3 August, 1944, and was shortly to be joined by the British 36th Division advancing south down the so-called 'Railway Corridor', so familiar to 3/6th Gurkha Rifles during Wingate's Operation THURSDAY in 1944.

In November, 1944, the brigades of 19th Division crossed the River Chindwin and began the advance to the Irrawaddy. The troops were on an all-pack basis and were marching between ten and twenty miles a day as they followed up the fast-retreating

Japanese. All supply was by air. Urged on by General Rees, a general who led from the front, on 16 December a patrol of the Royal Scots from 36th Division was encountered. It was the first contact 36th Division had had with other allied troops in six months' advance down the 'Railway Corridor'. General Slim was justifiably pleased with the rapid advance of 19th Division and is on record for telling some incredulous American staff officers that 'The Regiment's share in that march was historic'; it was his old Battalion which was setting the pace.

The 1st Battalion's advance to the Irrawaddy was chiefly hard slogging, almost entirely on foot, although on 1 December, 1944, it received its jeeps. However, this entailed improving the track to enable the jeeps to get forward, added to which Dropping Zones had to be cleared for the airdrop of supplies. Although the Japanese had taken a terrible beating at Manipur and Kohima, they still had a lot of fight left in them, as the Battalion was to discover on 4 January, 1945, when it had its first encounter with the Japanese rearguards. It cost the Battalion eight killed and eleven wounded. On 16 January the Battalion reached the Irrawaddy at Kyaukmyaung, having marched around 400 miles since crossing the Chindwin. At this point the river is 800 yards wide and 64th Brigade was to establish a bridgehead across the river. 62nd Brigade, with the 4th Battalion, was in reserve to protect Shwebo.

It might be thought from some acounts of the war in Burma that the Fourteenth Army's triumphant advance on Mandalay was unimpeded. In fact the reverse was true. The Japanese fought desperately to hold Mandalay and although Kyauk-myaung was only 45 miles north of Mandalay, from the moment the crossing of the Irrawaddy was made on 17 January there was very hard fighting, first to defeat Japanese counter-attacks against the bridgehead and then to fight their way south against suicidal Japanese opposition. It was only on 26 February that the 19th Division broke out of the bridgehead and it was not until 8 March that the pagodas crowning Mandalay Hill, outside the city, could be seen through the early morning mist, and there was still stiff fighting ahead.

Sadly, among the casualties suffered by the Battalion was that

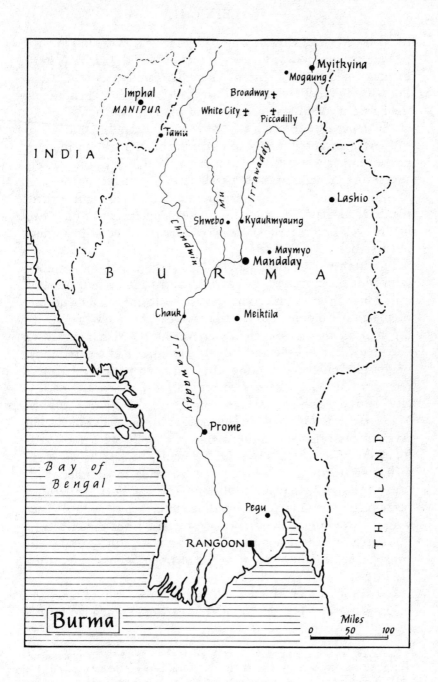

Myitkyina

Mogaung

Broadway ✝

Imphal
MANIPUR

White City ✝
Piccadilly ✝

Tamú

INDIA

Lashio

Chindwin

Mu

Irrawaddy

Shwebo • Kyaukmyaung

B U R M A

Maymyo

Mandalay

Chauk

Meiktila

Irrawaddy

Prome

Bay of
Bengal

THAILAND

Pegu

RANGOON ■

Burma

Miles

0   50   100

of Major Michael Cowan who had joined the Battalion in 1940 in Waziristan. He was the son of one of the 6th Gurkha's most distinguished officers, Major General D. Tennant Cowan, better known as 'Punch', who was at the time successfully conducting the battle at Meiktila in command of the 17th Indian Division.

The Japanese had originally intended to defend Mandalay 'to the last man and the last round' which, in Japanese military parlance, meant just that – no more and no less. But it was the success of General Messervy's IV Corps in defeating them at Meiktila that led to a change of mind. With Meiktila in British hands Mandalay was no longer worth defending, which was just as well because Mandalay would have proved a very tough nut to crack.

Firstly there was Mandalay Hill, 700 feet high, honeycombed with tunnels and passages, covered with pagodas and nearly a mile long. Even in peacetime the ascent to the summit up one of the four canopied stone stairways caught one's breath. By the time of the 1st Battalion's arrival on 10 March the 4/4th Gurkha Rifles and the 2nd Royal Berkshires had secured most of the hill but fierce fighting still continued with the Japanese remnants. Secondly there was Fort Dufferin, the former palace-city of the Kings of Ava, renamed for the Viceroy* when Mandalay was captured in January, 1886; he also added 'and Ava' to his title. Square in layout, the walls are 2,500 yards long, thirty feet high and four feet wide, backed by an earth wall and surrounded by a forty-yard wide moat filled with water. The city itself lay south and west of Fort Dufferin, a maze of brick and concrete buildings interspersed with flimsier wooden dwellings. Mandalay had suffered from the effects of Japanese and Allied bombing but there were still several well-constructed buildings to serve as strongpoints during street fighting.

It was on 10 March that the Battalion moved up to take part in the battle for Fort Dufferin. The Japanese defended fanati-

---

* The Marquess of Dufferin & Ava, Viceroy 1884–88; by a strange coincidence the 4th Marquess was killed in an ambush between Mandalay and Ava on 23 March, 1945, when serving with a Field Broadcasting Unit.

cally against attempts to scale the walls as in some medieval siege. The walls proved resistant to modern artillery and aerial bombing did little other than to burn wooden-walled houses within the Fort. A fullscale attack was planned for 24 March and the 1st Battalion was withdrawn to make the necessary preparations. It was relieved in the front line by the 4th Battalion, brought down from Maymyo for the purpose. Fortunately, however, the attack never took place, the Japanese pulling out during the night of 19/20 March. General Slim arrived on 21 March for the Union Jack to be hoisted once again over Fort Dufferin. After the parade General Slim visited his old Battalion and arranged for two Japanese 70-mm guns captured by the 1st Battalion to be flown to the Regimental centre at Abbottabad.

Although the war was far from over, the capture of Mandalay and the Japanese defeat at Meiktila marked a watershed in the 1944–45 Burma campaign. This is therefore the moment to consider how the 4th Battalion had fared since it crossed the Chindwin between 12 and 18 November, 1944, until it arrived to relieve the 1st Battalion outside Mandalay on 17 March, 1945. It served throughout in the 62nd Infantry Brigade together with the 2nd Welch Regiment and the 3/6th Rajputana Rifles. The Brigade's role initially was a long-range penetration one, following up the retreating Japanese and covering the flank of 64th Infantry Brigade on the left. The 98th Infantry Brigade, the other brigade in the 19th Division, came up eventually on the right of 62nd Brigade once they had broken out of the jungle and were within reach of Shwebo. It was taken on 5 January, 1945.

The 4th Battalion, during the advance to Shwebo, had had several brushes with the Japanese rearguards and on 8 January was ordered to secure the village of Kabwet on the west bank of the Irrawaddy, about 15 miles north of Kyaukmyaung where 19th Division was to secure a bridgehead on the east bank of the river. Local villagers had reported Kabwet as empty of enemy but it was, in fact, strongly held. The Battalion was involved in hand-to-hand fighting, repelling with kukri and bayonet a 'Banzai' charge led by three Japanese officers brandishing their swords, one of whom was dealt with by Naik Balbahadur Gurung, himself wounded, when the already wounded Japanese jumped into his trench. The Naik killed him with his kukri. When the Japanese returned a few days later to recapture Kabwet they found the Machine-Gun battalion of the 11th Sikhs well installed and suffered heavy losses. However, with the tenacity that was such a marked characteristic of the Japanese soldier, the remnants dug themselves in and it required a brigade attack and considerable air support to evict them.

4/6 GR crossed the Irrawaddy on 27 January, near Kyauk-myaung and, for the next few weeks, found itself involved in several hard-fought actions with the Japanese who were struggling to hold up 19th Division's advance on Mandalay, but to no avail. On 4 February it went to the assistance of the 1st Battalion which was hard pressed while returning to the bridge-head after a mission against the enemy. The 1st Battalion was covered in successfully. On 4 February the Army Commander visited the bridgehead where he was warmly received by the 4th Battalion, many of the Gurkha officers having previously served with him in the 1st Battalion before the war. It was a happy reunion.

A great many Japanese were killed as the Battalion fought its way south down the east bank of the Irrawaddy, as Mandalay drew steadily nearer. There were several casualties, the Japanese continuing to fight fiercely. 19th Division had the support of 254th Indian Tank Brigade which helped the infantry forward, although the 'going' was difficult for tanks until close to Mandalay itself.

On 5 March there came a change of direction. 62nd Brigade was to strike east across the mountains to take Maymyo, the 4th Battalion leading the way. This involved a climb of more than three thousand feet and almost freezing night temperatures. The advance was not opposed and on the night of 9 March the battalion entered Maymyo against light opposition. 62nd Brig-ade established blocks on the road to Lashio and to Mandalay, and Burma's principal hill station was now in British hands. It had been a virtually bloodless victory. There were a great many Gurkhas settled in and around Maymyo and the Battalion was therefore assured of the warmest of welcomes, which also included fresh vegetables and – luxury of luxuries – strawberries and cream!

For a brief period there was a halt to the endless marching but Mandalay was still untaken. On 16 March, 62nd Brigade was moved to Mandalay to take part in the assault that was being planned. On 17 March the Battalion was ferried forward by MT, the first time it had been lifted in the 500 miles it had marched since moving down to the Chindwin. But, as already recounted in the 1st Battalion's story, the Japanese slipped away from Mandalay and Fort Dufferin was occupied without any further fighting. The 4th Battalion then soon found itself following up the Japanese rearguards as the enemy withdrew southwards.

Although the back of the Japanese in Burma had been broken at Mandalay and Meiktila, there was still stiff fighting ahead, as well as a race to reach Rangoon before the monsoon broke in mid-May. Until the Japanese surrendered after the dropping of atomic bombs on Hiroshima and Nagasaki in August, 1945, both the 1st and 4th Battalions were chiefly involved in following up the Japanese forces withdrawing eastwards towards Thailand. There was a considerable amount of fierce fighting as the countryside turned into a swamp in the monsoon rains, and as the 28th Japanese Army, holed up in the Pegu Yomas, tried desperately to break out across the Rangoon/Toungoo highway to reach and cross the River Sittang.

The 1st Battalion ended the war at Shwegyin on the east bank of the Sittang; the 4th Battalion, after fierce fighting on the road to Mawchi, at Toungoo, where it was enjoying a well-earned rest. The 1st Battalion still had more than two years to serve in Burma. The 4th Battalion returned to India in April, 1946, and had a year still to serve before its final disbandment. It had lost, killed, in Burma five officers and 95 soldiers; 317 had been wounded and five were posted as missing.

Nearly four years of war had devastated Burma. What had been in 1940 a smiling and prosperous land had, by 1945, been turned into a desert. Bridges had been demolished, road surfaces wrecked, towns and villages burnt, railway lines torn up and, in many areas, the jungle had reclaimed the fields. Law and order had virtually vanished, providing every opportunity for the national pastime of dacoity, following closely on the two other Burmese national pastimes, cock-fighting and football. Certain areas contained more dacoits than mosquitoes, according to one Burmese civilian. Highway robbery was rife. Internal Security became the army's principal task, as the 1st Battalion was soon to discover.

With the countryside littered with abandoned arms and ammunition and completely devoid of police, it was 'open season' where dacoity was concerned. A notorious area for dacoits was around Mount Popa, a 5,000 feet extinct volcano, seventy miles east of the Irrawaddy, with a crater a mile in diameter. It lies roughly midway betwen Chauk on the Irrawaddy and Meiktila, in what was called the 'Dry Zone' in Burma, surrounded by a burningly hot and featureless plain, covered with dried-up scrub and patches of lentana. The Burmese believe Mount Popa to be the abode of *nats* (spirits) and it is holy ground. Not far away is the ruined city of Pagan, once the capital of the Kings of Ava. Local gossip has it that the crater is the home of hundreds of *Hamadryads* (King Cobras) which attack on sight.

In 1947 the 1st Battalion, then stationed in Maymyo, was sent to undertake a dacoit-sweeping operation around Mount Popa. Their camp was established in a kind of oasis that turned out to be infested with vipers and the Gurkhas had great fun chasing and killing them. Their joy was even greater when a nest of writhing vipers was discovered underneath the Commanding Officer's pillow. Various sweeps failed to disclose any dacoits but Burma Command believed the main dacoit HQ was on top of Mount Popa. At the same time Burma Command insisted that no one was to set foot on Mount Popa until all officers had received instruction in administering anti-snake bite vaccine, which was done.

The assault went in the next morning but in the interval the dacoits, warned presumably by local villagers, had flown. They had been there because the embers of a fire were still warm and the Buddhist temples had been well, and recently, used. It was

15. *"Since Gurkha soldiers were expected at that time to shave their heads, the felt hat worn double and with a stiff brim, at an angle and secured by a chin strap, was a smart headdress."* (p.16) Naik (Corporal) in Battle Order, 1939.

16. *"For a great many years operations on the North-West Frontier dominated the tactics and the thought of the Indian Army."* (p.19) Waziristan, 1931.

17. *"The North-West Frontier of India was a hard school in the teaching of most of the military virtues."* (p.40)

18. *"When war was declared on Germany on 3 September, 1939, the 1st Battalion was in the Malakand on the Frontier."* (p.45)

Rear: Lieutenants N.F.B. Shaw, N.E.V. Short, Major O.C.T. Dykes, MC, Captain J.A.R. Robertson, Major H.R.K. Gibbs, Lieutenant P.M.D. McLaughlin, Second Lieutenant A.G. Patterson.
Front: Major I.N. Macleod, Lieutenant-Colonel D. Tennant Cowan, MC, Lieutenant-Colonel H.V. Collingridge, OBE, Majors G.R. Ward, T.N. Smith.

19. *"At long last equipment was improving with the issue of 3" mortars, ..."*

20. *"... tracked carriers ..."*

21. *"... and the replacement of the Vickers-Berthier by the Bren."* (p.48)

22. *"The jeep, a war-winning invention if ever there was one."* (p.49)

23. *"All supply was by air."* (p.5(

24. *"4/6th crossed the Irrawaddy on 27 January, 1945, and, for the next few weeks found itself involved in several hard-fought actions with the Japanese."* (p.54)

25. *"It was not until 8 March that the pagodas crowning Mandalay Hill, outside the city, could be seen and there was still stiff fighting ahead for 1/6th."* (p.50)

26. *"The 3rd Battalion was raised in Abbottabad during the second half of 1940 by drafts from both the 1st and 2nd Battalions."* (p.59) British officers and Mess staff.

27. *"The battle for Mogaung, which began on the night 6/7 June, 1944 ... deserves to be engraved in letters of gold alongside that of Sari Bair."* (p.66) Tulbahadur Pun, VC at the Coronation Parade, 1953. At Mogaung members of 3/6th won two VCs, one DSO, one IOM, three MCs, two IDSMs and nine MMs.

28. *"Certainly the 2/6th established a formidable reputation for themselves during the later stages of the war in Italy."* (p.73)

29. *"The long years of waiting and training had ended and now all was to be put to the test."* (p.75)

30. *"Freyberg disagreed. 'They have short legs but they move them mighty fast. They'll keep up all right.' They did."* (p.82)

31. *"By 9 May, 1945, the day that Germany surrendered unconditionally, the Battalion was resting in the pleasant seaside village of Belvedere."* (p.83) Lieutenant-Colonel W.M. Amoore, DSO and his officers.

not until they had scoured the crater, which took several hours, and spent the night on the top of Mount Popa, that it suddenly dawned on them that not a single snake had been seen, let alone a *hamadryad*. It certainly cast some doubt on the *hamadryad* legend.

That night the Area Commander,* himself a 6th Gurkha, who had come down to see the fun of mopping up the dacoits, went to bed in his tent only to emerge considerably shaken. He had found a viper in his bed. This made the operation even greater fun where the Gurkhas were concerned!

It was while they were serving in Burma after the war that the 1st Battalion, together with the 2nd Battalion then in Dehra Dun, underwent what was probably the most traumatic event in the Regiment's long history. On 8 August, 1947, a signal was received stating that the 2nd, 6th, 7th and 10th Gurkha Rifles were to become part of the British Army. The other six regiments of Gurkha Rifles were to remain in the Army of independent India. 3/6th Gurkha Rifles was to remain in the Indian Army as a battalion of the 5th Gurkha Rifles; 4/6th Gurkha Rifles would be disbanded. A referendum was to be held in which each man was to declare whether he wished to serve on, take his discharge or be transferred to an Indian Gurkha unit. Although the referendum was almost immediately cancelled, some ninety per cent opted to serve on with the Regiment.

India became independent on 15 August, 1947, and, almost immediately, became engulfed in chaos. Meanwhile many British officers whom the soldiers knew left, either on demobilization or to join other British units, many ex-Gurkhas joining the Royal Artillery. It was a period of great confusion and not only in India and Pakistan. When another referendum was held in

---

* Brigadier O. C. T. Dykes, MC, always known as 'Sailor'. He joined 1/6th GR in 1929 after 7 years in the Royal Marines (hence the nickname). He commanded the Battalion from 1944–45 and after a short break in the USA returned to Burma again to command 1/6th GR in 1946. In 1947 he was promoted Brigadier as Commander North Burma Area. He retired in 1948. One of the Regiment's best known characters, a fine horseman and polo player, he eventually settled in South Africa where he died on 30 December, 1979.

December, 1947, although the majority of the 1st Battalion stood firm, the majority in the 2nd Battalion and Regimental Centre chose India. This came as a great shock to many of the British officers in all the Gurkha regiments. It had for long been a shibboleth among British officers in Gurkha regiments that the Gurkha soldier would serve only under British and Gurkha officers – under an Indian *never*! This was entirely disproved when put to the test. Gurkha officer after Gurkha officer and Gurkha soldier after Gurkha soldier opted for the Indian Army. India had intimated that Gurkha officers could hold full commissioned rank, no longer as Viceroy's Commissioned Officers, and this undoubtedly influenced many in their decision. In any case the British Army was an unknown quantity. Although the British soldier and 'Johnny' Gurkha got on amazingly well, there had always been a substratum of jealousy, perhaps envy, between the Royal Army (or British Service) and the Indian Army, going back to the days of the East India Company. The reasons for it are many but the feeling did exist, however much it may be glossed over by modern military historians. British officers of Gurkha regiments, who prided themselves on their professionalism, may have looked down on their somewhat 'amateurish' British Service contemporaries who, in their turn, considered their Gurkha colleagues as being completely besotted by their pride and affection for the Gurkhas they commanded: 'Mongolian Madness' it was called in some circles!

Be this as it may, on 1 January, 1948, the 6th Gurkha Rifles passed formally into the British Service. A completely new system of administration had to be adopted and there was a lot of cross-posting between regiments. The 1st Battalion moved from Burma to Malaya in January, 1948, the 2nd Battalion following in February. Meanwhile the new Regimental Centre for the Brigade of Gurkhas was established for the time being in Ranchi. The VCOs now became King's Gurkha Officers (KGOs) and the British non-commissioned titles replaced the old Indian Army ones. The Regiment became formally affiliated to The Rifle Brigade and 132 years' service in the Indian Army was ended.

CHAPTER FIVE

―――――∞――――――

Chindits

THE 3rd Battalion was raised in Abbottabad during the second half of 1940 by drafts from both the 1st and 2nd Battalions. The balance was made up with recruits and formation was completed by December, 1940. In March, 1941, the Battalion moved to Landi Kotal on the Khyber Pass and the best part of the two following years was spent on the North-West Frontier. It was the best of schools in which to toughen the Gurkha soldier and make him bullet-wise. It was also the ideal place in which to turn 800 or more individual officers and soldiers into a well-trained team, although at first the Battalion was principally occupied in digging and erecting defences against a possible attack by the Germans, launched from the Caucasus and directed against India, which seemed to be a distinct possibility at the time. However, in June, 1943, the Battalion moved to Jhansi to join 77th Indian Infantry Brigade in General Wingate's Special Force. This was regarded as a great honour and was greeted with acclamation.

Like another unorthodox soldier, T. E. Lawrence, Wingate has his critics as well as admirers, but there can be no doubt that he was an inspiring trainer of men, as well as being full of original ideas. He had already dispelled the myth that the Japanese were supermen when operating in the jungle with his Long Range Penetration Expedition in 1943, General Wavell commenting that 'the experience gained . . . was invaluable'. Now a much more ambitious operation was being planned involving no fewer than six infantry brigades, supported by three wings of the United States Army Air Force – fighters, light bombers and transport planes. The 77th Brigade was commanded by Colonel Michael Calvert, Wingate's devoted disciple, and consisted of the 1st King's, 1st Lancashire Fusiliers, 1st South Staffords and 3/6th Gurkha Rifles. The British battalions were all regular ones. Each battalion was organized into two Columns, each of Column Headquarters, HQ Company and one rifle company of four platoons numbered, in the case of 3/6 GR, as 63 and 36 Columns. The training in the jungles of Central India was intensive, to some extent intended to eliminate the weaker brethren, and culminating in an exercise extending over 140 miles of jungle and open country carrying a 60 lb pack, weapons, ammunition and equipment. In the case of the Battalion, not a single man fell out.

Much of the training was concerned with animal management, mules once again coming into their own, ground-to-air control, river crossings and air supply drops. Some of it was new to the Gurkha soldier but he took to it as to the manner born. There was nevertheless some relief when on 17 January, 1944, the move to Assam began. There training continued, particularly practice in loading men, mules and supplies in aircraft by day and by night. Some little time was wasted in trying to teach the building of *bashas* with bamboo which undoubtedly came as something new to the British soldiers, but on the Gurkha who, since childhood, had been accustomed to turning bamboo into huts, tables and chairs, and also much else with the aid of his kukri, the exercise was very largely wasted.

The main aim of Operation THURSDAY, as it was codenamed, was to dominate the so-called 'railway corridor' which ran west of the Irrawaddy between Shwebo and Myitkyina. This was the chief supply route for the Japanese 18th Division which was defending Myitkyina against General Stilwell's American-Chinese advance down the Hukawng valley from Assam. There were several subsidiary aims, Wingate's mind being fertile in this respect, some of them realizable, others less so, but it was the main aim that chiefly concerned the operations of Calvert's 77th Brigade.

Almost from his subaltern days onwards, Major General

Orde Wingate inspired controversy. The Army Commander, Slim, made no secret of his suspicion and dislike for what became known as 'private armies' and no army formation was more publicly 'private' than were Wingate's Chindits. However, once Operation THURSDAY had been agreed at the highest level, Slim gave Wingate his full and unstinting support. 'On the whole,' he has written, 'Wingate and I agreed better than most people expected, perhaps because we had known each other before, or perhaps because we had each, in our own way, arrived at the same conclusions on certain major issues; the potentialities of air supply, the possibility of taking Burma from the north and in our estimates of the strengths and weaknesses of the Japanese. Of course we differed on many things. It was impossible not to differ from a man who so fanatically pursued his own purposes without regard to any other consideration or person.'*

Perhaps Slim's most vital contribution to Wingate's operation was his decision that it should go ahead despite the apparent blocking of one of the three intended landing zones, PICCA-DILLY. D-Day for the fly-in had been fixed as Sunday, 5 March, 1944, and H-Hour was 1700 hours. There were gathered to wish the Operation 'God speed' a galaxy of senior officers which, of course, included General Slim. However at 1630 hours there landed at Lalaghat, one of the principal launching airfields, a light plane with recently taken photographs which disclosed that although BROADWAY and CHOWRINGHEE were clear, PICCADILLY was not. Wingate immediately assumed that in some way the enemy had come to learn of the operation and had therefore taken counter-measures. He exploded with rage and had to be taken aside by Slim who calmed him down. Although as concerned as Wingate by the various possibilities, Slim remained throughout his outwardly imperturbable self. He consulted Calvert, whose troops were standing by and waiting for the 'off', and Calvert was ready to go. Wingate was still unhappy, reminding Slim in insubordinate fashion that the final

* *Defeat into Victory* by Field Marshal Sir William Slim (Cassell & Company Limited) 1956, page 216.

responsibility rested with Slim, but Slim did not waver and not long afterwards 77th Brigade set off on the grand adventure, Calvert having said he was willing to use BROADWAY only. It transpired later that the blocking of PICCADILLY was part of a normal logging operation, the logs being laid out in the clearing in order to dry and the Japanese had had nothing to do with it. 77th Brigade's arrival in Burma came as a complete surprise to them.

None of this drama was, of course, known to the officers and riflemen of 3/6th GR in their bivouacs not far from the airfields. They were to follow on after the three British battalions, all of which were complete at BROADWAY by 7 March. The turn of 3/6th GR came in the night of 7/8 March and the account given in Volume II of the Historical Record of the 6th Gurkha Rifles is certainly worth repeating:

'Emplaning arrangements were excellent. Parties were called up by Tannoy from the flying control room, each planeful separately. The plane commander handed in his manifest showing exactly how many men, individually by name, and what stores were going into his aircraft. The Dakotas were lined up on either side of the runway at intervals of twenty yards. Mustang fighters were landing and taking off for operations all the time while our men were persuading mules and ponies into the planes. At last all stores were loaded and made fast to the satisfaction of the pilots, and the men fell out behind the aircraft and made tea. It was astounding to see how unconcerned the men were at the prospect of flying into Burma, for none of them had any flying experience. After a last cigarette and mug of tea the men climbed in and fastened their safety belts. As the aircraft became airborne there were exclamations of surprise and noses were pressed against the small windows, but before long everyone was asleep.'*

We are told that the flying was 'uneventful'; a tribute to the skill of the pilots and the hard work of the Engineers flown in during the early stages to level and improve the landing zone at

* Historical Record of the 6th Gurkha Rifles, Volume II, p. 123–4.

BROADWAY. But although there is no mention of this in the Historical Record, the mounting of Operation THURSDAY was, in fact, a miracle of staff work on the part of all those involved. '9,000 fighting men, 1,300 animals and 500,000 lbs of weapons and warlike stores had been flown into Burma without the loss of a single man or aircraft by enemy action. This was a remarkable achievement by any judgement.'*

The day after 3/6 GR landed at BROADWAY, Calvert set off to establish a block on the railway. He took with him his Brigade Headquarters, his personal assault company†, the 1st South Staffords and 3/6 GR. The route lay over the 3,000 feet Gangaw Range covered in dense jungle and involved crossing and recrossing the Kawkkwe Chaung, flowing slow, but deep, in the pre-monsoon months. Divided into two columns, 63 under Skone and 36 under Shaw, the Gurkhas were unsurpassed as marchers but even so the 'going' was so difficult that it took six days to reach their objective, the railway at Henu, which subsequently became known as WHITE CITY. This was because the trees surrounding the block became draped with scores of white parachutes.

The South Staffords had a fierce fight to seize Pagoda Hill, a dominating feature which the Japanese were turning into a defensive position. Calvert himself, rifle and bayonet in hand, together with 63 Column, came up to support the Staffords and

---

* *The Chindit War* by Shelford Bidwell (Hodder and Stoughton) 1979, p. 110.
† 'As a subaltern I was put in charge of the Chinese contingent of the Royal Engineers [in Hong Kong] in 1936. They had a long history but by that date they had deteriorated into a pool of Chinese technicians in uniform . . . I put them through the recruits' and trained men's musketry course, increased the strength to about 250 and drilled them until they could march past as Royal Engineers in the King's Birthday Parade to the huge delight of the Chinese onlookers . . . [They] gave a good account of themselves during the battle for Hong Kong in 1941 . . . Many of them escaped overland to India . . . I found them woebegone in Deolali Transit Camp in 1943. They were very pleased to see somebody they knew for they had not been treated well and were miserable. They volunteered *en masse* to join my Brigade [Chindits] as Defence Company for Brigade Headquarters. I paid them out of my own pocket until they were officially recognized. They did very well.'
(Calvert in letter to Author repeated in *Imperial Sunset* published by Macdonald, 1981, page 318.)

there was much hand-to-hand fighting with bayonet and kukri before the hill was taken. Lieutenant George Cairns of the Somerset Light Infantry, attached to the Staffords, received a posthumous VC for his gallantry that day, and the Staffords had 59 casualties, seven of them officers. Jemadar Khumbarsing engaged a Japanese officer in single combat, kukri against sword, in which the kukri won despite Khumbarsing's wounds. By then the Japanese had had enough and withdrew, but it was only a lull before the storm. They later made attack after attack against WHITE CITY but were repulsed. Calvert, as a Sapper, was a master of the art of fortification and he turned WHITE CITY into a veritable fortress.

The Japanese, taken by surprise in the first instance, fell back to Mawlu, one mile down the line, which they turned into a strong defensive position. 63 Column was sent to clear them out. At first unsupported they met dogged resistance but when the Mustangs of Cochran's Air Commando (USAAF) arrived in support, their bombing and cannon fire striking close ahead of the attacking troops, the enemy broke as the Gurkhas closed in with kukris and grenades. 77th Brigade was master of the field – for the time being at least.

It took some little time for the Japanese High Command to react to the Chindit Columns, so surprisingly landed in their midst. At the time their attention was fixed on their Fifteenth Army's assault on Imphal and Kohima. Meanwhile Stilwell's slow advance down the Hukawng Valley towards Myitkyina was being resolutely opposed by General Tanaka's 18th 'Chrysanthemum' Division which depended almost entirely on the railway for its resupply. It was essential to relieve the stranglehold on the railway imposed by 77th Brigade at WHITE CITY. Therefore the principal Japanese aim was to evict Calvert and his troops from WHITE CITY.

While the Japanese Burma Area Army Commander, General Kawabe, was scraping together troops from wherever he could find them, Calvert was extending and strengthening his position at WHITE CITY. It was during this period that the Chindits suffered the loss of Wingate, killed in an air crash on 24 March, which resulted in the appointment of 'Joe' Lentaigne, himself of the 4th Gurkha Rifles, to command Special Force. With Wingate's death, something of the bounce went out of the Chindits. Lentaigne was a good soldier but he was too 'ordinary' to be able to take the place of one of the most 'extraordinary' men ever to have worn the 'red tabs' of a British general officer; nor had he inherited Wingate's right to communicate directly with the Prime Minister whenever he deemed it necessary to do so. The Japanese reckoned that Wingate was worth several divisions, and although this could never be proved, they were probably right. The best choice to succeed Wingate would probably have been Calvert, but he was too junior in rank and age, and too much of a maverick, to have fitted the required bill.

After two months of marching and counter-marching, accompanied by some bitter fighting resulting in heavy casualties, particularly among the British officers, it was thought that the 77th Brigade would be flown out to India. Skone had had to leave owing to a damaged foot and N. F. B. Shaw took over command, with Major James Lumley as his Second in Command. General Stilwell had asked for 77th Brigade to remain in Burma, partly to continue the blockade of the railway and partly to assist Stilwell's American and Chinese troops in the taking of Myitkyina. Stilwell's known anglophobia, coupled with a singular failure to visit his troops, of whatever nationality, did not make it easy for Calvert, who was in any case exercised over the condition of his soldiers after four months' fighting in a severe climate and without adequate rest. Moreover, the monsoon was about to break when *chaungs* would become torrents and much of the country turn into swamp. 3/6 GR had received only one lot of reinforcements since landing at BROADWAY; the British battalions in the brigade had received none. By any judgment they were due for relief.

The units forming 77th Brigade were mere skeletons of their former selves. 3/6 GR totalled no more than 230 all ranks, many of them suffering from malaria, dysentery or trench foot. Although the airfield at Myitkyina had been taken on 17 May, the town itself, a few miles away, was still held by around 4,000 Japanese. Thirty-five miles south of Myitkyina was Mogaung, a

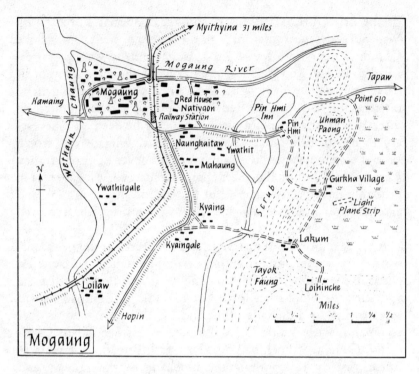

Mogaung

small town on the Mogaung River which was crossed by a railway bridge. The Japanese had still been operating the railway between Myitkyina and Mogaung. 77th Brigade was ordered towards the end of May to take Mogaung. Calvert said he would do so by 5 June, at the same time pointing out the debilitated state of his battalions. Then he sent his deputy, Colonel Rome, together with 3/6 GR, to march up the railway from BROADWAY to reconnoitre the approaches to Mogaung.

The battle for Mogaung, which began on the night 6/7 June, 1944, and which lasted for sixteen days until the Japanese withdrew, deserves to be engraved in letters of gold, alongside that of Sari Bair in the long list of Battle Honours granted to the 6th Queen Elizabeth's Own Gurkha Rifles. When the battle began Calvert's brigade was 2,355 strong; when it ended the figure was 806 effectives. Two Victoria Crosses were won by the Regiment at Mogaung, both of them immediate and one, sadly, posthumous. In his congratulatory signal to the Regi-

[66]

ment, the Commander-in-Chief, India, General Auchinleck, said the winning of two Victoria Crosses in one action was 'a most rare occurrence'. The citations of Captain Michael All-mand and Rifleman Tulbadur Pun are given in Appendix I.

The battle itself is not easy to describe. 'Mogaung was the very devil of a place to get at,' writes Bidwell. 'The west side of the town was washed by the Namyin and the north by the Mogaung River, running at six knots. The only approach was from the south-east along a narrow road built up on a causeway, with flooded ground, lakes and marshes right and left and a deep *chaung*, bridged only where the road crossed it, barring any flanking movement. From the ridge Calvert had chosen as his base of attack to the town lay two miles of open country studded with villages, all fortified in the Japanese fashion with bunkers cut underneath them and all able to bring interlocking fire to bear over the front. The Japanese garrison at the lowest computation was some 3,500 – a regiment of the 53rd Division, later reinforced by another battalion, and the service troops looking after the ammunition dumps and the hospital, where the very patients in the beds were armed with grenades.'*

The only way to tackle the problem was by a series of short and limited advances, preceded and supported by a barrage of mortar and machine-gun fire and accompanied by P-51 aircraft in the ground attack role. As each Japanese position was taken it served as the jumping-off position for the next attack. Quite apart from the targets presented by the attacking troops as they moved on such a narrow front amidst a nest of snipers, they were for much of the time wading up to their knees in clinging and stinking mud, and in some places sinking to their waists. Bearing in mind that the troops were already exhausted after their 160-mile march from WHITE CITY, it is remarkable that they could attack at all.

It had been hoped that the assault would be reinforced by a Chinese regiment, part of General Stilwell's force. The 114th Regiment did arrive on 18 June but the Chinese displayed no enthusiasm for joining in the fray. They had been fighting the

* Bidwell, *op. cit.* p. 268.

Japanese since 1937 and had developed their own tactics for dealing with such a formidable enemy. It had been their intention to by-pass Mogaung and it required much diplomacy to persuade them to participate in the attack. Moreover, time meant nothing to the Chinese. They were as likely to be late as to participate at all. However, they had with them four 77-mm guns which were manna from heaven to 77th Brigade that had until now lacked any form of artillery support.

The best account of the final stages of the battle for Mogaung is probably that given in Volume II of the Regimental History which (suitably edited) follows below:

'On 21st June 'A' Company, supported by mortars, put in a reconnaissance attack with the object of finding out more about the Japanese positions covering the railway line and bridge. This disclosed that the enemy was very strongly established in the brick buildings and that he had a high proportion of automatic weapons. One building in particular, known as the Red House, was noted as a likely trouble spot. Major M. G. Collins, who was acting as Mortar FCO, was unfortunately killed during this attack.

'On the night of the same day the Lancashire Fusiliers, supported by mortars and flamethrowers, succeeded in capturing Naungkaitaw, bringing the left flank of the Brigade almost up to the railway . . . During the night of 21st June, twelve hundred mortar bombs were fired on the Brigade's front in half an hour. Only the Lancashire Fusiliers advanced. The Japanese reacted violently and for several minutes fired off every weapon they had. In the early hours of 23rd June a similar bombardment was fired and the final assault on the railway line and bridge was launched at first light. *This was probably the greatest day in the Battalion's history.** 'C' Company, on the right, moved with skill and dash and drove on to the railway bridge. 'B' Company, in the centre, had a desperate task near the Red House and it was only after terrific fighting in which flamethrowers, grenades and PIATS were used that the house was captured. The epic feat of arms

* Author's italics.

[68]

by Captain Michael Allmand and Rifleman Tulbahadur Pun was chiefly responsible for the successful outcome of the attack. Allmand was suffering from trench foot which hampered his movements, but, moving forward alone over the muddy ground pitted with shell holes, he charged a Japanese machine-gun position single-handed and fell mortally wounded.

'Tulbahadur Pun was a rifleman in one of this Company's leading platoons attacking the Red House. Intense fire held up the attack and Tulbahadur's section was wiped out except for the Section Commander and Tulbahadur and one other rifleman. These three charged the Red House but almost at once the section commander and the other rifleman were seriously wounded. Tulbahadur seized the Bren gun and continued alone against the enemy, although with the dawn light behind him he presented a perfect target for the Japanese. He covered the thirty yards of open ground, which was deep in mud and made the more difficult by shell holes and fallen trees, still firing from the hip and closed with the enemy who were concentrating rifle and machine-gun fire on him. He killed three Japanese and put five more to flight and captured two light machine guns with a lot of ammunition. He then gave covering fire which helped the rest of the platoon to reach their objective. Tulbahadur and Allmand both received the Victoria Cross for their superb bravery and valour.

'Though Michael Allmand was moved to the hospital in the Gurkha village [see map], he died during the night of 23rd June while waiting for the plane which was to take him out to India. His death was as glorious as his valour was inspiring, but the Battalion grieved the loss of the bravest of men . . . Happily Tulbahadur survived.'*

Both the Lancashire Fusiliers and South Staffords suffered severe casualties in the fighting which followed to capture the railway rest-house but 'C' Company managed to hang on to their position on the bridge. Later, with air support, the

---

* Historical Record 6 GR, Vol II, *op. cit.* pp. 141–145.

Lancashire Fusiliers captured the rest-house. The Chinese now signified their intention to attack from the south of Mogaung at 1500 hours, but not surprisingly their attack was postponed. However, Calvert ordered the Lancashire Fusiliers and the Brigade Defence Company, supplied by 3/6 GR, to advance into Mogaung in support of the Chinese and this was done, but it met with severe opposition. 'A' Company was ordered forward in support and they were counter-attacked throughout most of the night of 25/26 June. On the morning of 26 June, 1944, they advanced cautiously into Mogaung to find the place deserted. The Japanese had had enough and had withdrawn, leaving the 3/6 GR to hold a small ceremonial parade when they hoisted the Union Jack on the most prominent building that remained standing. It had been a glorious, if dearly-won, victory.

It was the climax of the Battalion's service with the Chindits. On 5 July it marched out of Mogaung for fifty miles to the airstrip at Warazup where it emplaned in the aircraft flying in the 36th British Division. In three months of marching and fighting the Battalion had suffered 485 casualties and no fewer than eleven of its British officers had been killed or died, and a further nine had been wounded. Six Gurkha officers had been killed or died and eight had been wounded. Whether the Chindit operation in 1944 fully justified the enormous expenditure of effort put into it, or justified the casualties suffered by British and Gurkhas alike, will be debated by military historians far into the future, but in the words of one Chindit historian, 'In the history of infantry fighting the feat of the 77th Brigade is unsurpassed,' and this must remain the well deserved epitaph for the many who did not return.*

The Silver Star of the United States was awarded to three members of 77th Brigade, two of them to Subedar Rikhiram Ale and Naik Balbir Pun of 3/6 GR. The third went to Lieutenant David Wilcox of the South Staffords. Brigadier Michael Calvert was also awarded the Silver Star. Shortly afterwards the news was received that Special Force was being

* Bidwell, *op. cit.*, pp. 273–274.

broken up and volunteers were called for the newly formed Indian Airborne Division. The Gurkha units were willing to join provided they could retain their regimental identity but for some strange reason this was not allowed. The 3/6th moved instead to Ranchi where they joined the 23rd Brigade in reserve. As Chindits the battalion had won two VCs, two DSOs, three IOMs and six MCs. There were also four IDSMs and twelve MMs. It was no mean feat.

In June, 1945, the 3rd Battalion returned to Burma, at first to Rangoon but soon to join 89th Indian Brigade, where it found 1/11th Sikhs, old comrades as the 14th KGO Sikhs from Gallipoli days, and the 4/8th Gurkha Rifles which had been an Assam Light Infantry battalion more than a century previously. This was the period when the remnants of the Japanese army in Burma were trying to escape across the River Sittang and the Battalion had several brushes with them, losing one British and one Gurkha officer in these closing stages of the war. When the Japanese surrendered on 15 August, 1945, the Battalion had been earmarked to join 7th Indian Division and take part in the invasion of Malaya, but these orders were rescinded and instead it was flown to Bangkok in October.

After a spell in Thailand and Malaya the Battalion returned to India in February, 1946, to find the country in a very disturbed state. With Independence looming for both India and Pakistan, the soldiers' most unwelcome task of Internal Security was the Battalion's lot. Meanwhile British officers, Gurkha officers and Gurkha Other Ranks departed either on leave or demobilization, and rumours abounded regarding the future of the Gurkha Brigade. It was not a happy time. At last came the news that the 1st and 2nd Battalions of the 6th Gurkha Rifles were to join the British Army, but not the 3rd Battalion. It was to remain in the Indian Army as the 5th Battalion of those old friends from Abbottabad days, the 5th Gurkha Rifles, Frontier Force. This took effect from December, 1947, and carried with it the Chindit tradition into the Army of independent India.

As a postscript to this account of 3/6 GR in the Second World War it may be permissible to quote from a letter of Michael Calvert's to the Author dated 10 July, 1993: 'The 3/6

GR were the backbone of my brigade. The British battalions were not reinforced and wasted rapidly but the Gurkhas did receive one lot of reinforcements and were the only one of my units of any strength, weak though they undoubtedly were.'

They certainly served him well.

12. *"A truly great soldier, who was loved and admired by those who served under him, Bill Slim was also a great human being. The Regiment can be proud he always said he owed it so much."* (p.168) Portrait of Field Marshal The Viscount Slim, painted by Margaret Lindsay Williams in 1953.

13 & 14. *"In 1944 Captain Michael Allmand and Rifleman Tulbahadur Pun of the 3rd Battalion 6th Gurkha Rifles were awarded the Victoria Cross for conspicuous gallantry."* (p.187)

15. *"Manipur faded into the background until it became the scene of General Slim's great victory over General Mutaguchi's Fifteenth Japanese Army between March and July 1944."* (p.12) The sword of General Tanaka, commander of the Japanese 33 Division, received by General Slim at the surrender of Rangoon.

CHAPTER SIX

Italy

FIELD MARSHAL Slim has written that, 'Nothing looks as uniform as a Gurkha battalion, nothing looks more workman-like and few things look so formidable.'* Certainly the 2/6th established a formidable reputation for themselves during the later stages of the war in Italy, although they only arrived there on 1 August, 1944, together with the 2/8th and 2/10th Gurkha Rifles in the 43rd Gurkha Lorried Infantry Brigade.

The war began slowly for the 2nd Battalion. It was in the Malakand early in 1940 but moved in April to Delhi to join the 19th Indian Infantry Brigade in the newly forming 8th Indian Division. It was much under strength owing to drafts supplied to the forming 3rd and 4th Battalions and it required some time to build up its strength and, above all, to mechanize the Battalion after the departure of the horses and mules. Oddly enough, considering their primitive home background, the Gurkhas took readily to mechanization and showed themselves to be excellent mechanics, if, at times, somewhat too dashing as drivers. In August, 1941, they moved overseas, but not to Malaya as originally anticipated but instead to Basra and Iraq.

The campaigns in Iraq and Syria had been successfully concluded by the time of the Battalion's arrival at Basra but increasing German influence in Iran was giving cause for concern. It should be remembered that at this stage in the war the Germans, having cut through the Russians like a knife

* *Unofficial History* by Field Marshal Sir William Slim (Cassell, 1959), p. 218.

through butter, were driving south-east towards the Caucasian oilfields. It was seriously considered that they might continue this offensive either to seize the Suez Canal or drive through Iran and Afghanistan towards India, or both. It therefore became imperative to evict the pro-German Shah of Iran and his German advisers and establish control by the Allies over Iran. A subsidiary consideration was the fact that the main land link with Russia lay from the Persian Gulf through Iran. A joint operation was therefore carried out by the Russians coming from the north and the British from the south. General Slim commanded the British force which consisted of one brigade from his own 10th Indian Division and two other brigades, one infantry and one armoured. Slim described the operation as *opéra bouffe*. It was all over in four days with hardly any casualties – starting on 25 August, 1941. The 2/6th were little involved, apart from escort duties, but there were many lessons to be learnt regarding movement in the desert.

However, it provided a welcome relief from Zubair, the Battalion's bivouac area after arriving at Basra. The description given in the Historical Record bears repetition and will doubtless evoke memories in any reader who took part in the Gulf War in 1991, since it was fought over precisely the same area: 'The Battalion moved out to Zubair, some eighteen miles west of Basra and set about pitching camp in the desolate waste, devoid of everything except a few tired-looking trees. So devoid of features was the site that company areas were marked out by odd tins, minor bumps in the ground or even wheel marks. At that time of the year the heat was overpowering, the sun temperature averaging some 170°F by day; there was no shade. Inside the tents the temperature was normally over 120°F and touched 132°F. Nights were almost tolerable as the temperature usually dropped 35° or 40°.'

As it happened, the Battalion was to spend the next two years in the Middle East, retracing much of the ground covered by the 1st and 2nd Battalions during the First World War. It did not seem that weatherwise Iraq had much improved during the intervening years. It was while the Battalion was at Kirkuk digging defences for the oilfields that it was visited by General

[74]

Slim, then GOC 10th Indian Division in northern Iraq. He was clearly delighted to meet so many old friends. Only a few weeks later he was telephoned by General Quinan, the GOC-in-C in Baghdad, and told he must return to India within three days. On 13 March, 1942, he reported to General Alexander at Prome in Burma to assume command of what was to become Burma Corps (Burcorps) in the temporary rank of Lieutenant General. For once the army had found a square hole in which to fit a square peg.

The 2/6th soldiered on in the Middle East, moving to Shaiba in February, 1943, to join the 31st Indian Armoured Division as part of its Lorried Infantry Brigade. This was the Battalion's first contact with the 14th/20th King's Hussars which was later to be cemented in the comradeship of battle. It also acquired a new Brigade Commander, Brigadier A. R. Barker of the 2nd Gurkha Rifles, known throughout the Indian Army as 'Tochi' Barker. He was a very fine soldier who remained in command throughout the war with great success and wide popularity.

At this stage of the war in the Middle East units seldom stayed long in the same place, let alone in the same country. The Battalion's movements took it across the desert to Palestine, to Egypt, back again to Lebanon and Syria, forever moving and training. Then on 13 July, 1944, a welcome order was received. The Battalion was to move to Egypt, preliminary to going overseas to war. Italy was to be the destination and on 28 July, 1944, the 2/6th sailed from Alexandria for Taranto. The long years of waiting and training had ended and now all was to be put to the test. The 43rd Gurkha Lorried Infantry Brigade was to join the Eighth Army in the 1st British Armoured Division, then slowly battling its way north up the Adriatic coast in the face of very tough German opposition.

It is wasted effort by those who seek to compare the various theatres of the Second World War in terms of toughness, climate and so on. All war is tough. Burma was tough but so was New Guinea. The Western Desert saw some incredibly tough fighting but so did Normandy. Certainly Italy produced the full orchestra of tough fighting and climatic extremes – heat, snow, rain, tempest and the most rugged topography. And as for the enemy, they remained until the end some of the finest soldiers in the world. It never paid to take any chances with them.

After the fall of Rome on 4 June, 1944, the Allies pressed on until reaching the River Arno beyond Florence where they ground to a halt in mid-July. Partly this was owing to the removal of several divisions to take part in the landing in Southern France, partly to battle fatigue and partly to the weather. It rained and rained and rained. On the Adriatic coast, Ancona had been captured by the Poles but from Florence to Rimini stretched the Germans' Gothic Line, barring access to the plain of Lombardy. For many months past the 43rd Gurkha Lorried Infantry Brigade had been training in the desert for mobile warfare but once arrived in Italy the Gurkhas found themselves back on their feet. The conditions and the 'going' were such that only a man on his feet could be termed mobile and, of course, where a man could go without losing his feet, so could a mule. Mules, too, had come back into their own.

Early in the proceedings the 2/6th learnt they were to be supported by 60 Battery of 23rd Field Regiment, Royal Artillery. This was to continue with such confidence on the part of Gurkhas and Gunners alike that 60 Battery became 'our' battery and 23rd Field 'our' artillery regiment. This was first put to the test on 12/13 September, 1944, when 43rd Brigade was involved in the battle to capture the Passano Ridge to the south of Rimini. No fewer than three Allied divisions were involved, including 43rd Brigade. Unfortunately almost immediately after this successful operation it was decided to break up 1st British Armoured Division. The incessant rain had turned ground off the main roads into a quagmire, making the movement of tanks almost impossible. The Battalion regretted losing the White Rhino divisional sign and found itself now under the wing of 56th (London) Division with the divisional sign of Dick Whittington's cat.

The advance now continued towards San Arcangelo, a small town on the main highway between Rimini and Bologna. There was a fierce battle before the place was taken on 24 September, the Germans retaliating with prolonged shellfire causing many casualties. Major Andrew, commanding 'D' Company, was

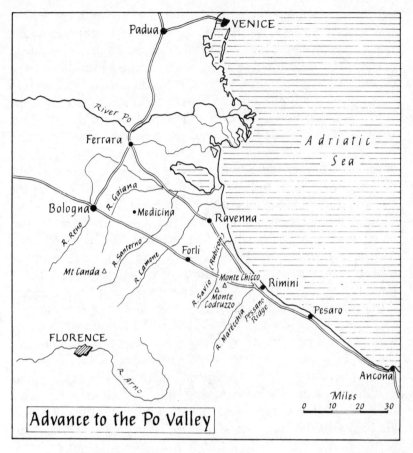

Advance to the Po Valley

badly wounded during this action but was most gallantly rescued by Lance-Naik Satbir Gurung who dashed through heavy fire to carry him back to cover where his wound could be dressed. Although the Canadians had taken Rimini on 21 September, and although San Arcangelo was only a short distance from the edge of the Lombardy plain, the Eighth Army would still have no fewer than thirteen rivers to cross in this flat and waterlogged region and no less than elements of ten German divisions to vanquish before the River Po was reached. And meanwhile it continued to rain – and the Gurkhas returned to their own element, the mountains!

On 6 October, 1944, the 43rd Brigade was transferred to 10th

[77]

Indian Division operating in the mountains above Bologna. The Battalion was now back to mule transport with orders to attack the 1300-feet-high Monte Chicco, 'protected by precipitous ravines and approachable along a narrow hogsback'. It was to be a night attack assisted by the artificial moonlight of search-lights. At 0300 hours on 11 October the Battalion crossed the River Rubicon that lay between the start line and the objective and began the tortuous ascent to the objective. The Germans, relying on the difficulties of the approach, were taken by surprise and after fierce fighting were driven out of the village of Montecodruzzo with bayonet and kukri on the way to the objective. The fiercest fighting took place around the White House, just short of Monte Chicco and it was only cleared after hand-to-hand fighting with kukris, grenades and bayonets.

The Germans' reaction was fierce and quick. They made frequent attempts to retake Monte Chicco and subjected the Battalion to very heavy shelling. There were many casualties by the time the 4/10th Baluch Regiment relieved the Battalion on the night of 22 October. The CO, Lieutenant Colonel Bulfield, had been wounded along with 59 others and 20 had been killed. Two DSOs and two MCs were awarded as a result of this action. According to the regimental history, 'The capture and holding of Monte Chicco against some of Germany's finest troops will be remembered for ever as one of the finest highlights in the Regiment's history.' It would be difficult to improve on that.

In a battle when all behaved so well, it may seem invidious to pick out one example of personal gallantry but Lance-Havildar Bhimbahadur Thapa's gallantry merits a mention in a record such as this. What follows is taken from the Historical Record of the Regiment 1919–1948:

'A platoon of "A" Company patrolling on the left flank was ordered to occupy a farmhouse, which it did, but our own shells were falling on it and the platoon was ordered back. As it began to withdraw heavy hostile mortar fire commenced. One section and Platoon Headquarters got away safely, but the second section was caught and all the men became casualties. The wounded were carried back into the house and the mortar fire . . . became intense, indicating an immediate counter-attack. Lance-Havildar Bhimbahadur Thapa called the remaining seven men together and gave his orders. "We cannot go away and leave our wounded so we must stay here until help arrives. Conserve your ammunition; don't fire except to kill. When your ammunition is exhausted use your kukris."

"The enemy came on in waves of twenty men . . . The first two counter-attacks were stopped, but when the third wave came our men's ammunition was running out and both Bren gunners were wounded. Bhimbahadur went out alone to meet the Germans. His section saw him shoot five Germans with his Sten gun and cut down three more with his kukri before he was overwhelmed by sheer weight of numbers. The surviving members of his section were overpowered and taken prisoner [two of them later escaping]." '

After a counter-attack by another platoon supported by artillery, the house was recaptured. They found Bhimbahadur's body lying in the open.

'He had been shot through the head and chest and, with blood-stained kukri in his hand, he was lying across the body of a German officer and surrounded by three dead and seven wounded German soldiers . . . Bhimbahadur Thapa's extremely gallant action was recognized by the posthumous award of the Indian Order of Merit (IOM), an award second only to the VC.'*

Individual acts of gallantry, such as Bhimbahadur Thapa's, have occurred time and again throughout the Regiment's history, and for that matter in all the other regiments of Gurkha Rifles. Those who performed them were only simple men from the mountains of Nepal, but they recognized their duty and were faithful to the Gurkhas' creed: '*Kafar hunne bhanda morno ramro* – Better to die than live a coward.'

The winter of 1944/45 was both cold and wet as the Eighth

* *Historical Record*, 6 GR, Vol II, pp. 90–91.

Army slowly fought its way forward out of the mountains into the Lombard plain. For the Regiment, serving for a time in the 2nd New Zealand Division and thereby renewing an old Gallipoli association, it was largely a matter of advancing from one water obstacle to the next; digging-in to withstand enemy counter-attack and patrolling forward again to reconnoitre yet another river line overlooked by high and thick banks, cleverly fortified and providing the enemy with excellent observation. This was infantry fighting at its most arduous, but the Gurkhas seemed to thrive on it. Surprisingly, the language barrier proved no problem, not even when serving for a time under the Polish Corps or when handing over to the Palestine Regiment's Hebrew. Italian (of a kind) was the lingua franca!

25 March, 1945, saw the end of this phase in the Battalion's history. It was to become mobile again with the issue of Kangaroos – turretless Sherman tanks to carry infantry into battle alongside the armoured squadrons. The Kangaroos were provided by 'A' Squadron of the 14th/20th King's Hussars, old friends from 'Polo Week' at Abbottabad and later from Syria and Iraq. This was the beginning of an association that was to become formally recognized, as will be described later in this history. From the outset relations between Hussars and Gurkhas was remarkable. 'While operating in their hangars our officers and men slept, fed, lived and moved as an integral part of the 14th/20th. With them, of course, were the Battery Commander and his OPs with their staffs. Cavalry, Gunners, Riflemen, all worked as one; it was on this that so much of the later successes hinged.'*

As spring came in 1945 and as the ground began to dry, the Allies prepared for the offensive intended to destroy the Germans and drive them out of Italy. Eighth Army (General McCreery) was on the right, Fifth Army (General Clark) on the left. Eighth Army consisted of XIII Corps (General Harding) and V Corps (General Keightley). 2nd New Zealand Division (General Freyberg VC), with 43rd Gurkha Lorried Infantry Brigade under command, was in XIII Corps. Ahead

* *Historical Record*, 6 GR, Vol II, p. 101.

was the German 1st Para Corps, the *élite* of the German Army, fanatical Nazis for the most part but first-class soldiers, well armed, dug in and supported by tanks and artillery. Even at that late stage of the war in Europe they were a formidable enemy.

The Gurkhas began to move forward behind the New Zealanders on 10 April, 1945. 8th Indian Division was on their left. Movement was slow owing to the need to cross numerous water obstacles which tended to canalize the advance and cause bad traffic jams. By 16 April the Battalion was closing up to Medicina, a small town to the north-east of Bologna. It was defended by part of the 4th Parachute Division who might have imposed a serious delay on the advance had they not been bounced out of the town by the speed of the Battalion's advance in their Kangaroos. Subedar Raghu Gurung, for example, was leading the way down a street supported by a tank. The tank was fired at by a bazooka but was missed. Realizing that a second shot might knock out the tank, the Subedar at once dashed forward under heavy Spandau fire and killed the firer with his kukri, before going on to capture the strong point. By nightfall Medicina was in our hands together with a great quantity of arms and equipment, which included one Mark V Tiger Tank and numerous artillery pieces. Over 70 prisoners were taken and the German dead were too numerous to count. General Harding who, many years later was to become Colonel of the 6th Gurkha Rifles, specially congratulated the Battalion on the successful taking of Medicina, now one of the Regiment's most prized Battle Honours.

Geoffrey Skellett, who was present at the battle, has left an interesting account of the 6th Gurkhas' part in it.

'We hit Medicina at dusk. There followed ten minutes of total chaos and confusion. The pursuit force in a single moment found itself translated from the wide open spaces of the Po Valley into the narrow tunnel-like confines of the town streets and in the descending gloom. On the other side, the enemy was unaware of any allied troops nearer than fifteen miles. The panic created by our arrival was almost comic.

The ten minutes of activity and near hysteria was marked by some remarkable shooting by the 14th/20th and some exceptional bravery by Gurkhas who countered the remarkable reaction of a few of the enemy Paras. With the descent of darkness, the enemy withdrew to the cellars and attics of the town. The pursuit group established control of the key points of the town, and started the systematic flushing of the enemy from their hideaways ... At daylight the following morning the remnants of the enemy crawled from their refuges and surrendered.'

There was, however, no time for celebrations. The New Zealand Division rapidly closed up to the so-called River Gaiana, the next obstacle on the way to the River Po. The Gaiana was more properly an irrigation ditch, of which there were many criss-crossing the Lombard plain; it crossed the Ravenna-Bologna road just beyond Medicina. It had straight, parallel flood banks fifteen to twenty feet high and a black muddy stream which could be waded by men but not crossed by tanks. It was a natural anti-tank ditch and the German paratroopers had dug themselves well into the flood banks. They were going to take some moving. New Zealanders and Gurkhas came up to this obstacle on 17 April.

General Freyberg held a conference on 18 April at which he decided to smash the Germans by the weight of his artillery fire. This would precede a night attack beginning at 2100 hours, by which time the Sappers should have set up the necessary bridges. Brigadier Barker, who commanded the Gurkha Brigade, wanted a slightly slower rate of advance than usual. 'My fellows have very short legs, you know,' he said. Freyberg disagreed. 'They have short legs but they move them mighty fast. They'll keep up all right.' They did.

Freyberg could muster some 192 artillery pieces, medium and field. They would fire about 100,000 shells which Freyberg reckoned meant about 100 shells for each individual enemy paratrooper. 'I wouldn't like to sit under that,' he said. The barrage was awe-inspiring, as were the Crocodile and Wasp armoured flamethrowers. The attack had been preceded by fierce hand-to-hand fighting the previous day during which Jemadar Harkabahadur led a charge with drawn kukris. This was against some 25 fanatical paratroopers dug in on the flood bank. The Battalion suffered severe casualties while trying to close up to the Gaiana but this was nothing when compared with the casualties suffered by the enemy on the night of the artillery barrage. 'Along these banks in the stream, in their trenches, in houses and holes behind, lay the massed dead. Few battlefields in this war can have presented the picture of carnage which the banks of the Gaiana showed that day.'* The German paratroopers had been literally pulverized.

After the forcing of the Gaiana the Battalion had a few days' well-earned rest. It received three IOMs, probably a record for one action, two MCs and four MMs; all were won in battle against the cream of the German Army who were at last beginning to crack. As the New Zealanders pushed on to reach the Po on 25 April, 1945, ANZAC Day, the thirtieth anniversary of the ANZAC landing at Gallipoli, the Gurkha Brigade followed more slowly, delayed by the constant traffic jams since both V and XIII Corps were following the same route and only one pontoon bridge had, as yet, been constructed across the broad river. The Gurkhas had had to swap their Kangaroos for lorries because the bridge was not strong enough for armoured vehicles. However, just before midnight on 26 April 2/6th Gurkha Rifles were across the Po, spending the rest of the night in the small town of Canda in pouring rain, the Gurkhas asleep where they sat in their vehicles. The next stop was to be Este, closely followed by Padua where they received a delirious reception. It was there that they received the welcome news on 2 May, 1945, that the German Armies in Italy had capitulated, but the advance north had to continue.†

By 9 May, 1945, the day that Germany surrendered unconditionally, the Battalion was resting in the pleasant seaside village of Belvedere, moving two days later to the outskirts of

---

* *The Race for Trieste* by Geoffrey Cox (William Kimber 1977) p. 112.
† The close comradeship between 6 GR and the New Zealanders had to wait over 40 years before it was officially recognized in 1987 by the affiliation of 6 GR with the 2/1st Royal New Zealand Infantry Regiment.

Trieste at Grado. They faced a very difficult situation because Tito's Partisan troops, advancing from Yugoslavia and laying claim to Trieste, found themselves confronted by the 2nd New Zealand Division. This was the beginning of a very tricky international situation that was not to be resolved until 1954 when Trieste became again an Italian city.

For the Battalion, however, the war was over at a cost of some 560 casualties, 141 of whom lie today in the Gurkha cemetery at Rimini. If the Battalion's conduct and record had lent lustre to the 6th Gurkha Rifles, it had not been without cost. On 9 July the Battalion sailed from Trieste for Haifa where it was to rejoin the 31st Indian Armoured Division, leaving the gallant dead to rest in Italian soil.

The remainder of the year was spent in Lebanon and Syria until in February, 1946, 2/6 GR embarked for India. They enjoyed a happy return to Abbottabad, prior to moving to Secunderabad to join up with the 31st Indian Armoured Division. This was to be only a short stay since in February, 1947, the Battalion moved to Delhi where it found a very tense internal security situation, added to which there was all the ceremonial of Viceregal duties. It was not a happy time for British and Gurkhas alike. The granting of independence to India and Pakistan meant, inevitably, the break-up of the Indian Army as the Battalion had known it since 1904. The air was filled with uncertainty and the situation was not helped by the departure of well-known British officers on demobilization. The long-drawn-out negotiations between the War Office, Foreign Office and the Treasury regarding the future of the Brigade of Gurkhas did nothing to help calm the situation.

According to Lieutenant Colonel J. A. I. Fillingham, who was a Company Commander in the 2nd Battalion, Lord Mountbatten was not the easiest master to serve. 'Mountbatten took a great interest,' writes Fillingham, 'especially in the ceremonial guard. He would appear on the balcony once a week after breakfast to voice his opinions on how the guard should be mounted. Fortunately [sic] they were Naval opinions which just did not fit in with our methods. Seldom constructive and often critical, nevertheless he would in the end bow to tradition.

However, he was forever demanding an increase in strength to compete with some visiting Maharajah. One had to be firm and this was accepted. The manpower was just not available.'*

On 14 August, 1947, when India and Pakistan became independent, the Battalion provided a guard of honour as the Union Jack was lowered over the Red Fort in Delhi. That Union Jack is now in the possession of the Regiment. And on 19 December, 1947, the battalion took part in the farewell parade of the British Infantry in Delhi. Besides the 2nd Battalion, the two other battalions involved were the 1st Battalion Royal Scots Fusiliers and 2nd Battalion East Lancashire Regiment. It was an historic occasion but for those British officers serving with the Battalion it must have been overshadowed by the knowledge that the majority of the Battalion had opted to remain in the Indian Army rather than join the British Army. It was, perhaps, the price that the 6th Gurkha Rifles had to pay for the British Government's over-hasty abdication of power. Less than 200 GOs, NCOs and riflemen opted to join the British Army.

* Regimental Association Report, Spring, 1988: p. 27. Fillingham had come from the 9th Gurkha Rifles, and later commanded a battalion of the 10th Gurkha Rifles.

CHAPTER SEVEN

―――⟩•☉•⟨―――

The Emergency in Malaya

THE British sometimes congratulate themselves on their success in disentangling themselves from Empire as compared with, say, the French. Certainly Malaya and Borneo ended in triumph after the inevitable ups and downs. However, the same cannot be said for Palestine and India where, by our hasty withdrawals, we created problems which have, if anything, grown worse with the years. Where the Gurkha Brigade was concerned the decision to leave India so hurriedly produced problems which came as a great shock to the serving British officers, some of whom believed their Gurkha soldiers would serve only under British and their own Gurkha officers.

The partition of the Indian Army between India and the newly-created Pakistan brought with it immense problems, while at the same time both countries were torn apart by communal strife. The future of the Gurkha regiments, recruited as they were in a country independent either of India or Pakistan, was in limbo. Lord Wavell as Viceroy had foreseen this problem when he warned that an independent India would be unable to employ all ten Gurkha regiments and he recommended that the balance of the Gurkha Brigade should be transferred to the British Army. This led to lengthy consideration in the War Office where the wheels of God grind slowly.

There followed negotiations between the British, Indian and Nepalese governments before a Tripartite Agreement for the employment of Gurkhas in the British and Indian Armies was ratified on 9 November, 1947. Four Gurkha regiments would

[86]

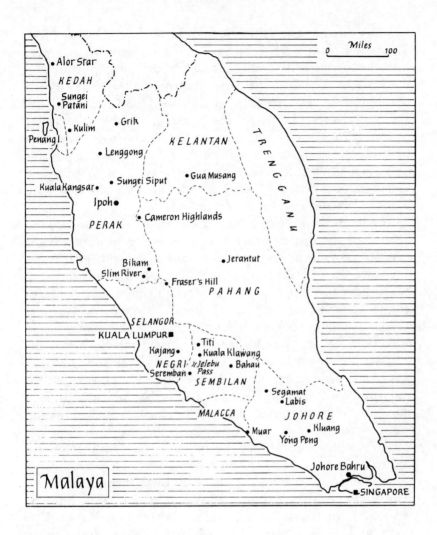

be transferred to the British Army, the balance going to India. The four British were to be two-battalion regiments and were to form the nucleus of a Gurkha Division for employment in the Far East. The War Office nominated only the 2nd Gurkhas, on account of that regiment's long and close association with the 60th Rifles. They left the selection of the other three regiments to Army Headquarters in New Delhi, specifying only that the recruiting area should be spread as widely as possible over Nepal, which meant two regiments of Magars and Gurungs, as in the 2nd Gurkhas, and two of Limbus and Rais, as in the 7th and 10th Gurkha Rifles.

At a time when shipping was at a premium with the demobilization of the British Army from overseas, it appears that the selection of Gurkha regiments for transfer to the British Army depended on their location at the time. The 6th, 7th and 10th had regular battalions in Burma under the command of Headquarters South-East Asia Land Forces. Only the 2nd Gurkhas had no battalions outside India but they had been specifically nominated by the War Office. It followed therefore that the 6th, who recruited Magars and Gurungs like the 2nd Gurkhas, was nominated for transfer to the British Army, as were the 7th and 10th with their Limbus and Rais. The choice came as a shock to regiments like the 5th Gurkhas, with a fighting tradition second to none, but the reason for it is clear.

It was not, however, easy to persuade the Gurkha officers and riflemen to opt to join the British Army. They had grown up in the Indian Army which was familiar to them. The British Army was not. The majority of them did not speak English, whereas Urdu was a second tongue. They were expected to make up their minds over-quickly between serving under either the British or Indian governments. It was to be a free choice, but those Gurkha officers opting to remain in the Indian Army would have one conspicuous advantage over those who opted for the British Army; they would be eligible for regular commissions as fully-fledged officers, whereas those joining the British Army would not. This undoubtedly influenced many of the Gurkha officers in opting for India and who could blame them; and, not surprisingly, they in their turn brought influence

16. *"The Subedar at once dashed forward under heavy Spandau fire and killed the firer with his kukri .... The ten minutes of activity and near hysteria was marked by some remarkable shooting by the 14th/20th and some exceptional bravery by the Gurkhas."* (p.81) The Battle of Medicina, 16 April, 1945, by Terence Cuneo

17. *"In 1990-91 Ian Thomas and James Cheshire served with the 14th/20th in the Gulf War."* (p.127) Captain I.N.A. Thomas 6 GR (4th right) with Major A.R.D. Shirreff and 'B' Squadron's war trophies, 1991, Iraq.

18. *"It was the helicopter that made all the difference in Borneo."* (p.114)

19. *"When the 1/6th returned to Hong Kong in August, 1964 ... they were once again a well-seasoned jungle battalion."* (p.118) Jungle range at Lundu.

to bear on the riflemen they commanded. In the event, the Indian Army retained the equivalent of VCOs in their own Army and the British Army awarded full commissions both to those Gurkhas trained at Sandhurst and to a few QGOs selected as Gurkha Commissioned Officers (GCOs).

In retrospect it must seem that the whole of this business was clumsily handled but the conditions under which decisions had to be taken in Army Headquarters should be borne in mind. The Indian sub-continent was in a state of chaos. The Indian Army was being broken up, the Sikh squadron of the 19th Lancers going to India, the Mussalman squadrons going to Pakistan, etc. There was the division of regimental memorabilia and funds between India and Pakistan, mayhem in the Punjab and Hariana, inexperienced Indian officers taking the place of British in Army Headquarters, the constant disappearance of experienced British officers in whom the soldiers had trust, as they joined their new British units or were demobilized. It has to be said that, given the conditions that prevailed, it is a miracle that things were not much, much worse.

Here due tribute should be paid to those British officers who stayed on to provide the necessary stability in such a time. Some had been overseas for five or more years; all had been through the wearying years of war. All were faced with an uncertain future, whether it be with the Gurkhas or in some British regiment, or as demobilized civilians. It was a time of flux when almost every month saw the disappearance of one familiar face and its substitution by another new one. The 6th Gurkhas owe a great deal to the British officers and to the Gurkha ones, who held the Regiment together in times as trying as any the Regiment had previously experienced. They should never be forgotten.

Amidst this difficult time of change from Indian to British administration, and the two were poles apart, the 1/6th arrived in Malaya from Rangoon on 28 January, 1948. The Battalion was commanded by Lieutenant Colonel 'Jim' Robertson who was a 6th Gurkha of 6th Gurkhas, having joined in 1931. During the war in Burma he commanded the 1/7th Gurkha Rifles for a spell before going on to command, as a Temporary Brigadier, the famous 48th Gurkha Infantry Brigade. After the war he reverted to Lieutenant Colonel in order to command his old battalion of the 6th. The 1/6th arrived in Malaya with only fifteen British officers and 330 Gurkhas. Their new home was to be Sungei Patani in the northern state of Kedah.

The 2nd Battalion sailed from Bombay for Malaya on 3 March, 1948, in an even more debilitated state than the 1/6th. It was commanded by Lieutenant Colonel 'Freddie' Shaw who had joined the 6th Gurkhas in 1932. He had commanded the 3rd Battalion with great distinction with the Chindits and had taken over command of the 2nd Battalion in Delhi. The battalion, open to every kind of propaganda while stationed in the Indian capital, opted in the main to remain in the Indian Army. This left the 2/6th with only eight British officers, three King's Gurkha Officers and 113 Gurkha other ranks. A draft of 192 ex-service recruits and another of 180 brand new recruits joined in February and March just prior to embarkation, which provided the CO with a difficult training problem. The only saving grace was that the 2/6th were intended to spend only 12 months in Malaya before moving to Hong Kong. In the meantime they were sent to Wardieburn Camp in Kuala Lumpur, which is described as being 'frankly depressing'.

As it happened both battalions had arrived in Malaya at what turned out to be the beginning of what came to be called the 'Malayan Emergency'. It began on 16 June, 1948, with the murder of an estate manager, a Mr Walker, closely followed by the murder of two other planters. The Malayan Government declared a State of Emergency on 17 June in the states of Perak and Johore and, the following day, throughout the Federated Malay States. It was to last for twelve years. The uprising, for it was no less, was largely fuelled by the spread of Communism in South-East Asia, strongly supported by the Soviet Union and encouraged, both morally and physically, by Mao Tse-tung's successes in China. In the aftermath of war and after three years' occupation by the Japanese, Malaya was awash with weapons, many of them supplied by the British in support of anti-Japanese activities; and in many instances the CTs (Communist Terrorists), as they came to be known, had been trained by British instructors parachuted into Malaya for the purpose.

The great majority were Chinese settled in Malaya but there were also some Malay and Indian sympathizers.

Although Malaya had not been ravaged by war as Burma had been, there had been a gradual breakdown in law and order. The Malays, being the predominant race, were reluctant to concede equal voting rights to the Chinese and Indians and there was a great deal of animosity between the three communities. Moreover, the original British colonial administration had taken a severe knock as a result of the Japanese victory and was slow in getting into its stride after the Japanese capitulation. What the country needed, but was not to get, was several years of peace while Malaya could be put back on its feet, the political situation overhauled and a new one instituted, and law and order introduced with the maximum vigour. There was an absence of 'get up and go' in the colonial administration which meant that when the Emergency first began the CTs had some easy successes. They were helped by the absence of an adequate Intelligence system country-wide, the most essential requirement in all counter-insurgency operations, and it was some little time before an efficient system could be organized.

From the start of the Emergency both battalions of the Regiment were involved, regardless of their recent arrival, low strength and acute shortage of trained soldiers. The 17th Gurkha Division was still in the process of being formed in Malaya. At the same time King George VI had signed a warrant ordering that the Corps of Gurkhas should be known as *The Brigade of Gurkhas* and their senior appointment was to be *Major General Brigade of Gurkhas*. The first holder of this apoointment, Major General Charles Boucher*, was the GOC Malaya District. In due course Major Generals Jim Robertson, Walter Walker and Pat Patterson successively held this appointment, which must surely be a record for the Regiment. They were also GOC 17th Gurkha Division. Another 6th Gurkha Colonel, Major General (later Lieutenant General Sir Derek) Boorman also held the appointment of Major General Brigade of Gurkhas, but combined with that of Commander British Forces, Hong Kong.

* General Boucher's regiment was the 3rd Queen Alexandra's Own Gurkha Rifles.

JAI SIXTH!

An interesting fact about the Regiment which is worthy of record is that from the time the 1/6th crossed the Chindwin in November, 1944, and the 2/6th landed at Basra in April, 1941, both battalions were virtually continuously on active service until the end of operations in Borneo in August, 1966. There were, of course, short breaks in Hong Kong and Tidworth and the tempo varied from hand-to-hand fighting with German paratroopers in Italy to ambushing CTs in the Malayan jungles. However, it is hardly surprising that the Regiment became so professional in its outlook and training. Of course it is not claimed that the 6th were in any way special in this regard. It could equally be applied to the Brigade of Gurkhas as a whole.

During the years of run-down of empire it seemed that each successive emergency, as it occurred, took the authorities by surprise. It was the same in Malaya, Cyprus, Kenya, Aden and so on. 'Business as usual' was the common reaction until some soldier like Templer or Harding was put in charge and knocked more than a few heads together. In Malaya it required a series of disasters including the ambushing and killing in 1951 of the High Commissioner, Sir Henry Gurney, before the home government pulled out all the stops, dispatched sufficient troops to do the job and found the man to give the lead in General Gerald Templer.

The Principles of War do not change, merely the conditions for their application. In Malaya, and later in Borneo, this meant dense jungle, poor communications and a fanatical enemy operating, on the whole, in small numbers but with the support, forced or willing, of the locals. There was also the climate, hot and humid, with often incessant and torrential rain. Jungle warfare demands its own techniques, differing from war in the desert or in the mountains, but above all it requires a very high standard of discipline, physical fitness, patience and perseverance and marksmanship in order to deal with fleeting targets. It is above all an infantryman's war for which the Gurkha rifleman is remarkably well suited, both in stamina and in courage.

The Regiment's record during the Malayan Emergency has already been covered in detail in Charles Messenger's *The*

*Steadfast Gurkha** and it would be tedious to repeat it again here. It was, on the whole, a campaign of small patrols, seldom over a company in strength, searching for, finding and, if at all possible, bringing to battle a skilful and brave enemy who used the jungle as home ground. Here it will be sufficient to describe a jungle patrol taken more or less verbatim from Messenger's book as an example of what it was like to serve in the 6th Gurkhas in Malaya between 1948 and 1960, when the Emergency was officially declared ended.

Originally it had been intended to waste out the British officers commissioned into the 6th Gurkha Rifles and replace them gradually by officers seconded from British regiments and by Sandhurst-trained Gurkha officers. This was abandoned in 1950 and a permanent cadre established. Officers joining it could do so after one year's secondment from a British unit or directly from Sandhurst; in the latter case they would serve a year's attachment with a British unit, in the Regiment's case the Rifle Brigade to which the 6th Gurkhas were affiliated, before joining the Regiment.† In the following year the Depot Brigade of Gurkhas was established at Sungei Patani where recruits were trained.

During the long years of the Emergency both the 1/6th and 2/6th acquired a wide knowledge of both Northern and Southern Malaya, for much of the time in the jungle, interspersed by short periods in the fleshpots of Singapore on Internal Security duties. The 1/6th had almost nine years of continuous operations against the CTs, not getting a break until 1957 when the battalion moved to Hong Kong and the 2/6th relieved them. One of the Brigade of Gurkhas' most distinguished officers, Lieutenant Colonel Walter Walker, took over command of the 1/6th in 1951. Originally an 8th Gurkha, he had commanded the 4/8th with great distinction in Burma. He was an inspired trainer and an outstanding leader who went

---

* *The Steadfast Gurkha: Historical Record of 6th Queen Elizabeth's Own Gurkha Rifles, Volume 3, 1948–1982* by Charles Messenger (Leo Cooper, 1985).
† Later the year's attachment was dropped in order to get new officers into action early.

on to achieve Four Star rank in the British Army with no less than two bars to his DSO. He realized that continuous patrolling in small numbers in the jungle, month in and month out, might have adverse effects on both discipline and morale, particularly for those who had had no let-up since Burma and he instituted a very intensive training programme whenever he managed to get the battalion together in Sungei Patani with, undoubtedly, excellent results.

As one example of what jungle operations entailed, the following account by Brevet Lieutenant Colonel 'Brunny' Short is well worth repetition. He was Second-in-Command of the 1/6th at the time to Lieutenant Colonel 'Speedy' Bredin,* a Dorset by origin but a dedicated 6th Gurkha by adoption. Short joined the 6th Gurkhas in 1937, winning the MC with the 4th Battalion in Burma, and went on to command the 1/6th from 1956–58. Retiring as a Brigadier in 1964 he became Secretary to the Speaker of the House of Commons and was knighted on his retirement from that appointment. He was Colonel of the Regiment from 1978–83, a very distinguished record.

'Most jungle operations seem to start off on the MT Park at 2 or 3 in the morning. This is because the way into the jungle invariably takes you through rubber estates, vegetable gardens, or tin mining land and, for security reasons, you like to get through this fringe before the labourers are up and about. There is therefore a preliminary drive, generally in an armoured 3-tonner with only minimum sized slits affording front visibility, through the hot airless night to the debussing point.

'Here the Platoon Commander takes charge; there are whispered commands, magazines are placed on the Bren guns and the leading section disappears some unidentifiable distance off the road to shake out for the move. You utilise this pause to struggle into your pack, probably with the help of the orderly. Knowing what it contains, you may experience a

---

* Lieutenant Colonel A. E. C. Bredin, DSO, MC, commanded the 1/6th from 1954–56. His book, *The Happy Warriors* (Blackmore Press, 1961) provides an excellent account of the battalion's adventures during the Emergency.

brief feeling of surprise that it isn't heavier ... This is an opinion you will have cause to revise before the day is much older.

'And so you start off, probably moving with Platoon HQ, your orderly trotting along a yard or two behind you. Weapons are carried differently from the old days – no longer balanced on the shoulder with the muzzle in the rear, as in Waziristan. The rifle, Bren, carbine or whatever is usually hitched under the arm, muzzle for'ard, the sling over the shoulder and the whole steadied by the hand. It is quicker to get into action when carried in this way and more manoeuvrable in thick jungle. You may decide at some stage to try slinging the rifle in the ordinary way, but after a brief and unproductive period in which the foresight gets entangled with every vine and creeper within range, you abandon the attempt and revert to the men's system.

'There is usually a pause on the edge of the jungle, whilst it gets light enough to see by. You can now observe what your companions are dressed in – you yourself also, for that matter – and it is not elegant. Basically there is little difference from the Burma kit, and the colour is the same. There is, of course, the jungle hat, a deerstalker affair whose major tactical advantage is its complete shapelessness – it presents no hard outline in the jungle, or indeed any visible outline whatsoever. It stays on by gravity, and sartorially speaking the only polite thing to do with a jungle hat is to look away. Then there are the jungle boots, rubber-soled and with canvas uppers, laced on the hook-and-eye principle, stretching half way up the calves. They are very useful when walking along the 2-foot iron pipes of the Kinta Intake Water Catchment area, which are met with from time to time in the jungle, but lack grip on a wet hillside. The final note of raffishness is added by 'Rags Sweat J. G. [Jungle Green]' worn round the neck, a dyed version of the domestic dishcloth, and possessing similar properties.

'Now you start moving through the jungle, and at this time of the morning it is not uncomfortable. The sun has not yet had time to make the ground surface the steam-bath it becomes later in the day. If you are lucky, the way will be through primary jungle, where the visibility is 30 yards or more, and the going reasonably good even without a track. Most of the trees are surprisingly small – a foot or so in diameter – though the occasional mastodon will rise to 200 feet or more. The foliage canopy is about 30 feet from the ground, and is penetrated by very little sunlight. Sometimes the space between the canopy and the ground is filled by the attap palm, making movement more difficult. Sometimes you get the even less welcome pandanus palm, with vicious saw-toothed edges. But on the whole movement through this sort of jungle is reasonably fast.

'Shortly after 9 a.m. you will hear mutters of "*Bhat pakaune*", and at the first suitable stream a halt is made, protective detachments are put out, and ration tins are excavated from the depths of packs. There are two types of ration, Gurkha and British. The Gurkha type provides two meals of rice and dal, with fish or meat as an adjunct, and tea at midday. The British provides two conventional meals for the early morning and evening, not unlike the wartime K-Ration. For the midday 'snack' it produces a sticky and highly unseasonable assortment of chocolate, Mars bars and other sweets that literally turn the stomach in the noon-day heat. Most of us carry one British to three Gurkha, using the British at breakfast time only.

'The "*bhat pakaune*" halt, which is a feature of the first day's operations only, is soon over. In a remarkably short time the debris is cleared away or concealed, and the platoon is once again on the move. By now the effect of the sun will have become increasingly apparent, and by 11 o'clock you will not have a square inch of dry clothing above the knees. The characteristic smell of sweat-drenched J.G. will start to assail your nostrils, and except for respites during the hours of darkness, will be with you now until the end of the operation.

'After a further period of climbing, during which your pack, the inner side saturated with sweat, glues itself to your back like a monstrous, over-weighted clam, the pace seems to slow down somewhat. Presently the ominous word *"bans"* is muttered from someone in front, and in no time you are in the thick of it. Bamboo everywhere, thickets quite impassable even to a cat, thin trailers with the strength and resilience of telephone wires, festooning the spaces between and worst of all the rotted broken-down stems that bar the way every few yards, just too high to be able to step over in comfort, and much too low to pass underneath except by going down on your knees. This process, constantly repeated, becomes exhausting, and you envy the men their low centre of gravity which enables them to duck under these obstructions with no more than a slight bend of the legs. After the top of your pack has been caught up for the tenth time, you lose patience, grit your teeth and shove. A slight splintering noise above indicates that the bamboo has given way, and in an instant your head and neck are overrun by red soldier ants, smarting with indignation at the destruction of their home, and by this time of the day in splendid fighting shape. With the help of your orderly and the rest of Platoon Headquarters they are eventually dislodged, but not before they have stung you in a dozen places or more. Next time you bend your knees.

'Shortly before half past twelve comes the "tea" halt, and as you thankfully wriggle out of your pack once more, the platoon signaller is already running out the aerial for the midday wireless call. During this call your platoon has to report position, not necessarily such an easy task as it sounds, particularly after a morning of hard going and limited visibility. A sort of *jirgah* now takes place between the Platoon GO, seated on his pack, the Platoon Sergeant and the Section Commanders standing round in a respectful semi-circle. If you are wise you keep out of this discussion: the Platoon Commander and the NCOs have much more practice in this kind of thing than you, and at this stage of the operation you will invariably be quite certain that you have travelled much further than is actually the case. So you let them get on with it and, in due course, a tentative answer is arrived at, subject to confirmation by the Platoon Sergeant who has meanwhile been sent off to a flank to make a visual recce.

'By now your orderly, who has been boiling water on a Tommy-cooker, using solid fuel which looks like white soap, has got the tea ready. The milk in the Gurkha type ration comes in the form of a semi-solidified concentrate, the appearance and texture of blancmange, from which the orderly cuts slices as required. These he throws into the tea, where they tend to melt rather slowly. As the undissolved residue presents a somewhat unexpected appearance when you suddenly confront it in the bottom of your mess tin, at a range of about an inch and a half, when finishing off your tea, you may prefer him to use the milk from your BT ration. This works on the toothpaste principle, and though it does not look attractive whilst being added to the tea, it does behave more predictably once in the liquid.

'*Milap* has now been established with Bn HQ and the signaller is about to pass details of the midday position when you become aware of a slight commotion. The Platoon Sergeant has returned from his recce, and it seems that through a gap in the trees he has spotted a hill that shouldn't be there. Bn HQ is abruptly told to 'wait out', the *jirgah* reassembles, and the whole business starts again.

'By 1.15, if you are lucky, you are on the move once more, with about a pint and a half of tea inside you and a mental note to keep a closer watch on the map than you have hitherto.

'For ease of navigation the Platoon Commander may decide to move along a stream for a bit. As a relief from continual hill-climbing you approve of this idea, until you actually get down to the stream bed. Here you find the atmosphere incredibly dank and airless, the hills close in on you from either side, shutting out the daylight, and a whole variety of fleshy, dark green aspidistra-like plants and creepers, stimulated by the waterlogged earth, flourish abundantly.

'Having crossed and recrossed the stream for the twentieth time, you are profoundly relieved when the Platoon Commander decides to make for the hills once again. By this time, however, the strain is beginning to tell somewhat. The pack tends to throw you off balance, your knees lack co-ordination, and any grip on the hillside which your jungle boots ever afforded has long since disappeared. On reaching the crest of the hill, you have to take a firm line with the platoon and order a five-minute halt, a possibility which would not otherwise have occurred to them.

'The last trick that fate has in store for you, before you stop for the night, is a *ladang* to move through. This is an old aboriginal cultivation, abandoned perhaps six or seven years ago, and extending for anything up to half a mile. Since sun and air have had uninterrupted access to it for a number of years, the secondary vegetation is considerable. By far the worst is a trailing fern which the men call *chungya*. It occurs also in Nepal where its only use, according to the troops, is to make bedding for new-born piglets. In the writer's opinion the pigs get a raw deal. The plant forms a solid wall nine or ten feet high, and as deep as you care to go. The task of forcing a way through it devolves on the unfortunate leading section, and progress is exceedingly slow. Needless to say the passage-way, when finally made, is a good deal too small for you yourself to negotiate in comfort, and your verbal observations after disentangling your rifle and pack for the umpteenth time are generally worth listening to. Finally, as you emerge into the open, a hanging creeper dexterously whips your jungle hat from your head and carries it smartly two or three paces to the rear. You watch it for a moment as you have watched it on twenty-nine previous occasions this day, oscillating gently just out of reach. Your orderly retrieves it for you, and you are glad to get into camp half an hour later.

'On arrival in camp, there is a good deal of activity. Two sections are probably sent off immediately on local patrol, carrying nothing but their arms. They will be back in half an hour or so, and meanwhile the remainder of the platoon set about making bivouacs. Your orderly will get busy with his kukri, and in no time a site is cleared, and a framework of branches erected to take the poncho cape overhead. On the ground goes about six inches of attap palm and over that, to your surprise, another poncho cape. As you only carry one of these, you enquire where the second one came from, and, if you are proud, order that it be restored to its rightful owner. Your orderly merely grins happily and leaves it where it is.

'Close by you will be the Platoon Commander, once again studying his map, for the evening wireless call is just about due. This time he has no doubt about the position at all. He has plotted progress throughout the afternoon, and finally fixed his reference by means of a stream running just below the camp – it is so close that you can hear the sound of the water. So that is that, and the co-ordinates in due course are passed over the air with firmness and decision. Shortly afterwards one of the patrols returns to camp and reports that the water is flowing the wrong way . . .

'At dusk, when everyone is in camp, Stand-To takes place – in complete silence, and actuated only by the faintest of whistles. After Stand-Down the Platoon Commander's orderly will bring you a mug with a large tot of rum in it, and another for him. Sometimes he will even accompany this with 'cocktail eats' – curried fish and bamboo shoots, *chippy alus* and so on, all of which go down exceedingly well. He is followed – or sometimes preceded – by the Platoon Medical Orderly, who gives you a tablet of Paludrine, and if you have sustained any cuts or abrasions during the day, decorates them with a purplish-brown fluid which he carries in his medical *jhola*. Finally comes the *bhat* – a whole mess-tin full, with *dal*, tinned fish or meat, mashed-up vegetables from your BT ration pack, anything that can be shovelled on. You can't normally cope with all this on the first day, but your appetite improves as the operation progresses, and by the third evening you are clearing your mess tin with the best of them.

'After dark there is little to do for the men. Sentries have been posted and orders for the next day *sunao'd*. They therefore turn in early, though subdued mutterings and sometimes chucklings can be heard beneath bivouacs for the next hour or so. You yourself will probably have another rum with the Platoon Commander, who by this time will be well away crossing the Irrawaddy or assaulting Mandalay

Hill. This goes on for a while, until eventually you both decide to call it a day.

'The evening chorus of jungle-bats and tree hoppers continues for a time, and then dies away. During the night, although you get plenty of sleep, you tend to wake frequently. Mostly you turn over and are immediately asleep again, though sometimes you may be diverted for a while by the gentle snoring of the GO alongside you, or the Chinese CLO [Civil Liaison Officer] talking in his sleep.

'Halfway through the night, when the moon rises and floods the jungle with an unbelievable radiance, you forget the sweat and the smells and the agonies of the day before, and can only thank your lucky stars for the troops around you, whose magnificent qualities are just the same as they were when you first got to know them – maybe many years ago – and just the same as they will always be.'*

If the campaigning was tough, so were the soldiers and the officers, British and Gurkha, who led them. They had to be since otherwise they would never have got the upper hand over an equally tough and resourceful enemy. Malaya achieved independence (*Merdeka*) on 31 August, 1957, but it was not until 31 July, 1960, that the Emergency was declared officially over. The 6th Gurkhas had made a magnificent contribution to the victory but in so doing had paid the price of 59 killed, who included two British and five Gurkha officers. In return the Regiment had accounted for well over 400 CTs. Nearly 7,000 had been killed altogether, and another 4,000 had surrendered or been captured.

The campaign in Malaya did not make much impact in Britain where people were still recovering from five years of war. Nevertheless, the campaign's importance for the newly-fledged 17th Gurkha Division cannot be over-emphasized. It is remarkable how quickly the Gurkha units adapted themselves to the peculiar nature of the Emergency; not only to the tactical use of jungle and rubber estate but also to the more exacting requirement of constant readiness to engage a fleeting foe whose

* *The Steadfast Gurkha, op. cit.* pp. 37–43.

whereabouts could seldom be pinpointed with any degree of accuracy. It is in this connection that the comments by Lieutenant Colonel A. S. Harvey* on the Malayan Campaign as a whole are very significant and, at the risk of a certain amount of repetition, they follow below.

'As has been explained earlier,' writes Harvey, 'Gurkha battalions in general, and 2/6 GR in particular, arrived in Malaya ill-equipped to perform any task. There were virtually no records, a motley collection of clerks and very few trained officers and senior NCOs. The immediate task for Colonel Shaw [the CO] was to forge a coherent and workmanlike unit and to do this he needed time. Fortunately he had some war-experienced officers who had refused, or had escaped, exchange to a British regiment, and some former 6th and ex-Gurkha Brigade Gurkha officers, several of them from 8 GR. A training Wing was established within the battalion and recruits began to arrive. Just as this was beginning to take shape the Emergency was proclaimed. 1/6 GR were not in such bad shape and were better placed to meet this new challenge.

'It is paradoxical that this new call to active soldiering proved to be the best way of resolving the problem. There can be little doubt that the Malayan Emergency welded together units which otherwise would have taken a considerable time to absorb previously unknown British officers, including those on attachment from British infantry regiments, as well as the virtually untrained rank and file. That the Gurkha regiments succeeded in doing this remarkably quickly must reflect the greatest credit on the Commanding Officers at that time, and also on their officers, British and Gurkha. The Sixth learned quickly and soon became very proficient in dealing with the tactical situation, as will be explained.

* Lieutenant Colonel Tony ('Tich') Harvey served in 5 RGR during the war and joined 2/6 GR in Delhi in 1947. He was among the handful of British officers who arrived in Malaya with the 2nd Battalion in March, 1948. He served in Malaya as a company commander and later commanded 2/6 GR in Borneo from 1963–66.

'The Malayan Campaign, all but unnoticed in the United Kingdom, was *not* another Burma war. The CTs were ordinary citizens of the country who had been trained by the British to assist in disrupting the Japanese occupation of Malaya. When victory over Japan was assured, these CTs buried the majority of their weapons and bided their time until they could rebel against another kind of occupation, that of the British, as well as against their so-called lackeys, the Malay rulers. Receiving every encouragement from Peking, they opted for the middle of May, 1948, to open their campaign. Their opening moves in the Malay States and in Singapore bore an uncanny resemblance to Northern Ireland today, viz: 'Hit and Run', then melt into the ordinary civilian background, which in Malay meant the jungle. Their Achilles heel was, of course, food supply and medicines, but by a sustained campaign of terror and extortion from the Chinese coolie population they overcame this problem until General Briggs resettled the Chinese squatters into villages behind barbed wire. This, combined with a vigorous 'Hearts and Minds' campaign, effectively closed the CTs' supply route and had a pronounced effect on the surrender rate.

'In the beginning the initiative lay with the CTs, the more so because the Intelligence Branch of government was hardly functioning. Moreover there was no overall direction of effort by the Security Forces and co-ordination was hard to achieve. This was only rectified when General Templer was appointed 'Supremo' and the success rate began to swing in our favour.

'The best way to employ the army was not easy to determine because every tin miner and rubber planter would have liked to have had a detachment of troops permanently located on their properties. In some areas Companies were given their own area of responsibility which they managed with the local District Officer and Civil Policeman. Although long-winded, this system was on the whole successful, but not until after the District War Executive Council system had been established, i.e., daily meetings of Civil Police, Special Branch, Military Commanders, from company level right up to national level.

'Another way was to deploy platoons in the worst CT-infested areas. In the beginning of the Emergency this had to be done because of the low state of civilian morale, but it was wasteful of manpower and led to dissipation of force. Military Commanders above battalion level seemed, on occasion, to feel left out of the fight and so periodically a great 'sweep' was organized by the local Brigadier, using all available troops and often with air and artillery support. "We will sweep the jungle!" was the cry, and so the Army did. On one of these 'sweeps' one British battalion passed through another in the jungle without either being aware of the fact!

'It is hard to explain how impotent one feels in the jungle. There is no 'Front', or back line. There is no obvious avenue of approach although jungle paths tended to be used. For much of the time one advanced on a 'one man front', the rest of the platoon/section following in single file. Leading scouts of patrols were relieved of all their kit save their arms and ammunition and would be changed every 20 minutes or so in order to maintain the requisite degree of alertness. He would be the one to get a chance with a snap shot. The rest of the patrol were unlikely to see the target. Ambushes were, of course, different. Jungle warfare veterans of Malaya find it easy to believe that many hundreds of hours were spent on patrol before a CT was sighted, and many hundreds more before a 'kill' was made.

'It was in this game of 'blind man's buff' that the Gurkha really came into his own. The Gurkha soldier's innate sense of discipline and unquestioning loyalty enabled him to go on jungle patrol after jungle patrol uncomplainingly, irrespective of the success rate or his own personal feelings; and apart from leave home after every three years, the Gurkhas were in the campaign from start to finish. The British, Australian, New Zealand, Fijian and other troops came and went but the Gurkhas were there throughout. This is why Malaya owes such a debt of gratitude to the Brigade of Gurkhas – and among them not least the Sixth! Since there were no pitched battles like Alamein or Meiktila, the people of Britain knew

32. *"As it happened both battalions had arrived in Malaya at the beginning of the 'Malayan Emergency'. ... It was to last for twelve years."* (p.90) General Sir Gerald Templer congratulates Major D.H. Houston, MC and A Company 2/6th for successfully destroying a terrorist camp, 1954.

33. *"Lieutenant-Colonel Walter Walker took over command of the 1/6th in 1951 ... He was an inspired trainer and an outstanding leader who went on to achieve Four Star rank with no less than two bars to his DSO."* (p.93) General Sir Walter Walker, KCB, CBE, DSO and two Bars, Dato Seri Setia.

34. *"It was not until 31 July, 1960, that the Emergency was declared over. The 6th Gurkhas had made a magnificent contribution to the victory ... had accounted for well over 400 CTs."* (p.101) Captured terrorist weapons and ammunition.

35. *"Fortuitously both battalions were in Malaya when the glad news* [of the award of the title 'Queen Elizabeth's Own'] *was received and they combined together to celebrate the event. There they were joined by the Colonel of The Regiment, Field-Marshal Lord Harding."* (p.105) With the British Officers, August, 1959, Ipoh.

36. *"The 1/6th, the first Gurkha unit to be stationed west of Suez since the Second World War, had been warned at Tidworth that it would be Borneo next. The Battalion arrived there in January, 1964."* (p.115)

37. *"Gil Hickey was the CO and he did not much care for the western half of the Third Division where everything seemed quiet."* (p.116)
Lieutenant-Colonel B.G. Hickey, MC and Bar (centre, flanked by Major (QGO) Lokbahadur Thapa and Major Henry Hayward-Surrey). He was awarded the OBE for his success on *'Claret'* operations.

38. *"Walker never lost sight of an internal rebellion, which is why he promoted an active 'Hearts and Minds' campaign among the local population."* (p.111) Major P.B.F. Robeson's C Company 2/6th built this bridge at Salilaran, together with the Assault Pioneer Platoon.

39. *"The inter-company competition held annually in 6 GR is for the Wallace Memorial Trophy, which commemorates this gallant young officer."* (p.113)

40. *"In September, 1964, the 2/6th returned for a second tour, this time commanded by Tony Harvey."* (p.118) Lieutenant-Colonel A.S. Harvey, MC and Bar, at Bario. His Highness The Sultan conferred on him the Most Honourable Order of the Crown of Brunei, to add to the OBE which he was awarded.

41. *"Sergeant Bombahadur Gurung received the MM."* (p.120) Bombahadur (right); with Colour Sergeant Amerbahadur Pun, MM, and Bar, accompanied by Lieutenant-Colonel and Mrs R.C. Neath, February, 1967, Kuala Lumpur.

42. *"The Colonel of the 14th/20th Hussars approached Major-General Robertson ... with the proposal that 2/6 GR should wear 'The Hawk'."* (p.126) 'The Hawk', in fact the Prussian Eagle, is worn on the right sleeve by all 6th Gurkhas and will be carried on the cross-belt pouch of The Royal Gurkha Rifles.

43. *"Both British and Gurkha Officers have enjoyed short attachments with the Hussars."* (p.127)Captain (QGO) Amarbahadur Gurung with Lieutenant-Colonel Frazer and the 14th/20th Guidon Party in 1965. The King's Royal Hussars now wear crossed kukris.

44. *"The amalgamation of 1/6 GR and 2/6 GR took place in Hong Kong on 14 June, 1969."* (p.131) Support Company marches past Lieutenant-Colonel R.N.P. Reynolds, MBE.

45. *"One of the arguments in favour of the retention of the Gurkhas had been the requirement to garrison Hong Kong."* (p.132) Lieutenant (QGO) Purnabahadur Gurung, Support Company 2/6th, on a 'hearts and minds' project, 1968. He is now Hon Lieutenant (GCO) and first Chairman of the Nepal Branch of the Regimental Association.

46. *"Public Duties in London; the diminutive Gurkha sentries, who barely came up to the chests of the burly Guardsmen, making up for it by their impeccable turnout and smartness of drill."* (p.135)

47. *"There was too the difficult problem of keeping out the many thousands who sought to escape across 'the Wire' from China."* (p.133)

little of the part played by the Gurkha regiments in restoring peace in Malaya – the more's the pity!'

It is doubtful whether the ordinary Gurkha rifleman cared very much about the lack of recognition by the British for whom he fought and often died. For him it was 'A Matter of Honour' to be a soldier and he was fiercely proud of the honour of his regiment and of his comrades.

There was great rejoicing early in 1959 when Her Majesty The Queen conferred on the Regiment the title of 'Queen Elizabeth's Own'. In future it would be known as the 6th Queen Elizabeth's Own Gurkha Rifles. Fortuitously both battalions were in Malaya when the glad news was received and they combined together in Suvla Barracks, Ipoh to celebrate the event. There they were joined by the Colonel of the Regiment, Field Marshal Lord Harding, under whom they had served when he was Commander-in-Chief in Malaya in 1949–51. He had succeeded Field Marshal Lord Birdwood as Colonel in 1951, the year Lord Birdwood died after 25 years as Colonel of the Regiment.

CHAPTER EIGHT

———◦◉◦———

The Confrontation in Borneo

THE Confrontation between Britain and Indonesia began on 8 December, 1962, with a rebellion in the Sultanate of Brunei, an independent state under British protection in Borneo. Brunei was ruled by a Sultan, Sir Omar Ali Saifuddin. He abdicated voluntarily in 1967 in favour of his son, the present Sultan Hassanal Bolkia. The Malay name for Brunei is Negara Brunei Darussalam. By virtue of the flourishing Shell oilfield at Seria on the seacoast Brunei is, for its size, one of the richest states in the world.

Borneo is one of the world's biggest islands, very mountainous and covered in dense rain forest. Politically it is divided in two. By far the largest part is Indonesian (until 1949, Dutch) and known as Kalimantan. Along the west coast and northern tip of the island are three territories that used to be part of the British Empire: Sabah (North Borneo) and Sarawak, which were administered as colonies and, between them, the British-protected Sultanate of Brunei. The indigenous population are commonly known as Dayaks. They are divided into many different tribes such as Ibans, Muruts, Kenyahs, Kelabits and the nomadic Punans, spread thinly throughout the island. They are chiefly jungle-dwelling agriculturists, living in kampongs or long houses close to the great rivers which are the principal means of communication in what is otherwise virtually roadless country. There is also a large population of Chinese and Malays, the former predominating except in Brunei where Malays make

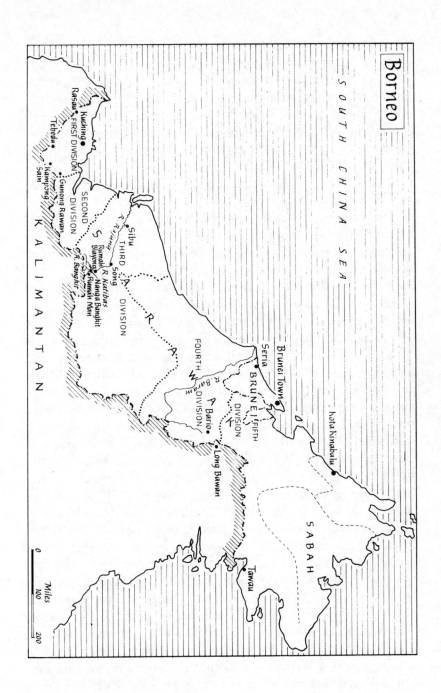

Borneo

SOUTH CHINA SEA

KALIMANTAN

Sain
•Kampong Rawan
Simong Rawan•
Tebedu•
Rasau•FIRST DIVISION
Kuching •

SECOND
DIVISION
R. Bangkit
THIRD
DIVISION
Sibu
•R. Katibas
Rumah \
Blavong\ Nanga Bangkit
Rumah Mau
Song

FOURTH
DIVISION

A. Bario•

Brunei Town
Seria•
BRUNEI FIFTH
DIVISION
DIVISION

Long Bawan•

kota Kinabalu•

SABAH

•Tawau

0
Miles
100
200

up 54% of the population. As in Malaya, the Chinese contained a large number of communist sympathizers.

For administrative purposes Sarawak is divided into five divisions running from west to east with First Division the westernmost. Brunei is sandwiched between Fourth and Fifth Divisions. Beyond Fifth Division is Sabah (formerly North Borneo) which is divided into four Residencies; Kuching in the First Division is the capital of Sarawak, Brunei Town the capital of Brunei and Kota Kinabalu (formerly Jesselton) the principal town in Sabah. The border with Kalimantan is 1,000 miles in length, running through dense jungle which is traversed only by native tracks and largely mountainous. Rain falls torrentially and the climate is hot and humid. It is almost certainly some of the most difficult campaigning country in the world.

For the greater part of their British connection the Borneo territories had seldom featured in the newspapers, apart, per-haps, from stories about head hunters in *Blackwood's Magazine* or accounts of piracy by the Sea Dayaks in the Sulu Sea in the *Wide World Magazine*. Even the seizure of Borneo by the Japanese army in 1942 rated little mention in the British Press and Borneo's recapture by the Australians in 1945 received little more. It was not until after Indonesia's and Malaya's indepen-dence that Borneo became 'news' and this was principally due to the conflicting ambitions of two men – President Sukarno of Indonesia and the Prime Minister of Malaya, Tunku Abdul Rahman. A further cause for confrontation between them was the spread of communism in South-East Asia. This was not solely confined to the Chinese population but found active disciples among the Malays as well. Sukarno himself was by no means unsympathetic and was receiving active support from both the Soviet Union and Communist China.

Sukarno had great ambitions for a 'Greater Indonesia' which would include not only the recently independent Malaya but also the Philippines. It would naturally include the whole of Kalimantan. Tunku Abdul Rahman thought otherwise and he had, in any case, not much time for Sukarno. The Tunku's ambition was a 'Greater Malaysia' incorporating the British Borneo territories and Singapore along with the newly independent Malaya. He first publicly announced this in a speech on 27 May, 1961, which caused a furore not only in Jakarta but also in the territories themselves. Union with Malaya aroused fierce resistance among certain of the Chinese and Malay population in Sarawak, Sabah and Brunei, where there already existed a movement called the North Kalimantan National Army, or TNKU. Their aim was to create a confederation of the three states outside Malaya, headed by the Sultan of Brunei whose wealth would provide an impressive figurehead. The head of this organization was an Arab/Malay called Azahari and on 8 December, 1962, TNKU struck.

The focus of the rebellion was in Brunei. The Sultan was to be seized and proclaimed head of a confederation. Police stations were to be raided in order to obtain weapons and the European employees at the Seria oilfields were to be seized as hostages or bargaining counters with the British government. The TNKU enjoyed an early success but the Sultan frustrated the rebel's plans by taking refuge with the armed police and asking for British aid. At the same time, with commendable speed, Headquarters Far East Command in Singapore dispatched the equivalent of an infantry brigade from Singapore to deal with the rebels. Hot foot after them went Major General Walter Walker, GOC 17th Gurkha Division, from Seremban, Malaya, who assumed the appointment of Commander British Forces Borneo (COMBRITBOR) on 19 December, 1962. His brief was to clear the TNKU from Brunei before Malaysia was established in August, 1963. This he accomplished by April in the same year.

No other general in the British Army could match Walker's experience of counter-insurgency operations in the jungle. He had served in Burma both during the retreat and afterwards, winning the DSO in command of the 4/8th Gurkha Rifles. At the beginning of the Malayan Emergency he raised and trained Ferret Force, intended to operate in small groups for long periods in the jungle. From 1951–54 he commanded 1/6th GR in Malaya, making it one of the best of the Gurkha units, but not without a good deal of 'blood, sweat and tears'. A forward-looking soldier with strong opinions, he had clashed

as Major General Brigade of Gurkhas with the MOD establishment over the intended reduction of the Gurkhas. This led the
Army Board to recall Major General Robertson, another 6th
Gurkha, from retirement to be the Board's adviser on Gurkha
matters. However, when Robertson flew out to Borneo to
see Walker, he received short shrift. Walker neither greeted
him on arrival nor saw him off on departure, although they
were old friends. But he did warn Robertson to keep his nose
out of the business of the Major General Brigade of Gurkhas,
as a somewhat discomfited Robertson later told the Army
Board.

Walker believed profoundly in the unified system of com-
mand (land, sea and air) recently introduced in Far East
Command by Lord Mountbatten. As Director of Operations in
Borneo he insisted on dealing directly with the C-in-C in
Singapore, an Admiral, thereby by-passing the Land Forces
Commander, first General Hewetson and later General Jolly,
both of whom outranked Walker. It is hardly surprising that
this should have led to some difficulties.*

Although the abortive rebellion in Brunei received considerable sympathy in Indonesia, Sukarno did not intervene on the
rebels' side, or at least not openly. However, the Tunku's
announcement of the intention to incorporate the Borneo
territories as 'East Malaysia' in a wider confederation with
Malaya, enraged him. He regarded it as a British neo-colonial
plot and set about disrupting it, both politically and militarily.
He had already heralded his intention on 12 April, 1963, by an
Indonesian raid on a village called Tebedu in the First Division
of Sarawak. At the time Walker was about to return with his
headquarters to Malaya but this was abruptly cancelled. The
rebellion might have been crushed in Brunei but war was about
to begin in Borneo.

Walker had warned of this beforehand but his warnings went
unheeded. But this was the least of his worries. In his opinion

---

* When the Author visited Singapore in 1965 on a mission from the MOD,
he stayed with General Jolly, whose GSO 1 he had been in BAOR. When
discussing the Borneo situation with Jolly he recalls him saying rather ruefully,
'Walter Walker's "bamboo curtain" effectively keeps me out!'

by far the greatest danger was a Malaya-style Emergency in East Malaysia among the Chinese population, supported actively from Kalimantan by the Indonesians. He had insufficient troops to deal with either contingency and too few helicopters to move the troops he had with sufficient speed to deal with incidents occurring along a thousand miles of frontier with the Indonesians. But throughout his control of operations in Borneo, Walker never lost sight of the prospect of an internal rebellion, which is why he promoted an active 'Hearts and Minds' campaign among the local population.

On 16 September, 1963, the Federation of Malaysia was established. Although this had received the blessing of the United Nations, Sukarno denounced the entire concept and threatened 'a terrible confrontation'. The British Embassy in Jakarta was sacked and burned and the Malayan Ambassador was packed off home. Meanwhile in the preceding June, 2/6th GR had arrived in Borneo from Hong Kong on the first of the Regiment's several tours in East Malaysia.

Half the Battalion under the CO, 'Slim' Horsford, was in the 99th Gurkha Infantry Brigade Group under Brigadier Pat Patterson, another 6th Gurkha. It was spread in platoon packets in Fifth Division and Brunei. One company was far away at Tawau on the south-east coast of Sabah, an important commercial and logging centre. The other half of the Battalion, under the Second in Command, Major Geoff Walsh, was in the western half of the Third Division under 3 Commando Brigade. The tasks were to deal with cross-border incursions, taking an active part in the 'Hearts and Minds' campaign and training the Border Scouts. These were recruited from local tribes and were useful as guides and trackers but not very effective as soldiers. The Border Scouts did not really come into their own until taken over by Lieutenant Colonel John Cross of the 7th Gurkha Rifles who turned them into an invaluable source of information as border watchers.

It was shortly after their deployment in Third Division that Walsh's half of the Battalion found themselves involved in a confrontation that was afterwards considered to mark the escalation of the cross-border campaign. It had its share of both triumph and tragedy and, for this reason, is worth describing at some length. It should, however, be borne in mind that this was very early in the Borneo campaign and some years had passed since the 2nd Battalion was last engaged in jungle operations in Malaya.

Nearly a week had passed before Walsh received a report of a border crossing in the vicinity of Nanga Bangkit. Some Ibans had been captured but one had escaped with the news. Walsh dispatched a patrol under a Gurkha officer to move up the Katibas River to investigate the report. While moving up-river the original patrol was increased by the addition of an SAS detachment, three Border Scouts, two policemen and the local District Officer. It succeeded in intercepting some refugees fleeing down the river in their longboats, among them the four Ibans who had been taken prisoner by the raiders. They said there were about 50 of them, well armed and in uniform. Their officers said their mission was to kill white men and keep the Malays out of Borneo. They were to be the spearhead of heavier attacks. 300 more raiders were to follow within a week and after them a further 600. All this was reported to Walsh despite poor radio communications.

Having ordered the patrol to base itself at Rumah Blayong Walsh decided to reinforce it, sending in by Belvedere helicopter 15 men under Lieutenant Hugh Wallace. Major Walter of the Parachute Regiment had accompanied the original patrol and the little force now split into two. Leaving a small base party at Blayong under the Kapit District Officer, Walter and Wallace set off upriver towards the border with a small platoon. Lieutenant (QGO) Matbarsing Gurung, with another small platoon but without a radio, set off on foot. At 1.00 p.m. on 16 August the boat party bumped the enemy and a firefight followed. Lieutenant Wallace set off in an attempt to outflank the enemy position, in the course of which he was badly wounded. The Iban boatmen, in the meantime, had decamped taking the patrol's kit but, fortunately, not the radio set. As darkness fell the firing stopped and the following morning Major Walter decided to retire to the base at Rumah Blayong, five hours of hard marching through the jungle. He reported by radio to Walsh who told him to remain where he was at Blayong and that reinforcements were being dispatched.

On 18 August Walter returned to the scene of action to search for Wallace, whose orderly reported that he had been seriously wounded. Walter found his body, as well as a lot of enemy equipment. Wallace had put up a good fight before the Indonesians killed him.* Matbarsing's patrol had, meanwhile, had its problems. It reached the long house at Rumah Man where it spent the night. The following morning, when about to eat a meal, they were approached by a body of enemy guided by a Kayan tribesman. There was yet another firefight and the patrol was pinned down for the rest of the day. Matbarsing withdrew his patrol to the high ground above the long house under cover of darkness. Later it withdrew to the patrol base at Blayong.

There is always muddle in war and there certainly seems to have been a fair share of it in this action. Walsh was not helped by very bad radio reception owing to a tropical storm. He moved his Tac HQ to Song to be nearer the scene of action and began to deploy more troops. He was convinced the enemy had not recrossed the border into Kalimantan and planned to bring them to battle before they did so. Wallace's body was recovered, an Indonesian was killed and at least three were wounded. Two other wounded enemy were captured. At this crucial moment – for Walsh certainly – higher authority intervened. Walker decided to move the 1/2nd Goorkhas into the Third Division and to concentrate the 2/6th in Brunei, Sabah and Fifth Division. 'We were not allowed to stay and finish the battle we started,' Walsh told his officers. 'Military movement plans remain the supreme medium for dispensing frustration!'

All in all, however, it was not quite so frustrating as originally appeared. The Indonesians lost 15 killed and had three taken prisoner by the end of August. Their aim was to capture Song on the great Rajang River and set the Third Division aflame. But they brought with them no maps, nor compasses, and

---

* The inter-company competition held annually in 6 GR is for the *Wallace Memorial Trophy*, which commemorates this gallant young officer.

expected to live off the land. The raid did, however, demonstrate how difficult it was to deal with small parties of the enemy in such difficult country, and without the benefit of powerful radios – and above all of helicopters.

It is very hard to convey to those who have never had the experience, the strain and stress never absent from war in the jungle – the constant demand for vigilance in case of ambush, the clinging vegetation that impedes both movement and sight, the heat and humidity which saps mental and physical energy – either dripping with sweat or soaked by torrential downpours, sliding and slipping in the boggy ground. And all around the noises of the jungle which may or may not be an enemy scout giving warning of your approach. Is it a monkey or is it a man? General Walker wanted his soldiers to live in the jungle like animals, but in the jungle the animal has sharper eyesight, better hearing and a keener sense of smell than any human.

Even the Gurkhas wilted after too long a spell in the jungle. It was infinitely harder on the British officers who led them. This was particularly so in the earlier stages of the campaign when it was a question of waiting for the enemy to take the initiative, with the choice of dozens of border crossings from Kalimantan. It was different when we were allowed to take the war to the enemy, leaving him to wonder where, when and how we would come. Jungle warfare, a Burma veteran once said, is like a gigantic game of Blind Man's Buff, played in a Turkish bath with one hand tied behind your back. It is not a bad simile. Certainly, in order to prevent the cutting edge becoming blunted, jungle operations in both Malaya and Borneo needed to be interspersed by frequent periods out of the jungle wearing dry clothes, doing normal things and behaving like humans instead of animals.

The problem where Borneo was concerned was that the frontage was so long, the jungle so thick and the communications so appalling that there were never enough troops to do the job until the campaign was almost ended. Had it been a war instead of a confrontation, Whitehall might have reacted very differently. As it was it wanted to keep Borneo low key.

It was the helicopter that made all the difference in Borneo.

There were never enough of them but those there were were flown brilliantly and bravely by their pilots. General Walker maintained that one battalion with six helicopters equalled one brigade without. One hour in the air equalled five days on foot. The RAF, with their insistence on the flexibility of air power, have shown themselves to be singularly inflexible when it comes to decentralizing control over helicopter operations. In Borneo, as in Aden in the Radfan in 1964, it was the Fleet Air Arm and Army Air Corps squadrons which showed the way. They would go anywhere at any time without referring everything back and in the end the RAF had to follow suit, although often under protest!*

Helicopters meant that soldiers could get swiftly into position within easy reach of their base within hours rather than days; if an LZ could not be prepared the troops could slide down on ropes. Vital resupply of ammunition could come by 'chopper'. 105mm artillery pieces could be placed in otherwise inaccessible positions slung under helicopters. Most important of all from the soldier's point of view, casualties could be lifted out and lives could be saved. But helicopters are noisy and very vulnerable to ground fire when hovering to land or pick up soldiers. They had to be flown very skilfully to take advantage of the terrain and they could be difficult to control in a tropical storm. However, nothing seemed to daunt the pilots and the 6th Gurkhas owed them a great deal more than could ever be adequately expressed in a history such as this. They were superb!

The 2/6th returned to Hong Kong in September, 1963, and were sped on their way by a congratulatory signal from General Walker: 'On your departure for Hong Kong I wish to offer my congratulations on your successful tour here.' The 1/6th, the first Gurkha unit to be stationed *west* of Suez since the Second World War, had been warned at Tidworth that it would be Borneo next. The Battalion arrived there in January, 1964,

---

* At one stage a Gurkha Air Platoon was formed. Captain Robin Adshead, Signals Officer of the 1/6th GR, was seconded to the Army Air Corps for the purpose.

leaving behind the families. The British ones remained there throughout the Borneo tour but the Gurkha ones were moved to Malacca in Malaya. Gil Hickey was the CO and he did not much care for the western half of Third Division where everything seemed quiet. He succeeded in obtaining a move for the Battalion to the First Division where life was much more interesting and Brigadier Pat Patterson was still in the driving seat. This was where the battalion first came to know about Operation CLARET, supposedly the best-kept secret of Confrontation.

The British Government was anxious to avoid outright war with Indonesia but it was bad for the morale of those on the ground to leave all the initiative to the enemy. Walker was well aware of this, as he was of the political situation, and in the end he succeeded in obtaining permission for limited and carefully controlled operations across the border in Kalimantan. It must have required the most persuasive argument on Walker's part but he may have been helped by the Indonesian raid on West Malaysia in August, 1964. This was by sea and was easily dealt with. It was followed two weeks later by an airborne raid near Labis, about a hundred miles from Singapore. It was not a success. Several of the planes failed to take off, or ran into an electric storm, and the 200 parachute troops were scattered all over the place. They were quickly rounded up by the 1/10th Gurkha Rifles and the 1st Royal New Zealand Infantry Regiment and virtually wiped out. It did, however, add a new dimension to Confrontation and may have been the cause for Whitehall's change of tune. It was now agreed that pre-emptive infantry attacks could be launched wherever an Indonesain attack was anticipated. By now the Indonesians were much better organized along conventional military lines and with much more sophisticated weapons. Their senior commanders, General Maraden Panggabean and Colonel Supargo, were both experienced fighting soldiers who had attended courses of instruction in the USA and Pakistan. Many of their subordinates had attended courses at the (British) Jungle Warfare School in Johore. They represented a much greater threat to East Malaysia than had been the case a year or two previously.

The rules governing Operation CLARET operations were nevertheless very tightly drawn. Every operation had to be authorized by the Director of Borneo Operations under the authority of the C-in-C Far East. Only trained and tested troops were to be used. Depth of penetration was limited and attacks were made to thwart the enemy intentions and never in retribution for a previous attack. Close air support was banned except in an emergency. Every operation had to be planned on a sand-table and rehearsed for at least two weeks. Maximum security was essential. Every man taking part must be sworn to secrecy. No traces must be left behind. Code-names only were to be used. Nothing could be discussed on telephone or radio, nor even in officers' messes. On no account must any soldier taking part be captured by the enemy – alive or dead.

It is remarkable how well this secret was kept. There were plenty of experienced journalists – British, American, Malay and others – sniffing around Borneo or in Singapore, but no leak ever appeared. Even the award of the VC to a Gurkha soldier involved in a CLARET operation was carefully camouflaged to give nothing away by the citation. One of the first CLARET operations was mounted by the 1/6th on 17 May, 1964. The commander was Captain (QGO) Damarbahadur Gurung who commanded 15 Platoon in D Company. He laid an ambush on a track recently widened and used frequently by Indonesians moving up the border. He had to move the original ambush position because it was given away by some women who spotted a sentry. The ambush was moved to another track. Damarbahadur left his platoon sergeant with eight men to establish a base. The rest of the platoon were deployed in the ambush. However, the platoon sergeant disposed his men badly and the base was surprised. Two Gurkhas were killed, as were two of the enemy. When he heard the firing, Damarbahadur moved back to the base where he found the four dead bodies and the packs of the base party. These were carried across the border. It was not a successful operation but at least two of the enemy had been killed. Damarbahadur got his revenge later on 25 July when a party of nine enemy walked into an ambush he had laid close to the border. Five were killed and four were wounded. The MC awarded to Damarbahadur was well earned.

Soldiers learn from experience provided they survive the previous mistakes. There was one such on 21 June when two platoons were caught unawares at Rasau, just on the friendly side of the border. Camped for the night in a disused patrol base, they were attacked by about 60 Indonesians and the ensuing firefight lasted for about five hours, killing five riflemen and wounding five more. WO2 Chandrabahadur Thapa was among the killed. The attackers had no casualties and withdrew across the border. There had been a failure to check the surrounding area adequately before settling down for the night. It had been a mistake to choose a resting place which must have been known to the enemy and there was a lack of cover. Although on the whole the Indonesians received more knocks than they gave, nothing could be left to chance when dealing with them. They were well-armed, well-equipped, brave and determined. They would stand and fight and, if needs be, come back for more. When the 1/6th GR returned to Hong Kong in August, 1964, to be reunited with their wives from Tidworth and Malacca, they were once again a well-seasoned jungle battalion, not easy to achieve when stationed in Tidworth or Hong Kong where jungle is conspicuous by its absence.

In September, 1964, the 2/6th returned for a second tour, this time commanded by Tony Harvey. Prior to leaving Hong Kong they had been presented with the last Union Jack to fly over the Red Fort in Delhi. Roger Neath, who gave it to the British Officers' Mess, had been present with the Battalion when the flag was lowered for the last time. The Battalion's new parish in Sarawak was the Fourth Division, a vast area of jungle-covered hills through which flowed the wide and muddy Baram River. The Battalion was accompanied by its families, British and Gurkha. 2/6th GR was, in fact, the only unit, British or Gurkha, which served in Borneo 'accompanied'. This turned out to be a mixed blessing. A unit serving in an operational theatre is much better off without having to worry about the welfare of its families. The Battalion was based at Medicina Camp at Seria (in Brunei) which was rented from the Shell Oil Company. The

British families accompanying the Battalion were well housed and the bachelor British officers even better in one of the Sultan's palaces. The Gurkha families, however, were poorly accommodated in what amounted to coolie-lines. This gave rise to domestic discontent, taxing to the full the tact and diplomacy of the Gurkha Major who had to handle such complaints.

Battalion headquarters was at first at Miri, on the coast and 60 miles from Seria. This was later shifted to Seria while a Tac Headquarters was established much nearer the border at Bario, 100 miles by air from Seria. Bario was also a Company Base. The plan was to rotate companies through Seria at approximately six-weekly intervals, giving them plenty of time to rest and rehabilitate after the toil and sweat of jungle patrolling. Unfortunately Companies, while supposedly resting and retraining, were called upon for such duties as providing ceremonial guards, etc., or reinforcing some other unit which had got into difficulties. Although Gurkhas suffer the inevitable muddles of the army with a great deal more patience than would be the case with British troops, even their patience is not inexhaustible. Too much of it can lead to a drop in morale.

From September, 1964, onwards the 2/6th were working hard to achieve their Commanding Officer's aim of complete domination of the border in their area. Here it should be made plain that the border when originally agreed by the British and the Dutch had been largely traced off a map with scant regard for the actual terrain, or for the tribespeople living in the area. After hostilities began families might find themselves divided by a border which previously had meant little to them. Trans-border movement by the locals was virtually impossible to control, as was the passage of information from one side to the other.

By the time the Battalion returned for the second tour in Borneo, the situation on the ground had changed considerably. Company bases were now strongpoints with deep-dug bunkers, trenches and all-round fire. They were formidably armed with 105 mm pack howitzers manned by the Gunners, medium machine-guns, 81 mm mortars and claymore mines. The approches might be protected by sharpened bamboos hardened by fire and deeply dug into the earth, *panjis* as they were known in Burma. Supplies were air dropped by RAF Beverleys and there might be a landing strip for light aircraft and of course an LZ for helicopters. The locals were friendly and the Gurkhas enjoyed drinking beer with them in the long houses, more often than not livening the mixture with liberal quantities of issue rum. Such Company bases were much more sophisticated than had previously been the case and attacks on them were welcomed by the occupants. Unfortunately the Indonesians seldom obliged.

Patrol actions in the jungle are confusing enough for those taking part in them. They are even more confusing to describe in a history such as this. The Battalion's first CLARET operation was launched at the beginning of December when an ambush was laid across the border near a stile used by the enemy. The ambush party led by Major Robinson were armed with shotguns in order to mislead the enemy into thinking they were local villagers. The ambush was not very successful but the ruse with shotguns was, the Indonesians concluding they had been shot by a party of Kelabits. Another less successful ambush was the occasion when a party of Indonesian Marine Commandos surprised a platoon engaged in collecting supplies after a resupply operation close to the border. Although surprised and losing a sergeant and two riflemen killed, the platoon rallied quickly, killing five of the enemy and wounding several more. As a result of this action Lieutenant (QGO) Ranbahadur Pun, the Platoon commander, was awarded the MC and Sgt Bombahadur Gurung received the MM.

For another CLARET operation it was decided to attack an Indonesian airstrip at Long Bawan, less than a mile from the border inside Kalimantan. 'B' Company was to carry out the operation with two 105 mm howitzers of 45 Field Regiment, RA, in direct support. The Gunners were old friends from Hong Kong. As a first step LZs had to be cleared on the knife-edged border ridge and the guns flown in by helicopter. They were slung under the 'choppers' and had to be lowered to the ground before being manhandled to the gun positions. All this had to be done without alerting the enemy. There was, of course, no question of previous registration which would have

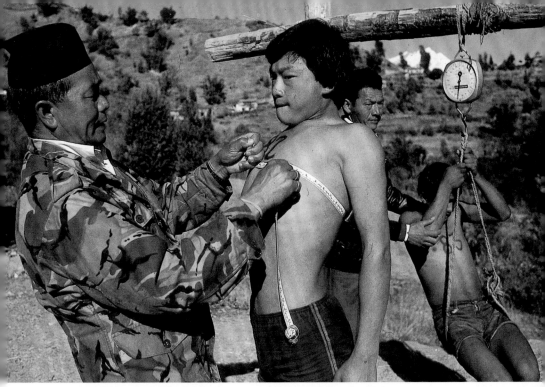

20. *"The Gurkhas were recruited into their several regiments after careful selection by officers who had knowledge of every shade of clan or sect and their qualities as soldiers at their finger tips."* (p.151) Hon Lieutenant (GCO) Bhirkaraj Gurung, late 6 GR, recruiting in Nepal. Few out of hundreds are accepted.

21. *"It is perhaps the Gurkha's imperturbability amidst the tumult of battle that makes it seem that he is unmoved by what is going on around him but he would probably look the same if poised on a precipice."* (p.154) Major Duncan Briggs and Corporal Rinchen Wangdi Lepcha, poised imperturbably on the summit of Annapurna South Peak (23,683 feet) in 1976, Nepal.

22. *"Sacrifices of living buffaloes and goats are decapitated by, hopefully, a single blow of a kukri."* (p.157) *Dasain*, October, 1993, Brunei.

23. *"The Gurkha is never happier than when playing games, preferably football, basketball and volleyball."* (p.134) The unbeaten 1985 basketball team with the Commanding Officer, Lieutenant-Colonel J.A. Anderson, and the Gurkha Major, Major (QGO) Gyanbahadur Gurung.

given the game away. Nevertheless the Gunners proved to be remarkably accurate when they opened fire at midday on 29 August. The Indonesians were taken completely by surprise. Their storehouses were wrecked and 'B' Company dropped down from the ridge to complete the damage. The enemy hastily decamped and withdrew a good ten thousand yards from the border.

As what might be described as the 'battalion in residence', 2/6th GR certainly had their fill of jungle operations by the end of 1964. They had undoubtedly fulfilled their CO's aim of dominating the border but had equally earned themselves a break in somewhat more civilized surroundings. One may get the impression from accounts of jungle operations in regimental histories that it is continuous activity, sometimes frenetically so, whereas the truth is usually different, viz; long periods of boredom interspersed by short periods of intense activity. Since living conditions in the jungle are never 'Five Star' and, more often than not, downright uncomfortable, morale could begin to sag after too long a time in the jungle. It paid to ring the changes.

Having been on operations for nearly a year, the 2/6th now concentrated at Seria for a well-earned rest. The 1/6th arrived in January, 1965, from Hong Kong and were sent to First Division. There were reports of an Indonesian build-up opposite First Division and the battalion was kept busy along the border, and on occasions *over* it, as in the case of the rescue of two wounded SAS men in February, 1965. Here is an account of what happened as provided by one of the soldiers involved:

'On the morning of 26th February, 1965, a small SAS patrol landed at Kampong Sain by helicopter from Kuching. This was a border village and was defended by 6 GR. We were given a briefing on the local area by the Gurkha commander, Captain Damarbahadur Gurung. The SAS task was to cross the Indonesian frontier by foot and recce the area of the Sungei Sekayan some five thousands yards inside Kalimantan.

'I was lead-scout of the patrol and around midday we set off by foot in the direction of Gunong Rawan, a mountain some 4,000 yards south-east of the village and over which the border ran. By five o'clock in the afternoon we were high on the slopes of Rawan but still in Sarawak and we decided to stop for the night. The following morning we continued upwards and by late afternoon on the 27th February we reached the border. We recced the area and again prepared to stop for the night.

'The following morning – Sunday, 28th February – our four-man patrol moved over the border and descended the water-shed of the Gunong. As we approached a small clearing we stopped to listen and then moved off very slowly. Suddenly we encountered a full frontal contact with fire to the flank. A bullet shattered my left hip and the patrol commander was hit in the pelvis. After a fire fight we managed to crawl out of the area leaving five Indonesians dead. Unfortunately I became separated from my commander. The other two SAS men were by this time over the border and on their way back to Kampong Sain and 6 GR for assistance as laid down in our SAS standing operating procedures.

'I, meanwhile, had crawled over the border and settled down for the night under an old tree in a pig hole. The following morning I was so very weak that I knew that unless 6 GR turned up soon I would die. I had nothing to lose so I fired three shots in the air every hour. Unknown to me help was on its way in the shape of Captain Damarbahadur Gurung and 6 GR. Wisely he did not return the shots but located my position and did a recce round me in case I was being used as ambush bait, before sending a section down to me with the two SAS men.

'Captain Damarbahadur then set up an all-round defensive position for the night. Next morning – 2nd March – the Gurkhas improvised a stretcher from a poncho and two poles and carried me, taking turns, non-stop for almost eight hours before stopping at a ridge-top where it was possible to get a helicopter in for a casualty evacuation. I was successfully lifted out and the Gurkha patrol all returned safely to base. The rescue operation had been planned and faultlessly conducted throughout and, although guided in by the two SAS men, had been conducted in its entirety by Captain Damarbahadur Gurung to whom I owe my life.

'The SAS commander had earlier been winched out by helicopter with the use of an air rescue beacon.'

The above account given by Mr Ian Thomson, now retired, was published in the 1993 edition of the Regimental Association journal. Sadly Captain Damarbahadur Gurung, MC and Bar, died in Nepal after his retirement. Although doubtless repeated elsewhere in Borneo during Confrontation, it was an amazing feat of endurance to carry a badly wounded man on a makeshift stretcher non-stop for eight hours up and down steep hills, across fast running streams and, all the time, through the thickest of the jungle. Perhaps only hillmen like the Gurkhas would have had the stamina to do it. Mr Thomson must have been pretty tough too!

In April, 1966, the 1/6th returned to Hong Kong after their third tour in Borneo. The 2/6th, back on operations after their break in Seria, moved to the Interior Residency in Sabah where life was reasonably quiet after the excitements of the previous two years.

There had been other changes. On 12 March, 1965, Walter Walker handed over as Director of Operations to Major General George Lea. There could be no argument regarding the magnitude of Walker's achievement in handling the problems of Confrontation but he was to receive little recognition for it, only a second Bar to his DSO and a second major general's appointment, this time with NATO. Even those with whom he had clashed, and there were not a few of them, felt he had been scurvily treated. Meanwhile, where the Gurkhas, who had borne the brunt of the battle, were concerned, their reward was to be reduced in strength, which meant in the case of the 6th Queen Elizabeth's Own Gurkha Rifles the amalgamation, in June, 1969, of the 1st and 2nd Battalions to form a single battalion regiment.

It has to be admitted that so far as the British people were concerned the war in Borneo was largely a 'silent' one. The aim in Whitehall was to avoid, at all costs, outright war with Indonesia and therefore security considerations were paramount. Moreover, during the later stages of Confrontation, the British position in Aden and South Arabia started to collapse, which the media found more telegenic than long patrols in the jungle. For the British the campaign in Borneo was a war in a faraway country in which they did not find themselves greatly involved. It was different, however, in Indonesia where the steadily deteriorating economy began to press hard on the lives of ordinary citizens.

The Indonesian generals too began to wonder what was the purpose of a struggle from which only the Communists seemed to benefit. Sukarno's 'Great Design' seemed so much tinsel. An attempted left-wing coup in September, 1965, was put down by the Army which then seized the opportunity to eliminate the Communists. Sukarno clung to power but he had lost the support of the Armed Forces. In March, 1966, they moved in against him and power passed to General Suharto. Sukarno remained President, but only in name, and the Communist Party was dissolved. In May an Indonesian delegation flew to Kuala Lumpur and negotiations began. Sukarno tried to sabotage them and was stripped of his title of President for Life. On 11 August, 1966, the Confrontation was ended by a Treaty between Indonesia and Malaysia, the only condition being that the people of Sabah and Sarawak should be given the opportunity to confirm their allegiance to Malaysia, which in due course they did. The last of Britain's 'colonial' wars had been brought to a satisfactory conclusion. For that the principal credit must go to Sir Walter Walker, but the 6th Gurkha Rifles had also played their part in containing, and then ending, the Confrontation.

CHAPTER NINE

'The Hawk' and Amalgamation

ALTHOUGH 6 GR has been on active service for much of
its existence it has, from time to time, come to rest in peacetime
garrisons such as Tidworth on Salisbury Plain, Church Crookham in Hampshire, Belize in the Caribbean and, of course,
Hong Kong which has been the 'home station' of the Brigade
of Gurkhas since Malaya achieved independence. All turned out
to be new experiences for the Gurkha riflemen who, in true
Gurkha fashion, took it all in their stride.

The conferment, by the Queen in 1959, of the title 'Queen
Elizabeth's Own' was naturally a source of great pride to
everyone in the Regiment, whether serving or retired. There
was similar delight in 1966 when the Regiment's affiliation with
the 14th/20th King's Hussars received official approval. The
story of how this came about is an interesting one.

At the end of March and in early April, 1945, the Allied
Armies in Italy were poised to break out into the Plain of
Lombardy and drive the Germans out of Italy. 2/6 GR, as part
of the 43rd Gurkha Lorried Infantry Brigade, was going
through the process of 'marrying up' with the British cavalry
regiment, the 14th/20th Hussars, whose Sherman tanks would
be supporting the Battalion during the forthcoming battle. For
part of the time the Gurkhas would be carried in Kangaroos,
turretless Sherman tanks driven by the Hussars. For several
days Gurkhas and Hussars lived together, sharing each other's
rations, conversing together as only Gurkha and British soldiers
can when neither really knows the other's language; and when

battle came the liaison was complete, as was evident when the 2/6th and Hussars thundered together into Medicina and hit the German defenders for six!

Together the Gurkhas and Hussars drove the Germans before them until the war ended at the beginning of May, 1945. Entirely unofficially the Hussars had taken to wearing the Crossed Kukris badge of the Gurkhas on their right sleeve. In return some of the Gurkhas did the same with 'The Hawk', as the 14th/20th Hussars called their cap badge. This was, in fact, the Prussian Eagle badge inherited from the 14th King's Hussars who were granted it in 1798 when they were given the subsidiary title, 'Duchess of York's Own'. The Duchess was Princess Frederica Charlotte of Prussia who married the Duke of York [Commander-in-Chief of the British Army], and the badge commemorated the connection with the Prussian royal house. Its use was dropped during the 1914–18 war but was resumed in 1931.

Some years after the end of the Second World War the then Colonel of the 14th/20th Hussars approached Major General Robertson, the Colonel of 6 GR, with the proposal that 2/6 GR should wear 'The Hawk' in recognition of the very close liaison the battalion had had with the Hussars. On consultation the Battalion said they would be delighted to accept. When the Hussars approached Field Marshall Slim for his views, he thought it a wonderful idea and proposed that, in return, the 14th/20th should wear the Crossed Kukris of the Brigade of Gurkhas. This was welcomed both by the Brigade and 2/6 GR.

The 14th/20th then approached Sir Richard Hull, as the senior serving cavalry officer for his agreement, which was not at first forthcoming. He was, however, persuaded by Slim but the distinction was only to apply to the 2nd Battalion and not the 1st. General Robertson believed it would be awkward to restrict the distinction to 2/6 GR and asked them if the First Battalion could be included. At first the Battalion was reluctant to agree; nor was the 1st Battalion any more anxious to accept, arguing that it was nothing to do with them. In the end, however, both 1/6 and 2/6 GR agreed, but there was a further snag. The Colonel of the 14th/20th wanted to restrict the distinction to the 2nd Battalion! In the end General Robertson's tact and diplomacy won over the various conflicting sides, including both Slim and Hull on a second approach and, in 1966, formal approval was received for the affiliation of the 14th/20th King's Hussars with the 6th Queen Elizabeth's Own Gurkha Rifles. It would never have happened without the persistence of General Robertson.*

Both the 6th and the 14th/20th were very proud of this affiliation. When the Hussars celebrated their 250th anniversary by a Regimental Dinner at Perham Down, General Robertson and Vivian Robinson were two of the only three guests; the third was General 'Tochi' Barker who commanded the 43rd Gurkha Lorried Infantry Brigade in the Italian campaign. At the 6th Gurkhas' 175th Anniversary Celebrations at The Tower of London in November, 1992, the last and previous Colonels of the 14th/20th, Major Generals Sir Michael Palmer and Peter Cavendish were there in their own right as Honorary Members of the 6th Gurkhas Regimental Association. So was Lieutenant Colonel Richard Shirreff, formerly seconded to the 6th and soon to be Commanding Officer of The King's Royal Hussars. Both British and Gurkha officers have enjoyed short attachments with the Hussars and in 1990–91 Ian Thomas and James Cheshire served with the 14th/20th in the Gulf War.† The Hussars were the armoured regiment in the 4th Armoured Brigade and saw plenty of action in what was to prove to be a very short war. Their only regret was that 6 GR was not one of the supporting infantry battalions. Some years previously at least one young cavalry officer had learnt what it was like to be an infantryman in the jungle when Lieutenant William Edge of the 14th/20th spent two months jungle-bashing with 'D' Company in Borneo.

The Regiment has also had a long affiliation with the Rifle Brigade since 1948, to whom they had then presented a silver

---

* In 1992 the 14th/20th King's Hussars were amalgamated with the Royal Hussars to form The King's Royal Hussars. The capbadge of the new regiment is 'The Hawk' and the affiliation with 6 GR has continued. It will pass to The Royal Gurkha Rifles on formation of that regiment.
† Jeremy Brade was attached to I RHF for Prisoner of War duties.

kukri, and who, in return, presented 6 GR with a silver bugle. When young officers were first gazetted to 6 GR it was usual for them to spend a year with the Rifle Brigade before joining either the 1st or 2nd Battalions. In 1966 the Royal Green Jackets were formed, in which the Rifle Brigade became the 3rd Battalion, The Royal Green Jackets. Although the old connection was preserved and, wherever possible strengthened, it is now with The Royal Green Jackets.

Field Marshal Lord Birdwood, who had been Colonel of the 6th Gurkha Rifles since 1926, died on 17 May, 1951. Throughout his Colonelcy he had shown the greatest interest in the Regiment which constituted for him a link with 'Gurkha Bluff' and Sari Bair when he was GOC the Australian & New Zealand Army Corps at Gallipoli. As his successor the Queen appointed General Sir John Harding on 17 August, 1951. At the time General Harding was GOC-in-C Far East Command in Singapore; both 1/6 GR and 2/6 GR were under his command in Malaya. He had had 2/6 GR serving under him in Italy when as GOC XIII Corps he had 43rd Gurkha Lorried Infantry Brigade as one of his formations. He was therefore no stranger to the Gurkhas and his appointment was warmly welcomed in the Regiment. He went on to become Chief of the Imperial General Staff and a Field Marshal. A staunch supporter of the Regiment at all times, Lord Harding of Petherton, as he became in 1958, remained as Colonel until 1961.

He was succeeded by Major General Jim Robertson who had first joined the 6th in 1931. In Burma he had for a time commanded 1/7th GR and, later, 48th Gurkha Infantry Brigade. From 1958–61 he was GOC 17th Division in Malaya and Major General Brigade of Gurkhas. He went to Aden in 1961 as GOC Middle East Land Forces, retiring in 1963. He was Colonel of the Regiment from 1961–68.

Jim Robertson was succeeded as Colonel by Pat Patterson, at the time GOC 17th Division and Major General Brigade of Gurkhas. He had joined the Regiment in 1938. It fell to him to implement the British Government's decision, made in 1964, to reduce the strength of the Brigade of Gurkhas from 14,500 to 10,000 by 31 December, 1969. In effect this meant the reduction of the four regiments of Gurkha Rifles from two to one battalion each although at almost the last minute the agreement by the Sultan of Brunei to pay for the Gurkha battalion stationed at Seria made it possible to provide a fifth battalion. As the senior regiment the 2nd KEO Goorkhas retained their second battalion – for the time being!

Patterson worked on four main principles in his dealings with the Ministry of Defence. Firstly, the rundown would not exceed 2,200 all ranks annually in order that the Resettlement Centre could cope. Secondly, the rate of rundown would be the same for all units, and no man would be declared redundant without a minimum of six months' warning. Thirdly, and looking to the future, a minimum of 300 recruits would be enlisted each year. Inevitably, perhaps, it was the financial terms that provided the principal difficulty. If the Gurkha has been described as 'most generous of the generous', the same could never be said of H. M. Treasury. The terms proposed took no account of the original Terms and Conditions of Service drawn up under the Tripartite Agreement of 1947 and General Patterson had to fight very hard indeed to obtain terms which were at least acceptable, if hardly over-generous.

The rundown came as a bitter blow after years of hard slog through the jungles of Malaya and Borneo, but the Gurkhas, with their customary good sense and instinctive self-discipline, carried on as usual. It was probably the British officers who felt it most keenly; not on account of the curtailment of a career perhaps but rather because they felt *their* country had let the Gurkhas down. After working them to the bone in Malaya and Borneo this was the cheapest of rewards.

There had, of course, been an immediate outcry when the intention to reduce the strength of the Brigade of Gurkhas was announced. A Gurkha 'lobby' emerged in which Walter Walker played a leading part. This brought him into conflict with the Whitehall Establishment and also with the three Gurkha Field Marshals, Slim, Templer and Harding, who were endeavouring to ensure that the proposed reduction in numbers would not involve a loss of identity for the eight existing Gurkha Battalions. Slim had been dispatched in haste on a supposedly 'secret' mission to obtain the King of Nepal's acquiescence to the proposed reduction, in which he succeeded.

Leaving aside the emotional aspect, the truth was that the arguments for and against the retention of Gurkhas in the British Army were finely balanced. Their value as soldiers had been proven time and time again. Moreover there was no problem about their recruitment at a time when the British Army were finding it increasingly difficult to recruit regiments to strength; every unit which went to the Gulf was a hotchpotch of several units to bring it up to strength. The Gurkhas would never have such a problem. This was a powerful argument for their retention.

On the other hand the retention of Gurkha regiments might involve the disbandment or amalgamation of British regiments; regiments of longer lineage and as distinguished a record as any Gurkha regiment. This argument could count on a good deal of popular support, as witness the successful campaign of the Argyll and Sutherland Highlanders to avoid disbandment. Some argued that political considerations limited the employment of Gurkhas anywhere in the world but this has no foundation in fact. The King of Nepal does not wish them to be used against Hindus; otherwise they can be used worldwide, as was evident when the 1/7th GR went to the Falklands. It would appear that it is the Foreign & Commonwealth Office which sees bogeys under every bush when ever the employment of Gurkhas is being considered, as the following story may demonstrate.

In 1968 the Author was serving at the British High Commission in New Delhi as Defence Adviser. As such he was involved in the handling of certain Gurkha matters between the Ministry of Defence in London and Indian Army Headquarters in New Delhi. Clearly the former feared an adverse reaction on the part of the latter when the size of the rundown was released and, in the event, the Author was directed to seek a meeting with the Chief of Army Staff, General 'Muchu' Chaudhuri in person, to whom the dreadful truth would be revealed. Chaudhuri's reaction was hardly as anticipated. After listening politely to the message from the CGS, he commented that it was a matter of indifference where the Government of India was concerned. In fact he rather welcomed such a reduction since it meant all the more Gurkhas for the Indian Army to recruit! He then changed the conversation to polo.

The amalgamation of 1/6 GR and 2/6 GR took place in Hong Kong on 14 June, 1969. The parade was deliberately kept low-key since it was, after all, a family affair – a case of joining like with like, although both Battalions had their own distinct personalities. The 2nd Battalion thought the 1st Battalion were inclined to be 'stuffy' and prided themselves on being much more 'laid back'. The Gurkha riflemen as might be expected, took it all in their stride, paying the same rapt attention to Gurkha Major Pahalsing Thapa's exhortation as they would have done to a briefing before setting out on a jungle patrol.

Eighteen months later the greatest 6th Gurkha of them all marched into history. Field Marshal the Viscount Slim, KG, died on 14 December, 1970. He had been Governor and Constable of Windsor Castle since 1963. Increasing frailty had led to his retirement a few months before his death. He was 79 years old. As a Knight of the Garter his funeral was held in St George's Chapel, Windsor Castle, in the company of many of his old comrades of the Burma Star Association. The 6th Gurkhas can be proud that it was in their ranks he came to maturity before going on to reconquer Burma.

Pat Patterson had fought valiantly for the Gurkhas both before and during the run-down. He handed over the Colonelcy of the 6th in 1974 to Brigadier David Powell-Jones who had joined the regiment in 1947 from the Rajputana Rifles. He commanded the 2/6th with distinction in Malaya from 1953–56 for which he was awarded the DSO. He died unduly young in 1981 but two of his sons served after him in the Regiment. Brigadier Sir Noel ('Brunny') Short succeeded him in 1978. He had joined the 6th in 1937 and won the MC in Burma with the 4/6th. Later in Malaya he commanded the 1/6th from 1956–58. He was the last of the pre-war vintage of British officers.

'Brunny's' Colonelcy terminated in 1983 and he was succeeded by Major General (later Lieutenant General Sir) Derek Boorman who was, at the time, Commander British Forces Hong Kong and Major General Brigade of Gurkhas. This provided the unusual situation of a Regiment serving under the *command* of its Colonel since in most instances the Colonel will be a retired officer. In 1989 Boorman, who was also Colonel of the Staffordshire Regiment, handed over to Brigadier (now Major General) R. A. Pett who had begun his career in the Lancashire Regiment (Prince of Wales's Volunteers) but who had served as a Company Commander in the 2/6th in Malaya and Hong Kong, when he acquired a great admiration and affection for the Gurkha soldier. After going on to command the 1st King's Own Royal Border Regiment from 1980–82, Ray Pett was promoted Brigadier to command the 48th Gurkha Infantry Brigade in Hong Kong. He is at present the Director of Infantry in the rank of Major General.

As the British Empire continued to fade away in the fifties and sixties, the few remaining colonies and dependencies acquired an importance quite disproportionate to their status before the Second World War. Most notable was Hong Kong which has become a byword for commercial prosperity, as well as for political complexity. The colonial government maintained a protocol and style not unlike that of the Viceroys in the great days of the Raj and there was a regular demand for guards of honour and other forms of ceremonial. With the shadow of the takeover by China in 1997 hanging over it, Hong Kong was a city in which everyone seemed to be in a hurry. It was either liked or loathed but it could never be ignored.

One of the arguments in favour of the retention of the Gurkhas had been the requirement to garrison Hong Kong. It was far cheaper to do this with Gurkhas than with British troops and the need for troops was obvious with the milling masses of Chinese striving to escape across the border from the Communist 'heaven' in Republican China to the Capitalist 'hell' of Hong Kong. The Brigade of Gurkhas Depot & Training Centre was established there in 1971 by Lt. Colonel Colin Scott (a son of General Bruce Scott) and the Major General Brigade of Gurkhas had his small headquarters there. Hong Kong was a peace station when compared with either Malaya or Borneo but it had its disadvantages. It attracted VIPs like moths to a lamp and there was a constant demand for the ceremonial needed to

[132]

greet them on arrival and departure. The Gurkhas took this with their usual aplomb – perhaps the additional allowances for service in Hong Kong may have something to do with it – but there were occasions when the British officers sighed for the jungles where 'spit and polish' was at a discount!

There was too the difficult problem of keeping out the many thousands who sought to escape across 'the Wire' from China into the New Territories. They came in all shapes and sizes; men, women and children, by land or by sea, many with weapons and all clamouring to be let through. Keeping them out was no easy task. It involved constant patrolling of the border, either in support of or in the company of the Hong Kong police. The scene has been dramatically described by one Commanding Officer who said that after dark it was 'a different scene as the majority of our manpower deployed to coves, inlets and vantage points to help counter the flood of illegal immigrants who tried to break in. They swam, came crammed in little boats, pushed sledges and scooters over the mud and floated in as hopeless corpses killed by cold or sharks. Women looked much the same as men, bedraggled, wet, mud-stained creatures in blue denims with bare feet ripped and bleeding on the rocks and shells. Some came carrying children, others heaved aged relations. All bent on sampling the good life and all determined to try again even if caught.'

It was not a pretty sight and, for the Gurkha, fond as he is of small children, it was often a heart-breaking one. The usual patrol consisted of a 'brick' of a Lance-Corporal, a radio operator and two riflemen. They had a rifle, a Federal Riot Gun which fired baton rounds, a stick each and their kukris. It was not an easy task and required not only determination but also good humour. For the most part those caught and handed over to the Police accepted it all philosophically but there were, from time to time, nasty incidents like that described in Chapter 12, when at Man Kam To 'D' Company of 1/6th found itself engaged in almost a pitched battle. This was in 1968 and it took some four hours to resolve a particularly tricky situation in which the Gurkhas behaved with great courage.

However, Hong Kong was not all crowd control and ceremonial parades. There were excellent opportunities for sport and the Gurkha is never happier then when playing games, preferably football, basket ball and volley ball. He also put paid to the belief that Gurkhas cannot swim. In addition, the Khud Race, at which the 1/6th and the 2/6th had excelled in the old days before the war, was introduced once more and won on several occasions in competition with the other Gurkha regiments, as well as with some of the British regiments in the garrison. It has its origins in the campaigns on the North-West Frontier. The key to mountain warfare is domination of the high ground, not always easy when the Pathan was the enemy. It involved sending up picquets very quickly to seize the heights in order to protect the column moving along the valley below. As the column advanced, the picquets were brought down. This had to be done fast if the withdrawing troops were not to be shot up by the tribesmen following hot on their trail. It required great physical fitness and very tight discipline. Planning the route up and down from a picquet was not always easy. The rule was to avoid re-entrants where ambush was easy.

The myth that Gurkhas would serve only under British or their own officers was exposed for what it was worth in 1947 when such a large number of Gurkhas opted to remain in the Indian Army. There was another myth, strongly believed by at least one senior retired Gurkha, that Gurkhas would never settle down to service in the United Kingdom. This was demolished in 1962 when the War Office decided to include a Gurkha battalion in the Strategic Reserve located on Salisbury Plain. The 1/6th were chosen for this experiment, arriving at Tidworth in May, 1962, to find themselves in 51st Infantry Brigade commanded by a 6th Gurkha, Brigadier Short. It was quite like old times! In fact the Gurkhas settled down as easily in Britain as they had done in Hong Kong, although they would have preferred a less damp and chilly climate. Later the UK battalion was located at Church Crookham in Hampshire where the always smiling Gurkhas soon became part of the everyday scene.

The 1/6th were to see a lot of the world during their time at Tidworth. One company took part in a NATO exercise in

Denmark and the Battalion, less a company, flew out to Aden
to exercise in mountains reminiscent of Waziristan. One of the
pleasures of the Aden trip was the presence there of General
Jim Robertson as the GOC. A joint exercise was held with the
Federal Regular Army (FRA), largely recruited from Arab
mountain tribesmen. It was notable that the Gurkhas were
outstripped by the Arabs when going up hill but, when descending, won the race easily.

The Battalion also played its part in Public Duties in London;
the diminutive Gurkha sentries, who barely came up to the
chests of the burly Guardsmen, making up for it by their
impeccable turnout and smartness of drill. They attracted
appreciative crowds to the 'Changing of the Guard' and, as
usual, made friends wherever they went.

Not surprisingly the sociological changes over the past thirty
years have had their repercussions in the Army as a whole.
There is, today, a more easy and relaxed relationship between
officer and soldier than once used to be the case. The soldier no
longer stands woodenly to attention, as if gasping for air, when
addressed by an officer but, as likely as not, will chat about
everything under the sun in the most relaxed fashion. And why
not? He is, probably, as avid a watcher of television as the
officer with whom he is talking and is, therefore, as competent
as his officer to argue the merits of leaving or staying with the
ERM. Both will have heard Jon Snow propound the arguments
for or against on Channel 4!

Similarly, there has been a change in the relationship between
the Gurkhas and their British officers. In the Indian Army of
the old days there was not a great deal of socialising between
the BOs and the *Jawans*, apart of course on the games field and
on special festive occasions. Few British officers made a practice
of dropping in to the VCOs Club for a drink and a gossip after
parade hours. This was less the case in Gurkha regiments,
perhaps, than in others but by no means in all of them.
Nowadays the Gurkha soldier is much more sophisticated than
his grandfather ever was and there are many Gurkha officers
holding the same Queen's Commission as their brother British
officers, and sharing the same officers' mess. Clearly this has

resulted in a much more relaxed attitude. One former CO says he frequently used the Gurkha Officers' Club for informal chats but insisted on being invited first by the Gurkha Major; nor would he do so if some entertainment of their own was in progress. 'The greatest gift of the Gurkha soldier,' he adds, 'is his ability to be free and easy off parade and to show no sign of it next morning.'

Those who have served with soldiers of many different races – Africans, Arabs, Burmese, Malays and so on – know it is unwise to be dogmatic about their many different characteristics, although the arguments raised in favour of the Sikh over the Mahratta, or of the Somali over the Kurd, can be repeated *ad nauseam*. In the Author's experience, however, there is one characteristic of the Gurkha soldier that seems to be repeated whenever and wherever he is met. This is an innate courtesy, just plain good manners. It is to be hoped that ever increasing sophistication will never change it.

24. *"During those 12 years (1982-1994) 6 GR ... has carried out Public Duties in London ..."*
26. *"... carried out duties in Aid to the Civil Power ..."*

25. *"... patrolled the Hong Kong Border with China ..."*
27. *"... and practised its jungle training in Brunei, Belize, Malaysia and Thailand."* (p.162)

28. *"It might be thought that Brunei, being somewhat off the beaten track, would have few visitors as compared with Hong Kong. This was not 6 GR's experience."* (p.164) Visit by HRH The Prince of Wales in February, 1984.

29. *"There was another Royal occasion on 24 February, 1989, when The Queen again visited the Regiment in Church Crookham."* (p.172) Her Majesty with Lieutenant Colonel D.H. McK Briggs and Major (QGO) Chintabahadur Gurung, MVO, left.

CHAPTER TEN

———◦·◦◦·◦———

'The Great and the Good'

IT is probably true to say that in the British Army it is the Regiment which is the focus of a soldier's loyalty. The same was, of course, true in the old Indian Army and is still jealously preserved in that Army today. In the British Army the Regiment, whether linked by its title to a County or known by a name like the Black Watch, represents an inheritance of two or three centuries, embodying a tradition which those serving in it value so greatly. Many men have died for the honour of their regiment.

No one is more fiercely proud of his regiment than the ordinary Gurkha rifleman. Gurkha regiments are all much the same, organized on the same lines, wearing much the same uniform and marching at the same rifle regiment's pace. And yet every Gurkha regiment prides itself on being, in some fashion, different and better, than the others. The 'Honour', or 'Izzat', of the regiment is more a matter of the Spirit than anything else.

For a great many years the 5th and 6th Gurkhas shared the amenities of Abbottabad. They both recruited Magars and Gurungs. Their British officers came from much the same backgrounds. The two regiments' comradeship had been sealed on many a bloody battlefield. But the 5th, once having been part of the old Punjab Frontier Force and bearing the letters 'FF' as part of their regimental title, doubtless felt that this entitled them to give themselves airs when it came to friendly rivalry with the 6th. The 6th might, on the other hand, have countered with the claim of being a more successful nursery for generals, in which they have been remarkably successful since 1939.

It would be wrong to assume that those regiments that produce many generals necessarily benefit from the fact. The Cameronians produced eight or more generals during the Second World War and in its aftermath but it did not save them from disbandment in 1968. It is, however, reasonable to expect a regiment which produces more senior commanders than the average to be more professional in its outlook than a regiment which produces none! Certainly the 6th Gurkhas have no reason to fear comparison in this regard. Between 1939 and 1945 they produced no fewer than four generals, one of them going on to become a Field Marshal; and between 1946 and 1994 they have produced four more, one of them of Four Star rank.

First and foremost must be, of course, Field Marshal the Viscount Slim, KG, the 'Uncle Bill' of the Fourteenth Army in Burma. No doubt the arguments will continue long into the future as to whether Slim or Montgomery was the greatest British field commander in the Second World War, although such debate is futile since they fought different enemies in widely different conditions. They were also totally different personalities. But one thing they did share. They both wore at one time the same regimental badge, that of the Royal Warwickshire Regiment, the old 6th Foot, Montgomery as a Regular and Slim as a Territorial.

Slim, born in Bishopston near Bristol in 1891, served throughout the First World War in the British Army. He went out to Gallipoli with the 9th Warwicks, a New Army battalion in the 13th Division, which landed at Cape Helles on 13 July, 1915. Some weeks later the 13th Division joined Birdwood's Anzac Corps as part of the operation to seize the heights of Sari Bair. Slim, only a subaltern, found himself commanding his company after the first day's fighting, the other officers having been killed or wounded on 7 August. After dark he pressed on upwards with some 50 men to join forces with 1/6th GR. They were pinned to the ground by the hellish artillery fire of the

Turks. Slim managed to find Allanson, commanding the 1/6th, and together they shared some raisins which Allanson had with him. At dawn the next morning, 8 August, the Warwicks moved forward with the Gurkhas in an attempt to seize the heights, but Slim was almost immediately wounded and had to be evacuated. He was so impressed by the bearing and the courage of the Gurkhas that he was to write many years later:

> 'I first met the 6th Gurkha Rifles in 1915 in Gallipoli. There I was so struck by their bearing in one of the most desperate battles in history that I resolved, should the opportunity come, to try to serve with them.'

After spending a long time in hospital in Britain, Slim managed to get back into the war, this time in Mesopotamia, where he was again wounded and awarded the MC. He ended the war in India in a staff appointment; he had been gazetted a regular commission in the West India Regiment but he managed to get a transfer to the Indian Army. On 27 March, 1920, he was posted as a captain to the 1/6th Gurkha Rifles. 'I spent many of the happiest, and from a military point of view, the most valuable years of my life in the Regiment,' he wrote later.

Slim was a first-class regimental officer who loved the 6th Gurkhas and his riflemen. He was a stern but always human adjutant of his Battalion, and served with it on the Frontier before passing top into the Staff College. Sadly there was no vacancy for him in the Regiment when the time came for him to command and he went instead to command the 2/7th Gurkha Rifles, but for little more than a year before he went to command the Senior Officers' School at Belgaum in the local rank of Brigadier. The rest is history, some of it recounted by his own pen in *Defeat into Victory*. A truly great soldier, who was loved and admired by those who served under him, Bill Slim was also a great human being. The Regiment can be proud that he always said he owed it so much.

Lord Slim achieved many 'Firsts' in the course of his distinguished career, but perhaps the most remarkable was his appointment in November, 1948, to be Chief of the Imperial General Staff at the War Office. He was the only 'Sepoy

General' in history to hold that prestigious appointment, and even more remarkably he had already retired from the army when recalled to succeed Field Marshal Montgomery. John Slim, his only son and now the 2nd Viscount, was commissioned in the 1/6th in 1945, serving in the Regiment for three years before transferring to the Argyll and Sutherland Highlanders, serving with them in Korea. Later he went on to command 22 SAS. He would undoubtedly have gone on to much higher rank had he not chosen to retire in 1972, becoming later a highly effective Chairman of the Burma Star Association.

In 1920, or shortly thereafter, the 1/6th were joined by two officers who, together with Slim, were to make a remarkable trinity. One was James Bruce Scott, the other David Tennant Cowan, universally known as 'Punch'. Both, under Slim as Corps Commander, were to fight as divisional commanders the long retreat from Burma in 1942. Seldom before, if ever, has a campaign been fought by three generals who had known each other since junior Captains, grown up together in the same battalion and, what is more, whose families had been close friends for a great many years. For them it was truly a family affair.

Bruce Scott, who arrived in Burma in 1940 to command the newly formed Maymyo Brigade was, and had always remained, the Author's *beau-idéal* of a soldier. He was smart, bright and friendly. He was also, as he had to be, clever at making bricks without straw in a Burma which was lacking in almost everything essential for the waging of war in the mid-20th Century. In the good times, and also in the bad, he was eminently approachable and encouraging. He joined the 33rd Punjabis (3/16th Punjab Regiment) in 1913, transferring to the 6th Gurkhas in 1922 after a spell as Commandant of the Tochi Scouts on the Frontier. 'Scottie' as he was known in the Regiment, was a great Frontier soldier, fluent in Pushtu as well as Urdu and Gurkhali, and he was officiating CO of the 1/6th during the 1930 operations in Waziristan. However, he went on to command the 1/8th Gurkhas and has been described as 'a superb trainer and a born leader'. In 1940 he went to Burma to form the 1st

Burma Brigade and was promoted to Major General in 1941 to raise the 1st Burma Division, an unenviable task since his Division was lacking in everything from guns to entrenching tools.

Somehow or other he brought his Division out of Burma after a retreat of more than nine hundred miles still in one piece although sadly depleted in strength. Scott himself was equally debilitated but later went on to be GOC Peshawar District, from which he retired in 1946. He died in 1974. His son, Colin, commanded the Regiment from 1973–75 and, after choosing early retirement became, among other tasks, Managing Trustee of the Gurkha Welfare Trust. To everyone's surprise and sorrow he collapsed and died on 13 January, 1986.

The third of the trinity to have survived as a senior commander the long retreat from Burma, was Major General David Tennant Cowan who first joined the Regiment in 1923. He is credited with having introduced Pipes and Drums into the 6th Gurkhas, which is hardly surprising since he began his service in the Argyll and Sutherland Highlanders. He commanded the 1/6th in 1939–40 in the Malakand. Considered to be one of the best officers for his age and rank in the Indian Army, he was posted to Burma just before the disastrous battle on the River Sittang when the Bridge was blown with over half the 17th Indian Division still on the wrong side of the fast-flowing river. Cowan was with the GOC, Major General 'Jackie' Smyth, when the terrible decision had to be taken to blow the bridge and he always contended that there was no alternative. However, it led to Smyth's removal from command and Cowan took over in his place. It was hardly a glad inheritance, with the 17th Division virtually decimated but somehow or other Cowan pulled the show together. He commanded the Division, known still today in the Indian Army as the 'Black Cats'* not only throughout the retreat, but later with conspicuous success in the advance from Imphal to Rangoon in 1944/45. He was later to command the Commonwealth Occupation Force in Japan before retiring from the Indian Army in 1947.

---

* The Divisional sign was a black cat, introduced by Cowan *after* the retreat.

'Punch' Cowan was a fine soldier who, like his Army
Commander, Slim, knew what it was like to endure defeat
before going on to achieve victory. He also had to endure the
private sorrow of having his son Malcolm killed while serving
with the 1/6th during the advance on Mandalay at a time when
Cowan himself was commanding the 17th Division in the
crucial battle at Meiktila, which broke the back of the Japanese
in Burma. He died in 1983.

Another 6th Gurkha who reached the rank of Major General
during the Second World War was J. G. Bruce, a cousin of
Brigadier General The Hon. C. G. Bruce, who took the 1/6th
to Gallipoli. Major General J. G. Bruce commanded the 2/6th
from 1936–39 and ended his army career as GOC Lahore
District. It was a remarkable record for a single, two-battalion
regiment in the Indian Army to produce no fewer than four
generals between 1939 and 1945.

The Regiment's record since 1945 has been no less remarkable
having produced in General Sir Walter Walker and Major
Generals 'Jim' Robertson and 'Pat' Patterson three GOCs of
the 17th Gurkha Division and three holders of the appointment,
'Major General Brigade of Gurkhas'. Robertson commanded
the 1/6th from 1947–48 and Walter Walker from 1951–54; he
was later to conduct the successful operations in Borneo and
reached the rank of full General as Commander-in-Chief, Allied
Forces Northern Europe from 1969–72, in which year he
retired. Patterson commanded the 2/6th from 1959–61 and
retired in 1972 after holding the appointment of Director of
Army Training.

There were, of course, a much larger number of 6th Gurkha
'characters' of lesser ranks maybe but who each, in their own
way, contributed to their Regiment's pursuit of excellence. But
to mention one must mean to mention all, which space does not
permit. The Hon. C. G. Bruce, for example, probably merits a
chapter all to himself, not only as a mountaineer and soldier but
also as an officer who had a particular empathy with the Gurkha
soldier. And there was also J. K. Jones, 'Jonah', of the 2/6th
who commanded the 1/1st Gurkha Rifles. Slim regarded him as
the epitome of the best kind of regimental officer. He survived

swimming the Sittang in 1942 and went on to be Commandant of the Indian Military Academy.

Mention must also be made of Brigadier A. E. C. Bredin, always known as 'Speedy' for his habit, as a young officer, of always turning up on parade at the very last moment. He joined the Dorsets from Sandhurst in 1931 and commanded the 1st Dorsets in Normandy. In between he had served with the 1st York & Lancasters in Italy and later still commanded the 5th Dorsets at the Rhine Crossing. He ended the war with the DSO and MC. In 1954 he was personally selected by Sir John Harding, then the Colonel of 6 GR, to command 1/6 GR in Malaya. He was a sensitive and sympathetic CO who was popular with British and Gurkha alike and has written a very interesting book about his time with them. He died, aged 80, in 1991.

It is hard to know where to draw the line over mentioning individuals in a history such as this, but there are at least two who merit more than a passing mention. They are Simon Fraser, 'Father' of the Regiment, who raised the Cuttack Legion in 1817, and Cecil John Lyons Allanson who came so close to winning the day on Sari Bair on 8 August, 1915.

Simon Fraser was born at Nairn in 1780. Like so many young Scots he set out when only 18 to win fame and fortune in the service of the Honourable East India Company. In 1799 he was appointed a Lieutenant in the 1/8th Bengal Native Infantry and by 1811 had reached the rank of Captain and was present at the capture of Java. During the Nepal War of 1814–16 he served in a battalion of Bengal Light Infantry and in May, 1817, was appointed to raise the Cuttack Legion in Orissa. He was promoted to Major in 1822 in the 2/6th Bengal Native Infantry but proceeded on furlough to Scotland after an absence of 22 years. He never returned to India although promoted to Lieutenant Colonel in the 41st Bengal Native Infantry, remaining on half-pay until his death in 1845. Lieutenant Colonel Simon Fraser Hannay was named after the founder of the Regiment. He joined the Assam Light Infantry on 14 May, 1838, later commanding the Regiment for 22 years. He died at Dibrugarh on 25 January, 1861.

JAI SIXTH!

Cecil John Allanson was a remarkable man. Born in 1877, son of a marriage that eventually broke up, he was educated at Bedford School and Sandhurst. A fine athlete, he held for some years the Army record for the two miles. He was commissioned into the Royal Artillery in 1897 and was posted to India in the Madras Garrison Artillery, serving later with an Elephant Battery in the Punjab. On 21 March, 1902, he transferred to the 42nd Gurkha Rifles which, a year later, became the 6th Gurkha Rifles and, in 1904, a regiment of two battalions. Allanson was Adjutant of the 1/6th for a short period before attending the Staff College, after which he spent most of the years up to the outbreak of war in 1914 on the personal staffs of the Lieutenant Governor of Bengal and subsequently the Governor of Madras, Lord Pentland, with only a brief return to his regiment. Consequently he never became fluent in Gurkhali although he spoke Urdu well enough.

It was not until July, 1915, that he was recalled to regimental duty to command the 1/6th in Gallipoli. He was commanding in the rank of Major when he so nearly seized the heights of Sari Bair on 8 August, 1915; it was owing to no failing on his part that he did not succeed. He was badly wounded, once in the thigh in the actual assault and later on 3 December, 1915, when he was temporarily blinded and as a result evacuated to hospital in Britain. Allanson was recommended for the Victoria Cross after Sari Bair but the War Office saw fit to change this to the DSO. An eye-witness account of this incident is given in the unpublished reminiscences of Lieutenant General Sir Reginald Savory, then serving at Gallipoli in the same infantry brigade as the 1/6th.

'While I was waiting at the dump for the mules to be loaded,' writes Savory, 'I looked in at brigade headquarters to learn the latest news and take up any fresh orders. In a very fragile dug-out sat the Brigadier, Major General H. V. Cox, with his staff, working by the light of a hurricane lantern. I had scarcely reported, when in came Major Cecil Allanson. General Cox had sent for him. Allanson had been wounded but was just able to get about. He made his report. The 6th

Gurkhas had indeed been blown off the top of Hill "Q" [Sari Bair]. They had suffered severely. No British officer remained except the regimental medical officer, Captain Phipson, who had taken off his red-cross arm band and taken over command of what was left of the battalion. General Cox told Allanson that he was going to recommend him for the Victoria Cross. Allanson replied that he had done the best he could, but was sorry to have failed. What an understatement! It was no fault of his. I regarded him then, as I do now, as one of the bravest men I have ever met, and the 1/6th Gurkhas as the outstanding battalion of the Gallipoli campaign. The Distinguished Service Order, which he subsequently received instead of the Victoria Cross, must surely stand out as being more than exceptional. I was fortunate in being present at this short meeting.'*

Allanson was some time recovering from his wounds and later served in France and on the staff in the War Office. He did not return to India until 1921 when he was appointed to command the 2/6th in Waziristan. He was still suffering from the effects of his Gallipoli wounds and he was wounded again – in the leg – in Waziristan. He was a very competent and much respected CO but seems to have been temperamentally unsuited to peacetime life in the Indian Army. He was not in favour of the 'Indianisation' of the Indian Army's Officer Corps and appears to have become disillusioned with the Indian Army. To the dismay of his friends and admirers he applied to retire at his own request in 1922. Had he remained in the service most people thought he would have become a general in due course. Allanson was one of the most outstanding officers ever to have served in the 6th Gurkha Rifles. He died in 1943 when working in Civil Defence in London. His diary, published in 1990 as *Allanson of the 6th*, edited by Harry Davies, also of the 6th, makes fascinating reading.

Like the British Army in the old days, the Indian Army had its fair share of eccentrics. They seem, as a breed, to have died

* Private papers of the late Lieutenant General Sir Reginald Savory by courtesy of Major A. C. S. Savory (his nephew).

out nowadays, probably as a result of the Staff College and 'sweating on promotion'. Certainly the Hon. C. G. Bruce must rank as one of the most remarkable eccentrics the Regiment has ever produced, as this story by the 1/6th's RMO at Gallipoli makes clear. Captain (as he then was) E. S. Phipson of the Indian Medical Service was the only British officer left unwounded with the battalion at Sari Bair. He removed his Red Cross armband and together with the Subedar-Major, Gambirsing Pun, proceeded to extricate what was left of the 1/6th from Sari Bair. He was later, along with Allanson, awarded the DSO. What follows is his story:

'In the month of December, 1914, the 29th Indian Brigade, and with it the 1st/6th GR, lay in a perimeter camp in Port Said, before moving on to Kantara.

'One evening the CO (Charles Bruce) was invited to dine at the 14th Sikhs' Mess, which was near our lines. It was a convivial party and after dinner Bruce entertained the Mess with some of his remarkable feats of strength.* Towards midnight he said farewell to his hosts and started to return to his own lines. It was pitch dark, and the pathway was beset on either side with tent pegs, and one of the subalterns, Reg Savory, kindly offered to light him on his way with a hurricane-*batti*. Bruce gratefully accepted his friendly offer, and the two made their way to Bruce's 40-pounder.

'Savory saw him safely into his tent and was saying goodnight when Bruce put his head outside the tent and called him back, and as he approached the fly of the tent, Bruce gave him a straight right on the point of the chin and knocked him down. Savory picked himself up and, feeling shaken and, naturally, indignant realized that any immediate protest would be useless, returned to his own Mess where he very properly reported the matter to his CO.

'The next morning the story got to the ears of Josh Ryan, the Adjutant, who came along and told me about it and we

---

* Charles Bruce was a man of remarkable physical strength. As a young man he would regularly carry his orderly up the steep slopes of the Khyber to keep himself in trim.

were both very worried. Bruce, to whom Josh recounted the events of the previous evening and whose memory of events was very hazy, was seriously disturbed, as well he might be, and went round at once to apologise to Savory and to his CO for assaulting one of his officers, and his apologies were generously accepted by the aggrieved parties.

'But to Ryan and myself, who were deeply concerned about the incident, Bruce was a menace and another such incident – and who could say how long Bruce's protestations of regret would be a guarantee of pacific behaviour? It might easily lead to formal representations to the Brigadier with results which might be disastrous. I thought it over some time, and decided that the only way of dealing with the CO was, if possible, to frighten him in probably the only way he could be frightened, that was to cast doubt on his physical fitness for command. I talked it over with Ryan, and he agreed that my proposal seemed to offer the only chance of avoiding a possible future scandal.

'So the next day I engaged Bruce in conversation and said I thought he was not looking as fit as he ought to and might I give him a medical examination? After some demur he agreed, and I made a full examination with certain tests which I could see puzzled him. Actually, of course, he was in robust health, but I felt it was my duty to him as well as to the Battalion to pretend that there were signs of "kidney-trouble" and, consequently, that unless he undertook to go on the water-waggon for three months, I should be compelled to ask for a Medical Board who, I felt sure, would relegate him to a post at the Base or on the L of C. This pronouncement, for which I hope I may be forgiven, had the desired effect and, after pondering over it for a time he capitulated and agreed to act on my advice.

'The next day, at my suggestion, he purchased a number of crates of Evian Water and began a strange daily régime of his own devising, which consisted of spells of hard exercise, such as skipping and running, followed by drinking quantities of Evian Water – I should say at least a dozen bottles a day. The most spectacular part of this régime was the Field Turkish

Bath. A hole five feet deep and four feet in diameter was dug in the camp site just in front of his tent, and this was prepared for use by lighting a wood fire in it like a field bakery. When the surrounding earth was hot enough he had the embers and the ashes removed, and he would lower himself into it so that only his head and neck protruded above ground-level and the annular space around his neck was filled in by a sheet of canvas, cut to fit. In the afternoons he would sit in this contraption and sweat profusely for an hour or more, and I can still see him sitting there, his face and neck scarlet, laughing and chatting with any BO, GO or Other Rank who might happen to pass by, and cracking jokes in (I should imagine) faultless Gurkhali.'*

Sadly, they don't come like that any more! Bruce took the 1/6th to Gallipoli and commanded the battalion with great panache until seriously wounded in both legs on 1 July, 1915. He was awarded the CB and made brevet Colonel for his services. After recovery from his wounds, and on promotion to Brigadier General, he commanded an infantry brigade in Waziristan, before going on to lead the Mount Everest expeditions in 1922 and 1924. He died in 1939 and it is recorded of him that 'He was a legendary figure whose name and exploits will never be forgotten. No man knew and understood the Gurkha better.'† Phipson remained with 1/6 GR in 1915 and 1916. Retiring from the Indian Medical Service as a Colonel in 1945, he died in 1973. His admiration for the Gurkha soldier, and for the 1/6th in particular, remained with him all his life. The Author, as a boy, used to listen enthralled as the old man told tales of Gallipoli and fought the battle of Sari Bair all over again!

In 1948 the Regimental Association was formed with the praiseworthy aims of keeping alive the comradeship formed after many years' service together in the 6th Gurkha Rifles, and to keep in touch with the Regiment. The Association publishes

* As recounted in *Memories of Port Said* in the Spring 1985 issue of the Regimental Association Journal, pages 16–18.
† *Historical Record of the 6th Gurkha Rifles*, Vol. II, P.13.

annually an excellent journal which has proven to be invaluable in the compilation of this history. The present Chairman is Brigadier Gil Hickey who commanded 1/6th GR in Borneo in 1963–66, and the Regimental Secretary is Lieutenant Colonel A. S. Harvey who commanded 2/6th GR, also in Borneo, over the same period. Gil Hickey went on to command 48th Gurkha Infantry Brigade in Hong Kong. Brigadier C. J. D. Bullock is co-opted on the Association Committee. He commanded 6 GR in 1978–81 and later became Brigadier, Brigade of Gurkhas, retiring to become Secretary of the Army Rifle Associaqtion.

A Nepal Branch of the Regimental Association was formed early in 1994, under the Chairmanship of Hon Lieutenant (GCO) Purnabahadur Gurung, with the aim of fostering contact amongst ex-6th Gurkhas in the hills of Nepal.

CHAPTER ELEVEN

'Johnny Gurkha'

OF all the many soldiers of different races, religion and colour who served the British Crown in the great days of Empire, it is probably the Gurkha who most captured the imagination and admiration of the ordinary British citizen. 'Johnny Gurkha', as he has always been known to the British soldiers who fought in battle alongside him, occupies a special corner in a great many British hearts, and not only the hearts of those British officers who served with him. His self-sacrificing gallantry, which has led to the award of an unusually large number of Victoria Crosses, may account for some of this admiration, but not entirely. His short stature, cheerful disposition and friendly nature has certainly contributed to his popularity among the British people.

It would be wrong, however, to regard the Gurkha soldier as some kind of plaster saint. He has his human weaknesses, among which wine and women figure prominently! One of the best descriptions of the Gurkha regiments has been written by a Gunner, Brigadier Shelford Bidwell, in his excellent book *The Chindit War*, which is quoted below with his permission:

'The Gurkha regiments were different again. The Gurkhas, or Ghorkas, of Nepal are Mongolian by race and Hindu by religion, but by an accident of history already accustomed to be ruled by Indians of the highest caste, and so had accepted, in their military life, the leadership of another kind of outsider, provided he came up to their own pitiless standard of courage. ("A good officer, Sahib, but not a Gurkha officer," was the polite formula by which the native Gurkha officers would invite their commanding officer to get rid of a British officer whom they had tried and found wanting.) The Gurkhas were recruited into their several regiments after careful selection by officers who had knowledge of every shade of clan or sect and their qualities as soldiers at their finger tips; Magars and Gurungs from Western Nepal; Rais and Limbus from the east; Puns, Thakurs and Chhetris. The 3/6th were westerners. The 3/9th and the 4/9th were Thakurs and Chhetris, these names indicating a claim to membership of the Rajput caste, famous for its military tradition. They were stricter in their adherence to the Hindu religion and so known to the other British officers as the 'High Church party'.

'As a class,' writes Bidwell, 'the British officers in the Gurkha regiments tended to be exclusive, narrow-minded, as professional as Prussians or the officers of the French Foreign Legion. Among them was a strong Scottish element, who had taught their mountaineers to accept the bagpipe as their regimental music. The biblical rhetoric of Wingate, though it struck a chord in the breasts of the British officers . . . meant little to the Gurkha officers and riflemen. By their own tradition, fighting was an end in itself. The "ninety-day" contract meant nothing to them; they were sworn, like the Legion, to "march, fight and die", and as long as their officers, British and Gurkha, led they were prepared to follow them until they dropped, as many of them did.'*

The description 'narrow-minded' may raise the hackles of many serving and retired British officers of Gurkha regiments but it is really just a bad choice of words. 'Dedicated' would be better. Partly on account of the nature of the soldiers they led and partly because of the isolated location of many of the Gurkha

---

* *The Chindit War – The Campaign in Burma 1944*, by Shelford Bidwell (Hodder & Stoughton, 1979, pp. 116–117). The Gurkha regiments referred to are the three Gurkha battalions, one from the 6th and two from the 9th, which served in Wingate's Special Force – The Chindits.

cantonments, British officers in Gurkha units were necessarily thrown in more on themselves than was the case in other British or Indian regiments. As is clear from John Masters' *Bugles and a Tiger*, there was much more socializing between British officers and the soldiers they commanded than was the case elsewhere in either the British or the Indian Armies.

It should be remembered that Gurkha units spent a great deal of the time on active service, even between the two world wars; and taking Malaya and Borneo into consideration, much longer since 1948. This meant separation for the families. Gurkhas may or may not marry young but during the first fifteen years of their service were entitled to only three years accompanied by their wives and children.

Gurkha officers of the old school were great upholders of tradition, turning themselves out immaculately whether in uniform or plain clothes. Doubtless they made allowances for the idiosyncrasies of the more senior British officers, with whom they had grown up, but junior officers were permitted no leeway. And not only, it may be said, in a Gurkha unit. The author remembers vividly being admonished by the Subedar-Major of the 4th Burma Rifles for appearing on parade in a badly polished Sam Browne belt!

The question which inevitably arises is how different is the Gurkha soldier of today from his forbears? He is obviously much more sophisticated with probably a bank account and credit cards. Most can speak and read English and are very keen on education, especially for their children. They have become worldly-wise, flying from continent to continent, reading English newspapers, watching English television and enjoying life in Hong Kong, that centre of capitalism. The old style Gurkha officers are gradually being phased out, their places taken by bright young men with ambitions to go to Sandhurst or to become a Gurkha Commissioned Officer (GCO). Of course there has been change.

One of the most remarkable characteristics of the Gurkha is his willingness to try his hand at anything. It came as no surprise to those who knew him that during the firemen's strike in 1977 the Regiment manned several of the antiquated 'Green

48. *First and foremost must be, of course, Field Marshal the Viscount Slim, KG, the 'Uncle Bill' of the Fourteenth Army in Burma."* (p.138)

49. *"He was a stern but always human adjutant of his battalion, and served with it on the Frontier before passing top into the Staff College."* (p.139)

50. Sergeant Jaibahadur Gurung and Rifleman Tulbahadur Pun, later Gurkha Major and Regimental Sergeant-Major of 6 GR and the Training Depot, Brigade of Gurkhas.

51. *"Having produced in General Sir Walter Walker and Major-Generals 'Jim' Robertson and 'Pat' Patterson three GOCs of the 17th Gurkha Division."* (p.142) Major-General J.A.R. Robertson, CB, CBE, DSO (right) with Colonel N.F.B. Shaw, DSO, OBE and the then Brigadier W.C. Walker, DSO, OBE.

52. Major-General A.G. Patterson, DSO, OBE, MC, presenting The Wallace Memorial Trophy in 1968, Kluang, West Malaysia. He was later made CB.

53. *"The Bisley results have been superb. To provide four Queen's Medallists in little more than ten years is, indeed, a proud record."* (p.161) Lieutenant (QGO) Dharmendra Gurung (1982 and 1993), WO 2 Khusiman Gurung (1985) and Rifleman Lalitbahadur Gurung (1992).

54. *"Allanson was recommended for the Victoria Cross after Sari Bair but the War Office saw fit to change this to the DSO."* (p.144) As CO-designate 2/6th, 1920.

55. " 'Brunei has hardly changed at all, and I am sure I speak for the
majority who relish the rather more relaxed way of life.' " (p.197)
Lieutenant-Colonel P.D. Pettigrew (sitting, second from left) with the
Colonel of the Regiment, Major-General (later Lieutenant-General Sir
Derek) Boorman (centre), the relaxed officers and their ladies, 1983,
Brunei.

56. "Patrols on foot, bicycles and vehicles were continuous." (p.165)
Lieutenant-Colonel R.F. Richardson-Aitken with the then Commander
Gurkha Field Force, Brigadier P.R. Duffell, OBE, MC, 1985, Hong
Kong-China Border.

57. "*On 8 November, 1988, a service of re-dedication* [of the Book of Remembrance] *was held. The Dean of Winchester officiated and there was an impressive attendance ... headed by Aileen, Viscountess Slim.*" (p.169)

58. "*Prior to returning to Hong Kong in April, 1989, the officers held a somewhat unusual Guest Night ... the guests were all past Colonels of the Regiment and former Commanding Officers of the 1st and 2nd Battalions.*" (p.169)

59. *"Twice in ten years [The Queen] has visited the Regiment … in Church Crookham. The first occasion was on 5 May, 1978."* (p.172) Lieutenant-Colonel M.J.F. Wardroper and Major (QGO) Toyebahadur Chand escort Her Majesty, watched by Major B.M. O'Bree.

60. *"When The Queen visited Hong Kong on 21 October, 1986, the Regiment once again had the privilege of mounting the Guard of Honour … This was commanded by Major Gopalbahadur Gurung, MBE."* (p.172)

61. *"There had, of course, to be a 175th Anniversary ceremonial parade which was carried out with immaculate precision."* (p.178) Lieutenant-Colonel N.A. Collett, Major (QGO) Padambahadur Gurung MVO and the officers on parade, rest on their laurels.

62. *"They are eager for education and their wives even more so — for themselves as much as for their children."* (p.183) Mrs Marie Pett, Mrs Sudha Rai (the 2IC's wife, 2nd left) and a group of 'elder sisters-younger sisters' with some of their children.

63. *"Major Harkasing Rai was one of the Regiment's first GCOs and also one of the Regiment's most redoubtable and venerated figures. In the course of his service he was awarded the MC and bar, the IDSM and MM which, even for a Gurkha, was remarkable."* (p.198)

64. *" 'The Almighty created in the Gurkha an ideal Infantryman ... brave, tough, patient, adaptable, skilled in fieldcraft.' "* (p.15) (Field Marshal Lord Slim). To 21164983 Rifleman Budhibahadur Gurung 6 GR, and all like him — ***Jai Sixth!***

Goddesses' which were brought out of mothballs to replace the
fire engines lying idle in the NFS Fire Stations. As one of them
with siren blaring passed by in a Berkshire lane, a grinning
Gurkha at the wheel, memory went back to Burma in 1942 and
an incident at Nyaunglebin, a small railway junction on the
main line from Rangoon to Mandalay. Rangoon was about to
be evacuated and everything that could be was being back-
loaded by rail to the north.

A Japanese air raid on the station had blocked the railway.
After the dead bodies had been cleared away there remained an
engine, still with steam up but without a driver who was
probably among the dead. A milling mass of people, desperate
to clamber aboard the next train that passed through, blocked
the platform. Every railway official had decamped. How was
the engine to be moved? At that critical moment a young
Gurkha Lance-Naik came out of the crowd, saluted and said he
would have a try. He had once travelled on the footplate of an
engine in the marshalling yard at Gorakhpur. All this in bad
Urdu as he also explained that he was looking for his unit
(1/7th Gurkha Rifles) from which he had been separated after
the Sittang Bridge disaster.

He climbed aboard as the stationmaster suddenly appeared.
Together they shovelled coal into the firebox and got up steam.
The Gurkha pulled the levers, there was a triumphant whistle
and slowly the engine moved forward. The crowd cheered. The
stationmaster ran ahead to adjust the points and then the line
was clear, just in time for the up-train from Rangoon to rumble
slowly past with every carriage crammed with fleeing passen-
gers. The Gurkha asked if he could now rejoin his unit but an
auxiliary engine driver was too valuable to lose at that juncture;
instead he was for the time being enrolled in the Defence
Platoon of Brigade headquarters with which he remained until
India was reached.

Shortly afterwards the Brigade Headquarters was visited by
the GOC 1st Burma Division, Major General Bruce Scott,
himself a 6th Gurkha. When he was told the story he smiled.
'Trust a Gurkha', was all he said.

When Professor R. L. Turner published his *A Comparative*

and Etymological Dictionary of the Nepali Language, he dedicated it to 'the stubborn and indomitable peasants of Nepal . . .
Bravest of the brave, most generous of the generous.' Few of
those who have served with the Gurkha soldier would disagree
with such a compliment. Bravery is the word most commonly
associated with the Gurkha, so much so that it is almost taken
for granted. It is perhaps the Gurkha's imperturbability amidst
the tumult of battle that makes it seem that he is unmoved by
what is going on around him but he would probably look the
same if poised on a precipice. He takes life as he finds it and has
a simple explanation for the most extraordinary occurrence.
When Lord Mountbatten visited 3/6th GR shortly before the
Battalion flew into Burma, he used a few words of Gurkhali in
the address he delivered to the troops. It made a considerable
impression, the conclusion reached being that Mountbatten
must have served in some other Gurkha unit. Like all men who
come from simple background, there is usually a simple explanation to account for anything out of the ordinary and there is
certainly no call to get excited about it.

The courage of the Gurkha soldier has become the stuff of
legend and, like all legends, may from time to time have been
exaggerated in the telling. Nevertheless there have been so many
well documented instances of such bravery – 'Above and
beyond the call of duty,' as an award of the US Congressional
Medal of Honour might describe it – that it may be safe to
assume that sheer physical courage is part of the Gurkha's
birthright. There is, for example, the story of the young Lance-
Naik Lilbahadur of 1/6th GR on the North-West Frontier
during operations against the Mahsuds in June, 1937.

Lilbahadur was commanding one of two sections withdrawing
from a picquet at the end of a day's duty. As he was running
down the hillside he heard the lever of the grenade he was
carrying in his pack click, followed by the noise of the fuse
burning. Without regard for his own safety he ordered the
section to keep away from him, running off diagonally in order
to keep clear of the other section coming down behind him. As
he ran he struggled to undo his equipment and was on the point
of throwing it away when the grenade exploded. He was

mortally wounded but no one else was hurt. It was a wonderful example of self-sacrifice by a very young and junior NCO. It also displayed courage of a very high order. The annals of every Gurkha regiment contain stories of like kind. They are very brave men.

A marked attribute of the Gurkha soldier is his ability to look neat and tidy in the most adverse of circumstances. He will also make himself comfortable when British soldiers abandon all hope of ever being comfortable again but always, in the Gurkha's case, within the strict limits of good order and military discipline. In the Spring, 1989, edition of the Regimental Association Journal there is an amusing account by Brigadier Guy Wheeler of the contrasting appearance of a Gurkha and a British platoon after a night of pouring rain and high winds during the final stages of the Italian campaign. Wheeler, who at the time was commanding a troop of tanks, had the British deployed on one side of him and on the other the Gurkhas. Of the British he writes: 'It appeared that the whole platoon had been washed out of their weapon pits and had spent the night vainly trying to keep themselves and the platoon equipment at least partially dry. Every stitch they had was sodden.'

On the other side of his tank the Gurkha platoon, 'who, clean and dry, fastidiously flicked specks of mud from their puttees and hosetops as they moved about repairing the reed thatch on their shelters and clearing the drainage ditches . . . Picking his way carefully through his platoon position, his boots and puttees spotless, his drill trousers and grey flannel shirt neatly pressed, the brim of his slouch hat stiff and level with chinstrap gleaming, came the Gurkha platoon sergeant.' The contrast with the dishevelled appearance of the British platoon must have lingered long in Wheeler's memory, as has a similar instance in the Author's.

A few days after the Sittang Bridge disaster on 23 February, 1942, while travelling north from Pegu in a 30cwt truck, the driver, a Burma rifleman, suddenly slammed on the brakes, pointing to the right of the road where a few dust covered *neem* trees were growing. Standing at the edge of them was a small figure dressed only in grubby singlet and khaki shorts but whose Gurkha hat was correctly angled. He stood at the salute as we went forward and was joined by three or four others similarly clad and, likewise, at strict attention. They were Gurkhas of the 2/5th Royal Gurkha Rifles who had, by some miracle, succeeded in crossing the swift-running Sittang and who had managed, by an equal miracle, to avoid the Burmese villagers who were cutting up stragglers wherever they found them. They had neither eaten nor drunk for several days and were obviously dehydrated but their faces were wreathed in smiles. All they wanted was to get back to their regiment. Turning the truck, we bundled them into the back and returned to Pegu where the stragglers were being collected. There chief regret appeared to be that they had lost their kukris, presumably while crossing the river. It seemed that otherwise their morale was entirely unshaken.

Gurkhas will eat every kind of meat with the exception of cows and female goats. In the matter of what they drink Gurkhas again, save Brahmans and Chhetris, have no scruples whatsoever and they have no hesitation in sampling wine, beer or any sort of spirits. It might be added that they also have incredibly hard heads. In their own homes they brew a kind of beer made from fermented rice, millet or Indian corn and they also drink a kind of spirit called *raksi*. But their favourite beverage is probably the ordinary issue rum which is remarkably potent, as many a British officer has ruefully noted after an evening's entertainment in the Gurkha Officers' Mess.*

The Gurkha soldier's relative freedom from caste prejudices, apart, of course, from the Chhetris, does not mean that he belongs to a completely classless society, if indeed such a society exists anywhere in the world. The Gurkha society is tribal and can be extremely clannish. The Magars, for example, are divided into six tribes – Rana, Thapa, Ale, Pun, Burathoki, and Gharti – of which the first three are supposedly superior to the remainder in physique and breeding. When left to their own devices Gurkha soldiers usually prefer to associate with those of their own tribe or clan.

The Gurkhas are, of course, Hindus or Buddhists, although

---

* The rum issue was regretfully abandoned when the Royal Navy gave up the free tot!

for the most part their religion sits lightly on them. They are, however, very fond of the displays of dancing, music and general fun which accompany most Hindu festivals, of which by far the most important is *Dashera* commemorating the victory of the goddess Durga over the monster Maheshur. This festival, which lasts for ten days, usually takes place in October, the actual date being determined by astrologers and dependent on the position of the moon. Festivities continue throughout *Dashera** but it is probably to the eighth, or *Astami* day, that the most importance is attached. This is the celebration of *Kalratri* in a splendid *Dashera Ghar*, erected and embellished under the eagle eye of the Gurkha Major, where the sacrifices of living buffaloes and goats are decapitated by, hopefully, a single blow of the kukri. Nowadays, however, by the King of Nepal's special dispensation, Gurkhas serving overseas are absolved from the animal sacrifices associated with *Kalratri*, a pumpkin being substituted instead, although on return to Nepal those concerned are supposed to undergo purification ceremonies by the Brahmans. The ceremonial at *Kalratri* is accompanied by much singing and dancing, the latter all-male. It is recorded in *The Steadfast Gurkha* that in 1982, during a regimental reunion in Hong Kong held over *Dashera*, the veteran *maruni*, Captain (QGO) Birbahadur Thapa, could still hold his own on the dance floor. *Maruni* is a male dancer but in a female dress.†

Twenty days after *Dashera* comes *Diwali*,‡ the 'Festival of Illumination' and sacred to Lakshmi, goddess of wealth and prosperity and consort of the god Vishnu. In Nepal, in the old days, this was chiefly popular for the opportunity to gamble in public, forbidden at other times. The Gurkha is a great gambler despite the fact that he is at the same time extremely money-

---

* In Gurkhali, *Dasain*.
† It is curious that in most primitive societies men and women do not dance together but only with their own sex. It is also surprising that among hillmen from widely differing parts of the world how similar are the steps and the various movements. For example, the Kachin soldiers in the Burma Rifles danced in much the same way as the Gurkhas and, even more surprisingly, so did the Arab soldiers from 'up-country' in Aden. The music and singing was, of course, very different.
‡ *Tihar* in Gurkhali

conscious. Perhaps it is a Mongolian trait? In the Burma Rifles the Burman soldiers would bet on anything – even the number of flies next to land on a piece of meat laid out for the purpose! They would wager away their uniform and equipment to such an extent that on the next pay day they would be marched to the pawnshops to redeem their kit before being paid the balance of their salary.

Up to the year 1914 the number of recruits required annually to maintain the twenty Gurkha battalions at full strength was about fifteen hundred and these were, with the sanction of the Nepal Government, recruited by Gurkhas specially deputed from the various regiments. British officers were regularly sent on these recruiting expeditions which provided them with a wonderful opportunity to meet the Gurkha in his home sur-roundings in some of the loveliest country in this world. All the trekking was on foot, up hill and down dale, to spend the eve-nings chatting with the old pensioners in their homes and talking about old wars. To climb out of the tent at dawn, a steaming mug of tea in hand and watch the slopes of Annapurna turn golden in the rays of the rising sun, was an unforgettable experience.

The numbers recruited were greatly increased as the war continued and the same was, of course, true during the Second World War. There was, however, no centralized training organ-ization until 1940. Previously each battalion had its Training or Depot Company which remained behind in Abbottabad when the battalion went off to the Frontier. On 15 November, 1940, the Regimental Centre was formed and became, in due course, the 6th Gurkha Rifles Regimental Centre. By 1943 the Centre was dealing with as many as five thousand recruits as well as maintaining all the Regimental Records. This included the 26th Gurkha Rifles, a garrison battalion composed of reservists too old to serve in the active battalions.

The principal credit for the expansion and successful organ-ization of the Regimental Centre must go to Colonel Hugh Walsh who joined 6 GR in 1917. He was responsible for everything from the initial training of recruits to the dispatch, on pension, of those soldiers time-expired or discharged on account of disability or wounds. Walsh really created the

Centre, but mention is also due of Colonel Norman ('John') Eustace who succeeded Walsh in 1945. It fell to him to run down the Centre after the war, move it from Abbottabad to Dehra Dun and to command the combined Centre with the 5th until the transfer came to British Service in 1947.

'John' Eustace joined 2/6 GR in 1921. In June, 1944, he was appointed to command 2/5 RGR during the bitter fighting to repel the Japanese attempts to take Imphal. He was the Battalion's third commanding officer within five days. Soon after he took over command his Battalion was subjected to a severe artillery barrage that temporarily severed communications. As soon as it was restored the Brigade commander, Brigadier Osborn Hedley, who had previously commanded the Battalion with great distinction, called up to query the state of play. 'It couldn't be worse,' replied Eustace, 'so it must get better!' Eustace was awarded the DSO later.

In order to wrest from the Japanese their so-called superiority in jungle warfare, the Army in India instituted an intensive training programme at the end of 1942. Two Divisions were formed to put the final polish on all recruits before they joined their active battalions. 6 GR, together with 5 RGR, formed 56 GR as part of 39th Indian Division, in which soldiers were trained in as near as possible to active service conditions before being dispatched to front-line units. 39th Division had formerly been the 1st Burma Division, of which Major General Bruce Scott had been the GOC throughout the withdrawal from Burma in 1942. It was located at Saharanpur in the Siwalik Hills on the way to Dehra Dun. The 56th GR were disbanded in 1946.

Early in 1947 it was decided to concentrate the Gurkha Rifles Regimental Centres at Dehra Dun which meant, sadly, the abandonment of Abbottabad. The move took place in August, 1947, to join up with the 5th Gurkha Rifles as the 56th Gurkha Rifles Regimental Centre.* It was not to last long because in the same month information was received that the 2nd, 6th, 7th

---

* It was not the easiest time for rail travel in India with the Punjab in a state of chaos, and the journey was particularly hard on the Gurkha families. A baby boy was born on the way and it was suggested to the proud mother and father that he should be named *Rail*bahadur!

and 10th Gurkha Rifles were to become part of the British Army. For the time being the regimental centres were to be concentrated at Ranchi in Bihar, but here again the move was only temporary. When finally it was decided to base the 17th Gurkha Division in Malaya, Sungei Patani became the Brigade of Gurkhas' base for the training of recruits etc. until the independence of Malaya in 1957, after which the Depot was moved to Hong Kong.

In Nepal itself there were recruiting centres at Dharan in the east and Pokhara in the west. They had not only to deal with the recruits arriving raw from their villages and get them into some sort of shape before sending them off to Malaya/Hong Kong but had also to deal with those going on pension. The Brigade of Gurkhas L of C was an elaborate one beginning with Malaya/Hong Kong and ending in Nepal, with a staging post at Barrackpore in Calcutta. It was a far cry from the simple days when the recruits came down from the hills to the Gurkha Recruiting Depot and Record Office at Kunraghat from where they were sent by road and rail to Abbottabad and the various other Gurkha garrisons. For many years Lieutenant Colonel H. R. K. Gibbs of 6th GR was the Deputy Recruiting Officer in Nepal and served the Regiment wonderfully well in that capacity – as well as in a great many other ways, not least as the Regiment's chronicler. 'Gibbos' is still alive as this is being written and only ninety-four years young!

The Gurkha has a very infectious sense of humour but can sometimes see the funny side of a situation which is not immediately apparent to the individual involved. Field Marshal Slim recounts the story of an incident on the Frontier when he was adjutant of 1/6th GR. A platoon was being sniped at by tribesmen and Slim went forward to investigate, in the course of which he had to cross a stretch of open ground before reaching the platoon. As he did so he was fired at, not once but on several occasions, and had to dodge from cover to cover. On reaching the platoon he found its commander beaming with laughter. When he angrily asked why he had not been given covering fire, the platoon commander replied, 'You looked so funny dodging about in the open!'

General Walker recounts the story of a Gurkha battalion which was celebrating its forthcoming departure from Borneo by one or two hectic parties in the British Officers' Mess. A newly arrived rifleman, on guard for the first time, was being instructed in his duties by the guard commander, a Sergeant. After the sentry's knowledge of the password and other procedures had been carefully checked, the Sergeant said, 'You are a sentry. It is one o'clock in the morning. Suddenly you see a figure crawling towards you through the long grass over there. What would you do?' Without a moments hesitation the sentry replied, 'Show him the way to the Officers' Mess!'

In 1964, in the Tokyo Olympics which Nepal had entered for the first time, 2/6th GR provided four of the boxers for the Nepalese team. They did not get very far unfortunately, but it was certainly an interesting experience. The Regiment always showed up well in the numerous sporting competitions held in Hong Kong and other garrisons but perhaps it is at Bisley at the annual meeting of the National Rifle Association that it has had, in recent years, a remarkable success. Coached and cheered on by Lieutenant Colonel 'Tich' Harvey, a former CO of 2/6 GR and now retired and the regimental secretary, the Bisley results have been superb. To provide four Queen's Medallists in little more than ten years is, indeed, a proud record.

It began in 1982 when Corporal Dharmendra Gurung won the Medal. He was followed in 1985 by Lance Corporal Khusiman Gurung. In 1992 Rifleman Lalitbahadur Gurung was the Champion Rifle Shot of the British Army and in 1993, for the second time, Dharmendra Gurung, now Lieutenant (QGO), won the Medal and received it from Her Majesty in person. A truly remarkable record.

CHAPTER TWELVE

The Last Twelve Years: 1982–1994

WHEN the last British soldier left the Indian Sub-Continent after Independence in 1947, there were many who thought that soldiering would never be the same again. Instead of the pre-war recruiting slogan, 'Join the Army and see the World,' there would be only a periodic exchange of Tidworth for BAOR, and vice versa. It is doubtful whether those who served in 6 GR from 1948 onwards would agree. From 1948 until 1966 both battalions were fully employed in active operations; they spent all too little time in peacetime garrisons. And since the end of Confrontation until today 6 GR has seen a good deal of the world and experienced more than a little excitement.

Charles Messenger's *The Steadfast Gurkha* has taken the Regiment's story up to 1982, when Lt-Colonel Paul Pettigrew was commanding the Regiment in succession to Lt-Colonel Christopher Bullock. What follows is an account of the following twelve years up to, but not including, amalgamation with 2 GR. During those twelve years 6 GR served at various times in Brunei (Seria), Hong Kong and Church Crookham in the United Kingdom. There was a second tour in Belize where 6 GR had been the first Gurkha unit to serve in 1978–79. It has carried out Public Duties in London, patrolled the Hong Kong border with China, carried out duties in Aid to the Civil Power, practised its jungle training in Brunei, Belize, Malaysia and Thailand, and exercised as far afield as Hawaii, Fiji and Papua New Guinea. It has had plenty of experience of ceremonial occasions, having mounted Guards of Honour for numerous visiting VIPs both in Hong Kong and Brunei and found the UN Honour Guard, South Korea. It has also had the honour of a second visit by Her Majesty The Queen whose title the Regiment so proudly bears. Nothing dull about all that!

In 1983, when this chapter begins, 6 GR was in Seria, having arrived there the previous November from Hong Kong. Lieutenant Colonel Pettigrew, commenting on the contrast with Hong Kong, has written, 'Brunei has hardly changed at all, and I am sure I speak for the majority who relish the rather more relaxed way of life to that experienced in Hong Kong. Certainly all our golf handicaps are improving!' Hong Kong was certainly 'all go' when compared with Brunei, but Seria provided a wonderful opportunity for the Commanding Officer to have his regiment all together and concentrated under his eye so to speak, with also the ability to concentrate on things regimental, as well as to brush up on jungle training, impossible to do in Hong Kong.

At first, however, there was some uncertainty whether 6 GR would enjoy a full tour in Seria. Brunei was about to become fully independent and negotiations were taking place between the Brunei Government and HMG. Fortunately the Sultan, HM Sir Muda Hassanal Bolkiah, expressed his desire for the continuance of a Gurkha battalion in Seria, and his willingness to pay for it. This provided the Gurkhas with a permanent commitment for as long as Brunei wished it to continue. 1984 was therefore an important year for the Brigade of Gurkhas as a whole, although the air was thick with rumours regarding the British Government's intention to reduce the strength of the Brigade of Gurkhas. 1984 also marked the end of Brigadier Sir Noel Short's Colonelcy of the Regiment and the last link with the pre-war Regiment was now severed. 'Brunny' Short had shown himself to be a very active and helpful Colonel and his departure was much regretted by the Regiment.

It was not until September, 1984, that the final agreement was signed between the Brunei Government and HMG. Much of the credit for the final conclusion must go to the British High Commissioner in Brunei, Mr Francis Cornish, and also of course to HM The Sultan. It is perhaps appropriate that before

Mr Cornish became a diplomat he was an officer in the 14th/20th King's Hussars, the 6th Gurkhas' affiliated regiment. Brunei celebrated its independence with great enthusiasm on 1 January, 1985.

It might be thought that Brunei, being somewhat off the beaten track, would have few visitors as compared with Hong Kong. This was not 6 GR's experience. In one month, February, 1984, it was visited by HRH The Prince of Wales and HRH Prince Dhirendra Devi Shah, brother of HM The King of Nepal. Others who can be placed on the VIP category were the Minister of State for the Armed Forces, one Field Marshal, five Generals, and Sir Edward Heath. There were in fact so many visitors to be programmed and cared for that an Assistant Adjutant was authorized for attachment to the Seria battalion. Lieutenant Rachael O'Meara, WRAC, was the first to be posted. The Gurkhas took a woman officer in their stride, as often calling her *sahib* as *memsahib*.

Some years later Rachael was followed by Lieutenant Anne Whittacker, WRAC. Army policy was that no WRAC officer could be permanently attached to the Brigade of Gurkhas but Anne found an excellent way to circumvent the ban. In her own words, 'The Adjutant of 6 GR whom I addressed nervously as "Sir" for my first month in office, later as "Griff" and more recently as "darling"', she subsequently married. As good a way of asserting women's rights as any!

A problem associated with single-unit garrisons is as old as the British Army. It is the absence of competition. The only other units in Brunei were the Royal Brunei Malay Regiment, probably the best equipped Infantry unit in the world, and the Gurkha Reserve Unit (GRU), raised, equipped and paid by the Sultan; but unlike Hong Kong there were no other British units with which to compete. It was nice to be on one's own for once but just as well that it did not last too long. There were plenty of visits to keep everyone on their toes including one from HM The Sultan on 11 October, 1984. The Sultan had not visited the Seria unit for several years and his decision to do so was regarded as being 'something of a coup' in 6 GR. It had been preceded by a visit by the Sultan's father, HRH Sir Omar, the

Seri Bagawan Sultan, in his capacity as Defence Minister. Both visits were very successful.

In November, 1984, the Regiment was back again in Hong Kong and finding little change in the border problem. Lieutenant Colonel Richardson-Aitken who had seen 6 GR through Brunei was soon to hand over to Lieutenant Colonel Anderson. This was some ten years after the time in the British Army's history when the members of the Army Board were engaged in playing the game 'What's in a Name?' Among other treasures that emerged from this contest was the abolition of 'brigade' and its substitution by 'field force'. This meant the disappearance of 48 Gurkha Infantry Brigade, a title unlikely to be forgotten by those who survived the retreat from Burma in 1942 when 48 Brigade so greatly distinguished itself. Fortunately 'field forces' as part of the army's nomenclature did not long remain and 'brigade' was resurrected, but not in Hong Kong until Brigadier Ray Pett re-titled the Gurkha Field Force as 48 Gurkha Infantry Brigade in December, 1986.

The problem of Hong Kong's border with China has long existed because the prosperity of Hong Kong has contrasted so vividly with China's poverty. The problem of keeping illegal immigrants out of Hong Kong has already been mentioned, but Chairman Mao's 'Cultural Revolution' enormously magnified the problem as people sought to flee the cruelty and corruption which accompanied the revolution. Tens of thousands sought to escape from the Communist 'paradise' and some of them were prepared to fight to the death in order to do so.

A 12-foot fence now ran the whole length of the border, illuminated and with intruder alarms which sounded if the wire was touched. Every piece of fence and pillar was numbered. Patrols on foot, bicycle and vehicles were continuous. In daylight, helicopter patrols were mounted, and they assisted in capturing illegal immigrants (IIs). The 6 GR Air Platoon, still under Robin Adshead, had accompanied 2/7GR from Malaysia to Hong Kong in 1967, as emergency reinforcements. 2/6GR subsequently relieved 2/7GR. The Air Platoon was later absorbed into the Army Air Corps under one of the Army's many reorganizations.

JAI SIXTH!

The 6th Gurkhas were no strangers to violence on the border. There was a particularly nasty incident in 1968 at Man Kam To involving D Company of 1/6 GR under Richard Lowe. A barricade had been erected on the bridge crossing the Man Kam To in order to close the border to all traffic. It was a metal sheet half an inch thick and 12 feet high. It completely sealed the bridge. There was a Section of riflemen in a sandbagged bunker on the Hong Kong side and the bridge was extensively wired with dannert. Orders were that the Chinese were to be prevented from entering Hong Kong across the bridge and from removing the barricade. The report continues:

'On a quiet peaceful Sunday afternoon, three of D Company's OPs simultaneously reported three separate groups of civilians and militia marching with banners towards the bridge. In total approximately 600 Chinese assembled on the Chinese side of the bridge and proceeded to demonstrate, demanding that the bridge be opened so that trade from China to Hong Kong could continue. Gradually the situation escalated to the point where the Chinese began to dismantle the barricade. A 48 Brigade helicopter reported that there were women and children in the crowd and orders were passed from 48 Brigade not to throw CS gas, but to hold the position. The position for the section in the bunker was beginning to become untenable as hand-to-hand fighting broke out. Lowe ordered CS gas but the Chinese donned masks and neutralized the thrown CS gas canisters with buckets of water. He therefore ordered white phosphorus grenades which successfully dispersed the demonstrators. The incident ended after about four hours, but not without A and C Companies being brought forward from barracks and several retaliatory high explosive stick grenades from the Chinese Communist Army; one rifleman in C Company was slightly wounded. Corporal Narbahadur Pun of D Company, the bunker commander, displayed excellent determination and devotion to duty, throughout the incident, holding the bridge under very trying circumstances.'*

* *The Steadfast Gurkha* pp. 117–118.

This was typical of the kind of incident which might blow up anywhere along the border. The Chinese, being both volatile and determined, would swiftly switch from good humour to savage hostility. The problem of the border reached its peak during the 'Cultural Revolution' but the construction of the border fence helped to control the influx.

According to Lieutenant Colonel Briggs, writing in 1991, 'During the past year the Battalion has spent twelve weeks on Border duty. The pattern of operations has changed from the tension of the early '70s and the influx of illegal immigrants in the '80s. The apprehension of illegal immigrants now requires much more skill and cunning. The outflow is not only southwards to the bright lights of Hong Kong. Nowadays a sizeable number of captures includes returnees en route to China, having been illegally working in the labour market in the Colony.'

There had been a time when a 'shooting war' might have broken out and proper defences were prepared, but the tension eased with Mao's death. Nevertheless illegal immigration if anything increased, to which was added later the pressure of the Vietnamese Boat People. As late as 1991 Lance Corporal Jamansing Thakali and Rifleman Tulbahadur Tamang were awarded Commander British Forces Commendations for disarming and arresting an armed illegal immigrant who was intending to shoot his way to freedom. He made two attempts to kill his captors, and both times his pistol misfired. He also failed to reckon with Gurkha resolve.

The soldiers lived rough for most of the time. There was scarcely enough manpower available to cover the spread of the frontier, so most got no more than two or three days rest in six weeks. The exhausting effects were made worse in summer by the high humidity and heat. All men, no matter how junior, had to operate radios, ride bicycles (for which they often needed training), work with Chinese soldiers of the Hong Kong Military Service Corps and their dogs, and often operate on their own. No firearms were carried but only light sticks (broom handles) and kukris. Many of the IIs carried weapons such as knives and pistols. Each Company deployed 'bricks' to locations along the frontier. The 'bricks' were four to six in strength, two often being Chinese dog handlers if allocated. Commanders were either junior NCOs or sometimes senior riflemen.

Operations were continuous with a minimum of two awake in each location at all times. At night there was little rest. Permanent locations were provided with metal towers from which to observe. Men lived in self-made shelters in the tops or bottoms of these. Temporary locations were suitable pieces of ground with cover from view, small rises with bushes and trees. Men in these lived under poncho capes, most locations being within yards of the fence.

Operations on the Frontier were often tedious and unpleasant, but involved some risk and had the odd splash of excitement and fun. Catching IIs involved using one's wits and gave the junior commanders the opportunity to command their men directly. British officers had the chance for a solid six weeks to live among their men and to learn operational planning on the job. Living conditions gradually improved over the years but little money was available. At times it could be insanitary and uncomfortable and perhaps only a Gurkha could have endured it all and still kept on smiling!

In Hong Kong the Border was only one problem, if the most important. There was also the problem of Internal Security within the Colony itself, 'Aid to the Civil Power', the most disliked of the army's many roles. In Hong Kong human beings are packed together as ants in an ant hill. Immense wealth lives side by side with abject poverty. Illegal immigrants proliferate. Boat People add to the swarm. Hong Kong is combustible and riddled with politics. A street riot can swell and grow like a prairie fire. 6 GR have more than once had to stand by to support the Police, but fortunately they have not been called on to open fire on a mob.

In 1987 6 GR moved from Hong Kong to Church Crookham to join 5 Airborne Brigade which has its headquarters in Aldershot. It consists of four battalions and supporting arms. Two are parachute battalions, one is Gurkha, and the fourth is Line Infantry. 5 Brigade constitutes the immediate 'Fire Brigade' of the British Army, ready to dash off at the drop of a

30. *"A 12 foot fence now ran the whole lenght of the border, illuminated and with intruder alarms which sounded if the wire was touched."* (p.165)

31. *"Those who successfully passed the course were given their parachutists' 'Wings' and were permitted to wear the coveted red beret of the parachute soldier."* (p.169) 6 GR 'Paras': Durgabahadur, Debbahadur, Narjang, Lalkaji, Yambahadur and Jagan Gurung.

32. *"Everyone ... was determined to make the 175th Anniversary an occasion long to be remembered... a ceremony at the Tower of London on 4 November, 1992, in the presence of HM The Queen and HM The Sultan of Brunei."* (p.174)

33. *"The Pipes and Drums of the 6th Gurkha Rifles were accompanied by the bands, trumpets and bugles of the affiliated regiments, 14th/20th King's Hussars and The Royal Green Jackets."* (p.175)

hat to extinguish the flames. While in 5 Brigade the opportunity was taken to put selected soldiers through the very tough parachute training course. There was no shortage of volunteers and the Gurkhas took to parachuting with aplomb. Those who successfully passed the course were given their parachutists' 'Wings' and were permitted to wear the coveted red beret of the parachute soldier – but only while serving in 5 Brigade.

In 1956 a ceremony had taken place in Winchester Cathedral whereby a Book of Remembrance commemorating those British Officers of 6 GR who had been killed in action since the raising of the Regiment in 1817 was placed in a glass case in the North Aisle of the Cathedral after it had been dedicated by the Bishop of Winchester. The dedication was attended by a distinguished assembly of Clergy and Guests headed by Field Marshal Slim. Sadly, some years later, both the badge and the book were stolen. It was only the sterling work of Lieutenant Colonel H. R. K. Gibbs (Gibbos), who was Secretary and Treasurer of the Association at the time, that enabled a copy to be made. Soon after the new copy had been placed in the Cathedral, the original book wrapped in brown paper was handed in to the Guard Room of the Royal Green Jackets by a man who refused to identify himself.

The original case had been vandalized and was a fitting memorial no longer. Mr Quin Hollick was commissioned to design and execute an appropriate plinth for the book, and on 8 November, 1988, a service of re-dedication was held. The Dean of Winchester officiated and there was an impressive attendance by both serving and retired officers. They were headed by Aileen, Viscountess Slim, and General Jim Robertson, and the ceremony has been described as 'simple, sincere and moving'.

Prior to returning to Hong Kong in April, 1989, the Officers held a somewhat unusual Guest Night of 3 March. It was probably a unique occasion because the guests were all past Colonels of the Regiment and former Commanding Officers of the 1st and 2nd Battalions. All the QGOs also attended, headed by Gurkha Major Chintabahadur Gurung who had returned from leave in Nepal just in time. It was a memorable evening.

[169]

Needless to say reminiscence was the order of the day (and night!).

One of the residual commitments of empire was Belize, known formerly as British Honduras. The Caribbean country about the size of Wales has been threatened on and off by Guatemala which laid claim to it. Belize became independent in 1975 and required British support if Guatemala was to be deterred from attacking it. Consequently, for the next 19 years, Belize's defence became one of the overseas defence commitments, the equivalent of an Infantry Battalion Group being deployed there. Recently, however, relations with Guatemala have greatly improved. Guatemala has formally revoked any claim to Belize; to the satisfaction of the Foreign & Commonwealth Office certainly, but probably not to the ordinary Belizean. However, Guatemala no long threatens Belize and the British garrison is to be withdrawn.

6 GR was the first Gurkha unit to serve in Belize. At very short notice, no more than three weeks, the Battalion, or most of it, was removed from running the NRA meeting at Bisley and dispatched to Belize in July, 1978. It returned in the following February. There is an account of 6 GR's first experience of jungle warfare – South American style – in *The Steadfast Gurkha*, pages 105 to 108.

In March, 1988, 6 GR was back in Belize for a seven months' tour with Lieutenant Colonel Duncan Briggs in the saddle. Divided into two battle groups North and South, two Companies with supporting arms were deployed in the North, and two Companies were in the southern group. Since much of the country is covered in thick jungle, and most of the remainder is mountainous, with torrential rain falling for much of the year, land communications between north and south are at best dodgy, but it was possible to carry out a complete battalion exercise. This was followed by a Force exercise which was somewhat marred by the Force Commander (not a 6 GR) being bitten by a fer-de-lance, a particularly poisonous snake.

Although social life in Belize did not compare with Hong Kong or Church Crookham, the Gurkhas got on spendidly with the local inhabitants, many of whom were of slave descent.

There was excellent sea bathing, fishing and sailing, and this is possibly the place to comment on swimming by Gurkhas. Brigadier Michael Calvert has said that the chief problem he experienced with Gurkhas in the Chindits was their inability to swim. This was a serious limitation in Burma where the numerous dry water courses became raging torrents in the monsoon. A great many Gurkhas were drowned when trying to get across the River Sittang when the bridge was demolished on 23 February, 1942, during the retreat from Burma. The same would no longer be the case today. Bathing is popular in Hong Kong, as it is in Brunei. So much so that the Gurkha ladies have taken to the sport and hold their own swimming galas!

6 GR were back in Hong Kong in 1991 when the sad news was received that the Brigade of Gurkhas was to be drastically reduced in strength as part of the overall reduction of the British Army as outlined in the Defence White Paper 'Options for Change'. The four regiments of Gurkha Rifles would lose their regimental identity, as would many other distinguished Cavalry and Infantry regiments in the British Army. To cope with this the Brigade of Gurkhas has established an extensive resettlement and re-employment organization in the United Kingdom, Hong Kong and Nepal. The aim is to find employment somewhere in the world for every soldier who leaves the Service. As it happened 6 GR provided many of the staff involved in the Resettlement Organization which was repeated within the Regiment itself.

Not surprisingly this task has overshadowed the early years of the 1990s but as ever the Gurkhas themselves have remained cheerful and resilient. Nevertheless they may be excused for beginning to wonder whether the word of the British Government is any longer its bond? One would need to be a super-optimist to answer that affirmatively. However, Lieutenant Colonel Duncan Briggs is confident of the survival of the Gurkhas in the British Army, and has gone so far as to say, 'I am confident that there will be a Regiment for my son to join in 1999 should he be acceptable'. Let us hope he is right!

From Hong Kong 6 GR moved to Brunei in May, 1992,

under the command of Lieutenant Colonel Nigel Collett. Ahead lay the preparations for the 175th Anniversary of the Regiment's raising in 1817, and the melancholy rundown in strength in readiness for the amalgamation with 2 GR in 1994. It says a great deal for everyone, from the Commanding Officer to the latest joined rifleman, that the morale of 6 GR was as high as ever. They are certainly remarkable soldiers!

The 6th Gurkhas' proudest boast is undoubtedly that they are 'Queen Elizabeth's Own'. No other regiment in the British Army bears the name of the reigning monarch. It can also pride itself in the interest shown by the Queen. Twice in ten years she has visited the Regiment in Queen Elizabeth Barracks (named after the Queen Mother) in Church Crookham. The first occasion was on 5 May, 1978, when the Queen visited all departments in the morning and afternoon, having lunched with the Officers. In the course of her 'Walkabout' she met Honorary Lieutenant (QGO) Tulbahadur Pun VC of Mogaung fame. At the end of her visit the Queen drove away behind the Pipes and Drums playing the regimental march, 'Queen Elizabeth's Own,' and through lines of smiling soldiers throwing flowers in her path.

When the Queen visited Hong Kong on 21 October, 1986, the Regiment once again had the privilege of mounting the Guard of Honour as it had in 1975. This time the Guard was commanded by Major Gopalbahadur Gurung MBE and a very nice letter was later received from the Royal Yacht *Britannia* congratulating the Guard on its smartness and drill. There was another Royal Occasion on 24 February, 1989 when the Queen again visited the Regiment in Church Crookham. It poured with rain but the Queen was indefatigable in carrying out her programme. This was intended to show her 6 GR both at work and at play and was clearly enjoyed despite the weather. The visit ended with the presentation by Gurkha Major Chintabahadur Gurung of a kukri brooch. It was pinned on the Queen's coat by the Commanding Officer, Lieutenant Colonel Duncan Briggs.

The last Royal Occasion in the Regiment's history took place in the Tower of London on 4 November, 1992, to celebrate the

175th Anniversary of the Regiment's raising. This is dealt with in greater detail later in the next chapter.

The last twelve years of the life of the Regiment have indeed been full ones, and they have been lived to the full by every member of the Regiment. For the true soldier there can be nothing more sad than the disappearance of his regiment from his army's order of battle, but nothing becomes the 6th Gurkhas better than their refusal to allow this to affect either their loyalty or their morale. Were the Regiment's motto to be changed to, 'To the bitter end,' it would truly reflect the 6th Gurkhas' spirit and the Regiment's attitude towards what lies ahead.

CHAPTER THIRTEEN

The 175th Anniversary

THE letter from the Major General Brigade of Gurkhas, Major General P. R. Duffell, to the Colonels of all Gurkha regiments, in which he outlined forthcoming changes in the strength and structure of the Gurkha Brigade, is dated 24 July, 1991. Instead of reducing from a current strength of 7,500 to 4,000, as had been previously agreed, the cut was to be to the much more drastic figure of around 2,500. The Brigade, as such, would disappear to be replaced by a totally new regiment of three and later only two battalions to be called The Royal Gurkha Rifles. This would involve the amalgamation of the 2nd Goorkhas with the 6th to form the 1st Battalion, and the subsequent amalgamation of the 7th with the 10th to form the 2nd Battalion. The Gurkha Engineers, Signals and Transport would be reduced to one Squadron each. The amalgamation of the 2nd with the 6th would take place in Hong Kong in 1994.

Naturally this came as a sudden blow to every serving and retired officer and rifleman but the sad news was received with the impeccable good sense and stoicism always to be expected from the Gurkha soldier. In the case of the 6th, the news was made more poignant owing to the fact that in May, 1992, the Regiment would be celebrating the 175th Anniversary of its raising. Everyone concerned from the Colonel of the Regiment down to the most junior rifleman was determined to make the 175th Anniversary an occasion long to be remembered, as will be evident from the account of it which follows.

The Regiment was in Brunei where it had arrived in May,

1992. The Anniversary celebrations were timed to coincide with a visit to the Regiment by its Colonel, Major General Ray Pett. It was preceded by a ceremony at the Tower of London on 4 November, 1992, in the presence of HM The Queen and HM The Sultan of Brunei. The Pipes and Drums of the 6th Gurkha Rifles were accompanied by the bands, trumpets and bugles of the affiliated regiments, 14th/20th King's Hussars and the Royal Green Jackets. The Pipes and Drums of the Regiment were carrying, in addition to those of the Queen and the 14th/20th, the pipe banners of former Colonels and Commanding Officers who were present. The 6th QEO Gurkha Rifles trumpet banner was carried by one of the 14th/20th trumpeters, which was noticed by the Queen.

There were 75 regimental guests who included the Lord Lieutenant of Greater London (Field Marshal Lord Bramall, KG, who was President of the Gurkha Brigade Association), the Constable of the Tower (Field Marshal Sir John Stanier), Colonels of all the other Gurkha Regiments and, to everyone's delight, the Gurkha Major of the Regiment, Major (QGO) Padambahadur Gurung MVO.

Retreat was beaten by the Regimental Pipes and Drums together with the bands, bugles and trumpets of the affiliated regiments. It was a moving occasion, superbly done, followed by a reception attended by the Queen. On the way to the reception the Queen signed the Regimental Visitor's Book and two portraits of herself which are to hang in the British and Gurkha Officers' Messes. In welcoming Her Majesty, General Pett said:

'May it please Your Majesty, my Lords, Ladies and Gentlemen. This is a Celebration! On behalf of the Regimental Association, I am delighted that you were able to join with us in celebrating our 175th Anniversary.

'It was a particular privilege for the Regiment that tonight's ceremony took place in the gracious presence of Her Majesty the Queen, in this the fortieth year of Your Majesty's reign. The Sixth Gurkhas have been intensely proud that we have borne Your Majesty's name in our title for almost 34 of those years.

'I would also like to take this opportunity to express our gratitude to the Constable and officers of Your Majesy's Tower of London and the Royal Armouries for allowing us to conduct tonight's celebrations in such a splendid and historic setting.

'For the last time the Bands, Trumpeters and Bugles of our affiliated Regiments, the 14th/20th King's Hussars and The Royal Green Jackets, have joined our Pipes and Drums in the Ceremony of Beating Retreat and we are most grateful to them and to the Regiments. We are delighted that our long-standing affiliations will survive into the future.

'Thank you all for sharing with us this special evening. Finally, as a very small memento of the occasion, and as an enduring mark of the affection and loyalty in which the Regiment holds Your Majesty, may I present this cere-monial Kukri of the 6th, Queen Elizabeth's Own, Gurkha Rifles.'

After the Queen's departure there was a splendid supper in the Sporting Armour Gallery at which many old friendships were renewed and many old tales told and retold far into the evening. It was agreed on all sides that it had been a really splendid occasion, which was confirmed shortly afterwards by a letter from the Queen's Private Secretary to the Colonel of the Regiment in which he said:

'The ceremony of Beating Retreat last night was a real triumph for the 6th Gurkhas and their affiliated Regiments, and Her Majesty much enjoyed both the ceremony itself and the Reception afterwards. The drill and music lived up to the highest standards of the Gurkha Brigade and both Her Majesty and The Sultan were greatly impressed by it. At the Reception, the Queen met several old friends and very much enjoyed herself. She was also very grateful for the magnificent kukri with which you presented her at the end of the Reception. Her Majesty has asked me to send you her warm congratulations and to request that you pass them on to all who were on parade and who organized a most enjoyable occasion.'

As a Royal accolade that would be hard to beat and the 6th could be satisfied that their 175th Anniversary celebrations had got off to a wonderful start. Something must be added about the weather, that perennial subject whenever two Englishmen meet. An early evening in November would not be everyone's choice for an occasion of this kind, but the Gods were kind and the rain held off.

The scene now shifts to distant Brunei where preparations for the celebration of the 175th Anniversary had been occupying most of 6 GR's attention for some little time. The programme, which was to last a week, began with General Pett's arrival in Seria in December, 1992, accompanied by his wife, Marie. After visiting Tuker Lines and spending four hours talking with the Gurkha officers and riflemen, he attended a barbecue and saw a pictorial presentation of the 6th's history, at which the CO, Lieutenant Colonel Nigel Collett, spoke to a packed audience:

'We decided to celebrate our birthday in a number of ways. First of all, for everyone who was in the UK in November, we celebrated at the Tower of London in front of HM The Queen by Beating Retreat. We also decided that we would hold two parties in Nepal; one at Kathmandu and the other at Pokhara, for all our pensioners. And because our regimental history is very important to us, we decided we would visit all the places that figure highly in our history. Therefore we sent parties to England, to our birthplace at Katak (Cuttack), to Assam and to places where we fought in and near Burma in World War II. We sent them to Pakistan, to Abhatabad (Abbottabad) and the NW Frontier. We visited places in Nepal where our recruiting started and Gallipoli where we won one of our great Battle Honours. Colonel Harvey, Seria's first garrison commander in 1963 and, therefore, 6 GR's first garrison commander in Brunei, has just returned from a visit to the site of the confrontation in which he fought with 6 GR in the early 1960s.'

Lieutenant Colonel Collett was followed by his Second-in-Command, Major Manikumar Rai, who spoke about the forthcoming merger with the 2nd Goorkhas:

[177]

'This is the last occasion in which we, as 6 GR, can celebrate anything in this sort of style. In the next eighteen months or so we are looking towards amalgamation with 2 GR. The next big parade will be our amalgamation parade so this week's celebrations are the great highlight before the name of 6 GR disappears into history and we become the 1st Battalion Royal Gurkha Rifles. There is, of course, an element of sadness. We look back with sadness that the name of 6 GR is going to disappear, but at the same time we are looking forward to the amalgamation and to carrying on the traditions not only of 6 GR, but also of the Brigade in the new Royal Gurkha Rifles.'

In a week's programme filled with interesting events there had, of course, to be a 175th Anniversary ceremonial parade which was carried out with immaculate precision in front of many distinguished guests including His Excellency the High Commissioner and his wife. Following the parade, and after presenting Long Service & Good Conduct medals to Colour-Sergeants Khusiman Gurung, Iman Kuman Gurung and Dukbahadur Gurung, General Pett as Colonel of the Regiment spoke on the British Forces Broadcasting Service of the way ahead.

'Obviously,' he said, 'I feel sad as the amalgamation approaches because the Regiment has established itself over many years and has a very fine reputation. There is a tremendous *esprit de corps* and family spirit, but, like the rest of the British Army, we are living in a different world where the whole of the Services are getting smaller as the nation's requirements for its defence services generally diminishes.

'But at least the Regiment will live on as part of the new Royal Gurkha Rifles. It is not as if we will simply cease to exist – we have had different titles in the past and in times of war we have had up to four battalions. However, although these were battalions of the same Regiment, they never served beside each other.* They were all very different. Each had

---

* The General was not quite correct. 1/6th and 4/6th served together in the 19th Indian Division in Burma although, admittedly, not in the same brigade.

its own personality but underneath they were the same. The soldiers came from the same part of West Nepal; and the officers all knew each other. And that is very much the same within the whole Brigade of Gurkhas.

'So, as we amalgamate with the other Regiments of the Brigade, we will primarily be going in with 2 GR who also came from West Nepal. Therefore our soldiers will have a lot in common and there will be a great deal of affinity with "the other half". The *esprit de corps* and the family spirit will carry on. If you like, the family will first of all get a bit bigger, then a bit smaller. But it will still be a family. The Brigade, as now, is a family beyond all challenge. We all take pride in beating each other in competitions but we would rather be alongside another part of the Gurkha family than thrown in beside somebody else'

The General ended with a stirring, '*Jai*, Sixth! *Jai* Royal Ghurka Rifles!'

As part of the proceedings there was a splendid Hunt Breakfast at which 'over one hundred of us, including the Queen's Gurkha Officers and their wives, sat down to Champagne, Mulligatawny Soup and breakfast before drinking the healths of the Queen, the Regiment and The King's Royal Hussars.' This was followed by a Sports afternoon which was, in turn, followed by a Christmas Dinner in the Mess, with games and disco dancing afterwards. There was also a 'Jungle Walk' to bring back memories of a different kind of jungle walk with, probably, a bullet or two of near misses. On this occasion, however, there were white tablecloths and tables flown in by the Regiment's Air Flight helicopters, together with gleaming table silver and excellent food. President Sukarno must have turned in his grave!

Similar celebrations were held in Nepal at Pokhara and Khatmandu. The former were planned by Major (QGO) Navinkumar Sahi, the Gurkha Major of BGP, who had been General Pett's orderly 26 years previously. There were some 145 guests which included Colonel Kishan Singh of 9 GR who commands the Indian Embassy Pension Paying Office in Pokhara. There was an equally successful celebration in Kathmandu organized by Major Tim Underhill, 6 GR. It was, according to report, 'A marvellous day to be remembered by all'.

All in all the Regiment had achieved all that it set out to do – to make the 175th Anniversary of the raising of the Cuttack Legion an occasion to remember. In true 6 GR fashion it had been done with complete efficiency, attention to detail and true family feeling. All the British and Gurkhas who were fortunate enough to attend, wherever it might be, were all of the same family and, like all Gurkha festivities of this kind, everyone had fun!

EPILOGUE

DURING the 177 years of its existence the Regiment has undergone many changes. The greatest of these have been in the fields of communications, transportation and weapon development. When the Cuttack Legion, in 1820, took the field against the Paicks and Kols, the 'Brown Bess' musket, with an effective range of about 30 yards, was only marginally superior to their adversaries' bows and arrows. They did, however, have the 'galloper guns', although only 3-pounders and inaccurate; but artillery, then as now, was 'Queen of the Battlefield'. Later, in the expeditions against Abors, Nagas, Lushais and other tribes on the north-eastern marches of India, it was superior discipline that prevailed against a brave but disorganized enemy. Only at Manipur, when the Manipuris had artillery, was the Regiment forced to retreat and, at that, shamefacedly. The only other time it was compelled to withdraw in the face of the enemy was at Sari Bair on the Gallipoli Peninsula, and that was one of the most glorious episodes in the Regiment's history.

The horse has left the battlefield, following after the elephant and the camel. Only the mule appears on rare occasions nowadays. The infantry soldier now rides into battle in armoured vehicles, leaving them only when within striking distance of the enemy. He has still to operate on his legs in the mountains or the jungle, but it is very unlikely that he will have to march 500 or more miles as the 1/6th and 4/6th did when advancing into Burma. The man down from the hills now drives vehicles of every kind, both soft-skinned and armoured, and on one memorable occasion the antiquated 'Green Goddess' fire engines.

Even more remarkable is the story of Corporal Pimbahadur Gurung of the Regiment, the first Gurkha pilot in the British Army. He received his Pilot's Wings on 5 March, 1993, from Lieutenant General Sir Peter Duffell.* He has since joined 4 Regiment Army Air Corps as a Gazelle helicopter pilot, taking with him the nickname bestowed on the course – 'Pilot Pim' or 'Douglas Bahadur'! Pimbahadur's story is indicative of the changes which the Gurkhas themselves are having to face in this last decade of the twentieth century. Pimbahadur's father, Dulbahadur Gurung, retired from 6 GR as a Corporal in 1973 but made certain his son had a good education. Pimbahadur joined 6 GR as a clerk in 1987 and underwent pilot training in Singapore and holds a Private Pilot Licence for Group 'A'. Before training as a helicopter pilot in the Army Air Corps he held a number of clerical appointments in the Regiment. He is married with a 2-year old son.

When 1/6 GR landed at Gallipoli on 1 May, 1915, they were dependent for inter-communication on the D-3 field telephone so often ruptured by shellfire, messages carried by runner, or ship to shore, or vice versa, by signal lamp flashing the morse code. Maps were few and far between, inaccurate and difficult to read. In the confusion of trenches men frequently got lost and were unable to indicate their position on the map. Contrast that with today when in the Gulf War, in featureless desert, a man could fix his position by an 8-figure map reference by immediate satellite communication.†

To cap it all there has been the incredible advance in weaponry. Since the days when the musket was abandoned for the rifle and, with it, the advent of smokeless powder, until today when the soldier has to operate surface-to-surface, and surface-to-air, weapons of great sophistication, and when the Gunner can drench a target with one salvo of Multi-Launch

---

* Sir Peter Duffell was Inspector General of Doctrine and Training. Himself a 2nd Goorkha, he is a former Major General Brigade of Gurkhas and, from 1 July, 1994, the first Colonel of The Royal Gurkha Rifles.
† The Global Positioning System (GPS) satellite navigation system.

Epilogue

Rocket Systems (MLRS), the ordinary infantryman has to learn to operate a bewildering array of weapons. It is no longer sufficient to march far and to shoot straight. War has become much more complicated and the Gurkha soldier has risen to the challenge. He has shown himself to be capable of adapting to the change going on around him but without losing his inherent characteristics of toughness of spirit and remarkable stamina. And, so far, he has not lost the qualities that led Field Marshal Slim to describe the Gurkha as 'an ideal infantryman.'

It would, however, be a mistake to assume that the Gurkha soldier of today is the same simple-minded peasant boy who has come down from the hills to enlist. His background may still be simple, and his home life sufficiently arduous to ensure that only the toughest youngsters reach manhood, but the Gurkha soldier today is world-travelled. The majority can speak and read English. They can find their way around London, Singapore and Hong Kong. They are eager for education and their wives even more so – for themselves as much as for their children. They will not find it all that easy to adjust when they return to the hills. Gurkhas drive cars, ride motorcycles and fly helicopters. They operate computers. They can still shoot straight, as witness their success at Bisley, and can still probably march the average British soldier off his feet! But like the rest of us they are having to adjust to changes no one could ever have visualized when Simon Fraser raised the Cuttack Legion 177 years ago. It is only to be hoped that, as he advances into the 21st century, the Gurkha will retain his inherent virtues of courage, courtesy and good humour. They are beyond price.

Writing this book has been a revelation for the author who thought he knew the Gurkha well enough to start with, and who could count among his friends many who had served as officers in the Gurkha Rifles. What has come as a surprise is the remarkable number of awards for gallantry won by the 6th, British and Gurkhas alike. It is clear that the ordinary Gurkha rifleman expected a great deal of his officer, British or Gurkha, and it is equally clear that, throughout, his officer lived up to the requirement – to the bitter end in some cases. This account of the Regiment's history over 177 years is in a sense a salute to

[183]

JAI SIXTH!

them all, Officers and Riflemen who, together, made the 6th Queen Elizabeth's Own Gurkha Rifles a regiment *Second to None*!

GOD SAVE THE QUEEN

34. "'Johnny Gurkha', as he has always been known to the British soldiers who fought in battle alongside him, occupies a special corner in a great many British hearts." (p.150) Lance-Corporal Dhanbahadur Thapa (front) and Rifleman Balbahadur Gurung.

35. "During the 177 years of its existence the Regiment has undergone many changes. Even more remarkable is the story of Corporal Pimbahadur Gurung of the Regiment, the first Gurkha pilot in the British Army." (p.181)

36. *"A most moving Presentation Parade was held in Hong Kong on 22 July, 1991 ... many distinguished guests included Professor and Mrs Christopher Allmand and Mrs Marguerite Murphy, Brigadier Michael Calvert who commanded 77th Brigade at Mogaung, Honorary Lieutenant (QGO) Tulbahadur Pun VC and Major (QGO) Khumbahadur Burathoki who had been present at Mogaung."* (p.187) All except Mrs Allmand shown here. On the right is Major Paul Griffin, late 3/6 GR.

37. *"The Colonel of the Regiment ... passed the Victoria Cross to the Gurkha Major who, with an escort of two Senior Non-Commissioned Officers and the Pipe Major, trooped the medal along the front rank of the Parade to the Tune 'Allmand VC'."* (p.188) Major (QGO) Lalbahadur Thapa takes the VC.

GLOSSARY

——◦◦◦——

Gurkhali/Malay/Urdu/Burmese

Basha	(B)	Hut – usually constructed of bamboo.
Bhat	(G)	Cooked Rice
Bhoj	(G)	A small celebration, usually on a company basis, including drinking and dancing.
Burho Sahib	(G)	An old veteran, British or Gurkha officer.
Burra Khana	(U)	Banquet or special dinner.
Chaung	(B)	A watercourse, often dry in summer but a torrent in the monsoon. Also *nullah* in Urdu and *wadi* in Arabic.
Chippy Alus	(G)	Chip Potatoes
Dal	(G)	Lentil Soup
Dashera	(U)	The main annual Gurkha religious festival. *Dasain* in Gurkhali.
Dashera Ghar	(U)	The structure, usually tented, within which the main *Dashera* celebrations take place.
Gunong	(M)	Mountain in Malay.
Izzat	(U)	Honour, personal or collective.
Jawan	(U)	A Hindi word meaning 'village lad', used by the BOs in the Indian Army as an affectionate word for their soldiers.

[185]

Jirgah	(U)	A conference of elders as used in Pushtu on the North West Frontier.
Jhola	(G)	A haversack.
Kaida	(G)	Custom, tradition
Kalratri	(G)	The eighth day and climax of *Dashera/Dasain.*
Khud	(U)	Steep, stony and rocky hillside
Kisan	(U)	Peasant farmer.
Ladang	(M)	Cultivation in the jungle.
Lashkar	(U)	A tribal armed force.
Maruni	(G)	Male performer at a *nautch*, but in female dress.
Milap	(U)	Co-operation, contact.
Nat	(B)	Spirits
Nautch	(G)	Dance of a formal kind as distinct from *bhoj*
Pakaune	(G)	Cooking
Shikar	(G)	Hunting
Sowan	(U)	Soldier
Sunao'd	(G)	[message] delivered
Syabas!	(G)	Well done!

APPENDIX ONE

———⊷⊶⊷———

The Victoria Cross

IN 1944 Captain Michael Allmand and Rifleman Tulbahadur Pun of the 3rd Battalion 6th Gurkha Rifles were awarded the Victoria Cross for conspicuous gallantry. Allmand's, unfortunately, was a posthumous award; he died of his wounds. Tulbahadur Pun, VC, now Honorary Lieutenant (QGO), survived the Battle of Mogaung and is now on pension. In his congratulatory signal to the Commandant, the Commander-in-Chief, India, General Sir Claude Auchinleck, said:

'Congratulate the Regiment most warmly on winning two Victoria Crosses in one action, a most rare occurrence.'

The Official Citations are given below.

Through the most generous decision by the Allmand family, Professor Christopher and Mrs Bernadette Allmand and Mrs Marguerite Murphy, to present the Victoria Cross of their late brother, Michael, to the Regiment, the unique collection of the only two VCs awarded for the Battle of Mogaung to members of the 6th Gurkhas, now reside together in the Regimental Quarter Guard.

A most moving Presentation Parade was held in Hong Kong on 22 July, 1991, in the presence of the Governor, Sir David (now Lord) Wilson and many other distinguished guests. They included Professor and Mrs Christopher Allmand and Mrs Marguerite Murphy, Brigadier Michael Calvert who commanded 77th Brigade at Mogaung, Honorary Lieutenant (QGO) Tulbahadur Pun VC and Major (QGO) Khumbahadur Burathoki who had been present at Mogaung. The date had been chosen in order to coincide with a visit to the Regiment by General Pett, Colonel of the Regiment.

The combined Band of the Brigade of Gurkhas and the Battalion Pipes and Drums marched on at 7.30 a.m., followed by the Battalion in No. 3 Dress. After the Governor had inspected the parade and had delivered a short address, Mrs Marguerite Murphy moved forward and presented her late brother's VC to the Colonel of the Regiment, with the following words:

'It is with great pleasure that I present, on behalf of my brother and myself, this Victoria Cross awarded to our brother Michael Allmand after the Battle of Mogaung; and I would particularly like to associate with his name those of Tulbahadur Pun VC, Brigadier Michael Calvert and Major (QGO) Khumbahadur Burathoki who showed similar valour and courage in that great battle, and who are present with us today.'

The Colonel of the Regiment received the medal and formally thanked Mrs Murphy and Professor Christopher Allmand for their generosity in presenting the medal to the Regiment. He then passed the Victoria Cross to the Gurkha Major who, with an escort of two senior Non-Commissioned Officers and the Pipe Major, trooped the medal along the front rank of the Parade to the tune 'Allmand VC', composed for the occasion by the Pipe Major. The trooping ended at the Regimental Quarter Guard, where the medal was placed next to the Victoria Cross and medals of Honorary Lieutenant (QGO) Tulbahadur Pun. The battalion then marched off to 'All the Blue Bonnets are Over the Border', 'Young May Moon' and 'Queen Elizabeth's Own'.

Professor Allmand, writing later on behalf of his sister and himself, said: 'Our brother's medal is now where it should be and we are both very happy at the way things have turned out.' It was a very moving occasion.

The Citations are given below:

Captain Allmand

'Captain Allmand was commanding the leading platoon in

a company of the 6th Gurkhas in Burma on 11th June 1944, when the battalion was ordered to attack the Pin Hmi Road Bridge. The enemy had already succeeded in holding up our advance at this point for twenty-four hours. The approach to the bridge was very narrow as the road was banked up and the low-lying land on either side was swampy and densely covered in jungle. The Japanese, who were dug in along the banks of the road and in the jungle with machine guns and small arms, were putting up the most desperate resistance. As the platoon came within twenty yards of the bridge, the enemy opened heavy and accurate fire inflicting severe casualties and causing the men to seek cover. Captain Allmand, however, with the utmost gallantry charged on by himself hurling grenades into the enemy positions and killing three Japanese himself with his kukri. Inspired by the splendid example of their platoon commander the surviving men followed him and captured their objective.

'Two days later, Captain Allmand, owing to casualties among the officers, took over command of the company and, dashing thirty yards ahead through long grass and marshy ground swept by machine gun fire, personally killed a number of enemy machine gunners and led his men onto the ridge of high ground that they had been ordered to seize.

'Once again on 23rd June, in the final attack on the railway bridge at Mogaung, Captain Allmand, although suffering from trench foot which made it difficult for him to walk, moved forward alone through deep mud and shell holes and charged a Japanese machine-gun nest single-handed, but he was mortally wounded and died shortly afterwards. The superb gallantry, outstanding leadership and protracted heroism of this very brave officer were a wonderful example to the whole Battalion and in the highest traditions of his regiment.'

Rifleman Tulbahadur Pun

'Immediately the attack developed the enemy opened concentrated and sustained cross-fire at close range from a position known as Red House and from a strongly placed position two hundred yards to the left. So intense was this cross-fire that both leading platoons of 'B' Company, one of which was Rifleman Tulbahadur's, were pinned to the ground and the whole of the section wiped out with the exception of himself, the section commander, and one other man. The section commander immediately led the remaining two men in a charge on Red House but was at once badly wounded.

'Rifleman Tulbahadur seized the Bren Gun and, firing from the hip as he went, continued to charge on the heavily bunkered position alone in the face of the most shattering concentration of automatic fire directed straight at him. With the dawn coming up behind him he presented a perfect target to the Japanese. He had to move thirty yards over open ground ankle deep in mud, through shell holes and over fallen trees.

'Despite overwhelming odds he reached the house and closed with the Japanese occupants. He killed three, put five more to flight and captured two LMGs and much ammunition. He then gave accurate supporting fire from the bunker to the remainder of the platoon, which enabled them to reach the objective. His outstanding courage and superb gallantry in the face of odds which meant almost certain death were inspiring to all ranks and were beyond praise.'

(Extracts from the *London Gazette, 26 October and 9 November, 1944*)

APPENDIX TWO

————⊸⊙⊶————

Colonels of the Regiment 1904–1994

Lieutenant General J. P. Sherriff CB	1904–1911
Major General H. O'Donnell CB DSO	1911–1925
Field Marshal The Lord Birdwood of Anzac GCB GCSI GCMG GCVO CIE DSO LLD	1926–1951
Field Marshal The Lord Harding of Petherton GCB CBE DSO MC	1951–1961
Major General J. A. R. Robertson CB CBE DSO DL	1961–1969
Major General A. G. Patterson CB DSO OBE MC	1969–1974
Brigadier D. L. Powell-Jones DSO OBE	1974–1978
Brigadier Sir Noel Short MBE MC	1978–1983
Lieutenant General Sir Derek Boorman KCB	1983–1988
Major General R. A. Pett MBE	1988–1994

APPENDIX THREE

Commanding Officers

The Regiment before the formation of a Second Battalion.

Captain	S. Fraser	1817–1823
Captain	A. McLeod	1823–1827
Captain	J. B. Neufville	1828–1830
Lieutenant	A. Charlton	1830–1831
Lieutenant Colonel	A. White	1831–1839
Lieutenant Colonel	S. F. Hannay	1839–1861
Major	H. M. Garstin	1861–1867
Colonel	T. Rattray CB CSI	1867–1873
Lieutenant Colonel	J. P. Sherriff CB	1873–1884
Lieutenant Colonel	A. D. Butter	1884–1886
Lieutenant Colonel	A. T. Davis	1886–1888
Lieutenant Colonel	C. McD. Skene DSO	1888–1891
Lieutenant Colonel	E. C. Elliston	1891
Bt. Colonel	A. G. B. Ternan DSO	1891–1893
Bt. Lieutenant Colonel	C. R. MacGregor DSO	1893–1899
Lieutenant Colonel	H. O'Donnell DSO	1899–1904

1st Battalion

Lieutenant Colonel	H. O'Donnell DSO	1904–1907
Lieutenant Colonel	C. M. Crawford	1907–1908
Colonel	J. B. Chatterton	1908–1914
Colonel, The Hon.	C. G. Bruce CB MVO	1914–1918
Colonel	W. C. Little	1918–1922
Lieutenant Colonel	G. M. Glynton DSO	1922–1926
Colonel	R. J. B. Yates DSO	1926–1930

Lieutenant Colonel	H. M. M. Hackett MC	1930–1934
Lieutenant Colonel	G. C. Strahan OBE	1934–1937
Lieutenant Colonel	H. V. Collingridge OBE	1937–1940
Lieutenant Colonel	D. Tennant Cowan MC	1940
Lieutenant Colonel	G. R. Grove	1940–1944
Lieutenant Colonel	O. C. T. Dykes MC	1944–1947
Lieutenant Colonel	J. A. R. Robertson DSO OBE	1947–1948
Lieutenant Colonel	E. P. Townsend DSO OBE	1948–1951
Lieutenant Colonel	W. C. Walker DSO OBE	1951–1954
Lieutenant Colonel	A. E. C. Bredin DSO MC	1954–1956
Lieutenant Colonel	N. E. V. Short MBE MC	1956–1958
Lieutenant Colonel	W. M. Amoore DSO OBE	1958–1961
Lieutenant Colonel	W. B. Standbridge OBE	1961–1963
Lieutenant Colonel	B. G. Hickey OBE MC	1963–1966
Lieutenant Colonel	W. D. McNaughtan MBE	1966–1968
Lieutenant Colonel	J. Whitehead MBE	1968–1969

2nd Battalion

Lieutenant Colonel	F. C. Colomb	1904–1908
Lieutenant Colonel	C. M. Crawford	1908–1912
Lieutenant Colonel	F. F. Badcock DSO	1912–1918
Lieutenant Colonel	G. A. Preston	1918–1919
Lieutenant Colonel	B. A. McH. Rice DSO	1919–1921
Colonel	C. J. L. Allanson CMG CIE DSO	1921–1922
Lieutenant Colonel	G. P. Sanders DSO OBE	1922–1927
Lieutenant Colonel	A. W. D. Cornish DSO MC	1927–1931
Lieutenant Colonel	E. C. Brown	1931–1934
Lieutenant Colonel	T. C. E. Barstow OBE	1934–1936
Lieutenant Colonel	J. G. Bruce DSO MC	1936–1939
Lieutenant Colonel	G. H. Pulling	1939–1942
Lieutenant Colonel	G. F. X. Bulfield DSO	1942–1944
Lieutenant Colonel	W. M. Amoore DSO	1944–1946
Lieutenant Colonel	R. R. Proud	1946–1947
Lieutenant Colonel	N. F. B. Shaw DSO OBE	1947–1950
Lieutenant Colonel	R. R. Griffith OBE	1950–1953
Lieutenant Colonel	D. L. Powell-Jones DSO OBE	1953–1956
Lieutenant Colonel	P. B. Winstanley MC	1956–1959
Lieutenant Colonel	A. G. Patterson OBE MC	1959–1961
Lieutenant Colonel	E. T. Horsford OBE MC	1961–1963
Lieutenant Colonel	A. S. Harvey OBE MC	1963–1966

Appendix Three

Lieutenant Colonel	R. C. Neath	1966–1968
Lieutenant Colonel	R. N. P. Reynolds MBE	1968–1969

3rd Battalion

Major	F. S. Massy	1917
Lieutenant Colonel	E. B. C. Boddam	1917–1918
Lieutenant Colonel	A. E. Jewett	1918–1920
Lieutenant Colonel	N. Hurst MC	1940–1941
Lieutenant Colonel	N. Skone DSO	1941–1944
Lieutenant Colonel	N. F. B. Shaw DSO	1944–1947

4th Battalion

Lieutenant Colonel	T. R. Harrison	1941–1944
Lieutenant Colonel	K. W. Ross-Hurst	1944–1946

56th Battalion

Lieutenant Colonel	R. R. Proud	6 GR
Lieutenant Colonel	H. Skone DSO	6 GR
Lieutenant Colonel	T. R. Harrison DSO	5 RGR
Lieutenant Colonel	G. E. I. Stone	5 RGR (later 6 GR)

The Regimental Centre

Colonel	H. Walsh	1941–1945
Colonel	N. Eustace DSO	1945–1948

The Regiment after the Amalgamation of the 1st and 2nd Battalions

Lieutenant Colonel	R. N. P. Reynolds MBE	1969–1970
Lieutenant Colonel	J. N. Kelly MC	1970–1973
Lieutenant Colonel	C. J. Scott	1973–1975
Lieutenant Colonel	M. J. F. Wardroper	1975–1978
Lieutenant Colonel	C. J. D. Bullock OBE MC	1978–1981
Lieutenant Colonel	P. D. Pettigrew	1981–1983
Lieutenant Colonel	R. F. Richardson-Aitken	1983–1985
Lieutenant Colonel	J. A. Anderson	1985–1988
Lieutenant Colonel	D. H. McK. Briggs	1988–1991

Commanding Officers

Lieutenant Colonel	N. A. Collett	1991–1993
Lieutenant Colonel	N. J. H. Hinton MBE	1993–1994

Officers officiating during the temporary absence of a permanent commanding officer have not been included.

Decorations shown are those held whilst in command or earned as a direct result of command. Decorations earned elsewhere after relinquishing command have not been included.

APPENDIX FOUR

Gurkha Majors 1948–1994

1st Battalion

1948	Maj (KGO) Pahalman Gurung MBE OBI
1948–52	Maj (QGO) Lachhiman Gurung MBE
1952–57	Maj (QGO) Nainasing Gurung MBE
1957–62	Maj (QGO) Lalbahadur Thapa MVO MC
1962–65	Maj (QGO) Lokbahadur Thapa MBE
1965–69	Maj (QGO) Partapsing Gurung MVO
1969–69	Maj (QGO) Pahalsing Thapa MVO

2nd Battalion

1948–50	Maj (QGO) Kulbahadur Gurung IDSM
1950–51	Maj (QGO) Nandalal Thapa MBE
1951–55	Maj (QGO) Hiralal Gurung MBE
1955–59	Maj (QGO) Dhanbahadur Gurung
1959–62	Maj (QGO) Jumparsad Gurung MBE
1962–66	Maj (QGO) Khusiman Gurung
1966–69	Maj (QGO) Amarbahadur Gurung

6th Gurkha Rifles

1969–71	Maj (QGO) Pahalsing Thapa MVO
1971–74	Maj (QGO) Kholal Ale
1974–78	Maj (QGO) Toyebahadur Chand
1978–82	Maj (QGO) Dalbahadur Gurung MVO

1982–84	Maj (QGO) Jaibahadur Gurung MVO MBE
1984–87	Maj (QGO) Gyanbahadur Gurung
1987–89	Maj (QGO) Chintabahadur Gurung MVO MBE
1989–92	Maj (QGO) Lalbahadur Thapa
1993–94	Maj (QGO) Padambahadur Gurung MVO

APPENDIX FIVE

A Jungle Patrol

THE Gurkha in his home environment is a great hunter. As a hunter of wild game he possesses the advantages of keen eyesight, great patience and almost inexhaustible stamina. Many of them are also excellent trackers. The CTs in Malaya were scrupulously careful to leave no trace of their movements and tracking them was a long, and frequently hopeless, business. What follows is an account of a patrol led by Major Harkasing Rai of 1/6 GR.

Harkasing Rai was one of the Regiment's first GCOs and also one of the Regiment's most redoubtable and venerated figures. In the course of his service he was awarded the MC and bar, the IDSM and MM which, even for a Gurkha, was remarkable. He joined the 6th from 10 GR in 1952 and quickly made a name for himself as an officer of great ability and determination. He retired from the Army in 1968 and lives in Darjeeling. In January 1956 he was commanding 'C' Company of the 1/6th in jungle operations against the CTs in Malaya. On 2 January, 1956, he received a report about a CT party in the vicinity and set out to track them down. The account of what followed has been taken from Brigadier 'Birdie' Smith's *Britain's Brigade of Gurkhas* with his kind permission. The CTs were believed to number around fifty:

'Temporary resting places were found but it was clear that these had been used four or five nights previously and that the CTs had moved towards the west. The Company then performed a most remarkable feat of tracking. Major Harkasing realised that he was on the trail of a well-trained party, led by a high ranking Communist who obviously enforced rigid discipline on the march and at their night stops. The CTs covered their traces well and on several occasions the Gurkha patrols lost the tracks and had to cast around up to 600 yards before finding a small clue which showed in which direction the CTs had moved. It took perseverance and it demanded patience and self discipline; it also required a commander who had faith in the ability of his men to narrow the gap between the quarry and themselves. Led by Harkasing, 'C' Company did this and by 9 January they knew that they were within a day's march of the CTs.

'At midday the leading scout spotted a hut through the gloom of the dense jungle. He signalled the information back but as the leading men began to get into position they were fired on by a sentry, whereupon they rushed forward into a small camp. Its one occupant, an aborigine, was promptly killed but then the Gurkhas realised that fire was being directed at them from the main camp some 200 yards ahead. Quickly reforming, they charged into this camp and killed three more CTs. By this time the main body of the bandits had withdrawn in a disciplined manner across the nearby river and from there they directed heavy automatic fire on to Harkasing and his men. As the leading Gurkhas tried to cross the river, a particularly fearless Chinese bandit, armed with a tommy-gun, covered his comrades' withdrawal and forced 'C' Company to deploy before he moved back. He was chased for over 1,000 yards up the far slopes of the valley. During the chase this brave man frequently turned and fired a few shots at his pursuers. He managed to escape in the end.

'For a short time 'C' Company lost contact with the CTs. A 'landing area' was cleared and a helicopter came in to take away the bodies of the dead bandits and a lot of valuable documents found in the camp. On 11 January, 'C' company were on the move again, following two-day old tracks up to a knife-edge ridge 3,000 feet above the valley. Here they found the CTs had split into two parties of equal strength, one going north and one south. 'C' Company concentrated on the southbound trail but found their already difficult task now well-nigh impossible. Having abandoned their packs in the previous camp, the bandits had thereafter moved with the wary stealth of hunted animals. They knew they were being pursued; they slept in caves, leaving only the smallest traces of their stay. They crawled like insects along the faces of cliffs, up crevices and down waterfalls and yet, carefully though they moved, they left some all but imperceptible sign of their passing. These were seen by the Gurkhas, expert hunters of game in their own country . . . Next day, a small patrol saw about 15 CTs in a temporary camp. One rifleman was sent back to call up the Company Commander. When he arrived, only about ten minutes daylight remained so that he decided it was too late to attack. He ordered his men to lie where they were; there was to be no sound, no smoking, no cooking – the enemy were only a stone's throw away.

'Next morning before dawn, 'C' Company began to edge forward; moving inch by inch they crawled silently in an attempt to surround the camp when, just before light, a sentry challenged them. The whole company 'froze'. Minutes passed and the Communist sentry relaxed. By now it was light and Harkasing considered the cordon was about half-way round the camp when the same sentry challenged again, but this time he did not wait for any reply before he fired a long burst. Two Gurkha soldiers fell wounded and in a flash the CTs were up and away. In terror they scattered and split into groups of two or three men. Harkasing appreciated that they would now make for an area where they could contact local sympathizers and obtain food and help – for it was clear that they were in a bad way. He reported by radio to his Commanding Officer ('Speedy' Bredin) and accordingly other companies from the battalion were deployed in the north, to the south and in 'stop' positions on the jungle edge to the west. These companies had further contacts with the CTs benefitting from 'C' Company's efforts.'*

* *Britain's Brigade of Gurkhas* by E. D. Smith (Leo Cooper, 1973) pp. 159–161.

It was a remarkable feat of tracking on Harkasing's part; as well as an equally remarkable example of the patience and determination required to keep on the trail. The Gurkha's skill as a tracker was of immense value when operating in dense jungle, although some of them were much better at it than others. It was during this operation that three important CTs were killed and Harkasing's initial contact had destroyed what had been intended to be a permanent camp. He was awarded a bar to his MC.

It would be wrong to assume that every patrol was as successful. As often as not patrols spent days and days in the jungle without seeing anything. It is interesting to speculate whether, as the Gurkha soldier becomes more sophisticated, he will lose the skills of primitive man, such as tracking. Such skills may be inherited but they require regular practice if they are not to atrophy and such practice will be hard to get on Salisbury Plain.

APPENDIX SIX

———◦◦◦———

The Royal Gurkha Rifles

IN 1947 there were ten Gurkha Rifles regiments in the Indian Army, of which six remained in the new Army of India upon Independence. On 1 January, 1948, four regiments transferred to the British Army to form the Brigade of Gurkhas: the 2nd, 6th, 7th and 10th. All four combine to become The Royal Gurkha Rifles on 1 July, 1994.

The 2nd King Edward VII's Own Goorkhas (The Sirmoor Rifles) were raised at Sirmoor in 1815, the second of the four friendly corps which took service with the East India Company. The Ram's Head on their shoulder belts commemorates the assault on Koonja Fort in 1824. In the Indian Mutiny, the Sirmoor Battalion (as they were then titled) were the first to raise their weapons against the mutineers and greatly distinguished themselves in 1857 at the Siege of Delhi, where began their long association with The King's Royal Rifle Corps (now part of The Royal Green Jackets), marked by adopting scarlet facings 'in memory of the English Riflemen with whom the Goorkhas served side by side in the stress of the Delhi siege'. In honour of their conduct in the Mutiny, they were awarded an extra Colour, replaced on the order of Queen Victoria by the unique Queen's Truncheon when the Regiment ceased to carry Colours on becoming a Rifle Regiment. The Regiment became the 2nd (Prince of Wales's Own) Goorkha Regiment (The Sirmoor Rifles) in 1886 and acquired its present title in 1936. It enjoys a fighting reputation which is second to none.

The 7th Duke of Edinburgh's Own Gurkha Rifles was

formed at Thayetmyo in 1902 as the 8th Gurkha Rifles, becoming 2/10th in 1903 and the 7th Gurkha Rifles in 1907, recruiting mostly from the Rais and Limbus of East Nepal. On joining the British Army in 1948, the Regiment served briefly in Malaya as 101st and 102nd Field Regiments, Royal Artillery (7th GR) but was soon re-converted to infantry for the remainder of the Emergency. The Royal title was awarded in 1959 in recognition of the Regiment's distinguished service in the Second World War. Both battalions saw frequent action during Confrontation in Borneo. The 1st Battalion served in the Falklands campaign in 1982, instilling extreme fear in the Argentinean soldiers opposing them, through their awesome reputation and total domination of no-man's land. The Regiment's affiliation with the Queen's Own Highlanders was marked by a Cameron of Erracht tartan flash on the Gurkha hat, whilst that with The Cameronians (Scottish Rifles) (disbanded in 1968) is commemorated in the pipers' trews and plaids.

The 10th Princess Mary's Own Gurkha Rifles began in 1890, at Mandalay, when Indian personnel of the 10th Madras Infantry were replaced by the mostly Gurkha complement of the Kubo Valley Military Police Battalion, becoming the 10th Gurkha Rifles in 1901. The Regiment recruited exclusively in East Nepal but remembers its origins in its arm badge: a rock fort placed on the back of an elephant, the former for the defence of Amboor in 1767, whilst the elephant commemorates their part in the Duke of Wellington's victory over the Mahratta Confederacy in 1803. The 10th Gurkhas fought alongside the 6th in Gallipoli and Mesopotamia in The Great War and earned more gallantry decorations in the Second World War than any other Indian Army regiment. The Royal title was awarded in 1950, when the Regiment also became affiliated to The Royal Scots (The Royal Regiment), who had also fought alongside them in the Gallipoli campaign. The 10th Gurkhas accounted for more terrorists than any other regiment during the Malayan Emergency, while Lance Corporal Rambahadur Limbu won the Victoria Cross in Borneo.

The 2nd and 6th Gurkhas will amalgamate to form the 1st Battalion of the new Regiment, whilst the 7th and 10th will simultaneously become the 2nd and 3rd Battalions respectively, merging a few years later when Gurkhas leave Hong Kong for the last time. In due course, the 1st Battalion will be predominantly manned from western Nepal, and the 2nd Battalion from the eastern clans. They will then rotate between the United Kingdom and Brunei for the foreseeable future.

The new cap-badge, illustrated below, will be a simple one whilst some of the distinguishing features of the founder regiments will still be worn. The officers' cross-belt will incorporate four principal battle honours for each of the regiments; in the case of 6th Gurkhas these will be Burma 1885–87, Sari Bair, Medicina and Burma 1944–45. It will also carry the 2nd Goorkhas' Ram's head as a whistle boss and the 10th Gurkhas' elephant and rock fort badge; the 14th/20th 'Hawk' will be worn on the pouch. The red 'touri' or pom-pom of the 6th will be worn on the full-dress Kilmarnock cap, whilst the Hunting Stewart patch of the 10th will remain on the felt Gurkha hat and the 7th's affiliation with The Cameronians will be marked by pipers' trews and plaids in Douglas tartan. The Sirmoor rifles' red facings, or 'lali', will be echoed by red piping on Number One Dress and tropical Mess Dress.

The Royal Gurkha Rifles will thus absorb much of the ethos of the founder Regiments and will maintain the existing affiliations, forged in battle, with British Regiments. As Her Majesty has written at the beginning of this book, 'the indomitable spirit of the Gurkha Officers and soldiers of Nepal, and the traditions and standards of the 6th Gurkhas, will live on in the new Regiment.'

'Jai Sixth! Jai Royal Gurkha Rifles!'

BIBLIOGRAPHY

Historical Record of the 6th Gurkha Rifles, Vol. I, 1817–1919, by Major D. G. J. Ryan, Major G. C. Stahan & Captain J. K. Jones (privately published, 1925)

Historical Record of the 6th Gurkha Rifles, Vol. II by Lt Col H. R. K. Gibbs (Gale & Polden, 1955)

The Steadfast Gurkha: Historical Record of 6th Queen Elizabeth's Own Gurkha Rifles, Vol. III by Charles Messenger (Leo Cooper, 1985)

Allanson of the 6th by Harry Davies (Square One Publications, 1990)

The Chindit War by Shelford Bidwell (Hodder and Stoughton, 1979)

Bugles and a Tiger by John Masters (Buchan & Enright, 1986)

Britain's Brigade of Gurkhas by E. D. Smith (Leo Cooper, 1973)

Fighting General by Tom Pocock (Collins, 1973)

Slim: The Standard Bearer by Ronald Lewin (Leo Cooper, 1976)

Defeat into Victory by Field Marshal Sir William Slim (Cassell, 1956)

Burma: The Longest War 1941–45 by Louis Allen (J. M. Dent, 1984)

Better to Die by Edward Bishop (New English Library, 1976)

A Pride of Gurkhas by Harold James and Denis Sheil-Small (Leo Cooper, 1975)

The Gurkhas by W. Brook Northey and C. J. Morris (Bodley Head, 1928)

A Matter of Honour by Philip Mason (Jonathan Cape, 1975)

Burma: The Turning Point by Ian Lyall Grant (The Zampi Press, Chichester, 1993)

'A Hell of a Licking': The Retreat from Burma 1941–2 by James Lunt (Collins, 1986)

The Indian Army 1822–1922 by T. A. Heathcote (David & Charles, 1974)

The Indian Army by Boris Mollo (Blandford Press, 1981)

Eastern Epic, Vol I by Compton Mackenzie (Chatto & Windus, 1951)

British Social Life in India, 1608–1937 by Dennis Kincaid (Routledge & Kegan Paul, 1973)

The Profession of Arms by General Sir John Hackett (Sidgwick & Jackson, 1983)

Imperial Sunset by James Lunt (Macdonald, 1981)

Unofficial History by Field Marshal Sir William Slim (Cassell, 1959)

The Race for Trieste by Geoffrey Cox (William Kimber, 1977)

Happy Warriors by Lt Col A. E. C. Bredin (Blackmore Press, 1961)

INDEX

Index

Index